PRAISE FOR

How One Parent Engaged Addiction

"Deni's book contains such emotion and truth, and should be read by anyone with an addicted child or loved one. Not everyone is capable of sharing so honestly the path she traveled to get to her goals."

—Anne Salter, LCSW, Family Addiction Specialist
author of *Family Stew – Our Relationship Legacy*

"This book offers more than ten years of heart, soul, and honest self-revealing commitment to the struggle a parent can dedicate to the fight against addiction. No quick fix pitches, no patented methods to purchase. Rather—the depth of a mother's love and strength of intention applied to one of the most wrenching, tormenting problems a family can face: addiction. The fight, in which, one is asked to relinquish it all in order to discover true self."

—Alex Kronstadt, Ph.D. Clinical Health Psychologist

"Well written and inspiring. I could feel this mother's pain and relate to it. Deni faces her own demons, while her son faces his. She learns to "let go" in order to save both her child and her SELF. This true story helps the reader understand what needs to be done in order to restore sanity through some tough decisions. This book is written with much creativity, heart, hope, love and suggestions for the reader."

—Roxy Jentes, Recovering Codependent

"This book is not only heartfelt, but truly an inspiration. As the parent of an addict, understanding that I, and my feelings are not alone–is invaluable. By Deni bearing her soul and giving an honest look at her part in her son's addiction has helped me to see how we all have to take a look at ourselves before we can sit in judgment of another. More than anything, she helped me to see how addiction is a family disease and we all play a part. I highly recommend this great book."

—Claudia Cayne, RN, Parent of an Addict

"What an incredibly powerful story—it needs to be told. When strong, successful women share past adversities—it inspires so much hope in others who are currently dealing with similar situations. I love it!"

—Melody Gustafson, Pastor, The Shepherd's Bridge, Davie, FL

"What an eye opener! You are a gift to our society by allowing us to see and to feel the pain thru your lenses of the reality of a modern plague. Thank you for such a vivid recount of your experience."

—Reina Sang, Pianist

"If you are searching for answers or HOPE, then this book provides both. My favorite quote from the book is, "My son's laughter is better than any drug I have ever taken." This quote comes from Deni's son, Ryan, who is speaking about his own, beautiful child. Deni's story takes you from hell to heaven! This is a MUST read for all struggling parents of addicts or for anyone who is codependent."

—Jaime Steel, President, *Steel Aviation*

"I have the privilege of working with many different kinds of families and believe that Deni's book can provide insight for all parents, whether their children are addicted or not. Familial dysfunction and codependency manifests in other forms of negative behaviors aside from addiction and alcoholism. This dysfunction may be why so many children are finding so many challenges both at home and at school. Deni's book can provide support for parents to make the changes they want, so that they might affect change in their children."

—Pam Newman, Youth and Family Specialist

"Deni B. Sher reports from the trenches of motherhood and middle age in the pages of this sincere memoir. While the content of Sher's story is not new, her presentation is. Inspired to create not only a journal-like narrative, but also a musical production to honor her family's experience, Sher offers a unique memoir that's part diary, part poetry, and part musical theater. While readers may wish for further refinements in Sher's storytelling choices, they will never doubt her message about the power of perseverance and a positive outlook."

—Sheila M. Trask, *Clarion ForeWord Reviews*

How One Parent Engaged

ADDICTION

A Mother's Healing Journey Through Her Son's Addiction

A Memoir

DENI B. SHER

WESTON PUBLISHERS
Weston, Florida

[Handwritten inscription:]

Linda,

May my journey from darkness into light become a beacon of light in your life on your own journey!

So glad we met.

Love Deni

10.15.15

HOW ONE PARENT ENGAGED ADDICTION

A MOTHER'S HEALING JOURNEY THROUGH HER SON'S ADDICTION

Weston Publishers books may be ordered through booksellers or by contacting:

Weston Publishers
304 Indian Trace #535
Weston, Florida 33326
www.westonpublishers.com

ISBN: 978-0-9913941-2-8(softcover)

Printed in the United States of America.

First published by IUniverse in 2014

Weston Publishers rev. date: 07/21/2014

AUTHOR'S NOTE

Deni Boehm Sher asserts the moral right to be identified as the author of this work.

This is a true story. To the best of my ability, I have re-created events, people, locales, and situations from my memories of them. In order to maintain the anonymity of others, in most instances I have changed the names of individuals, places, and the details of events. I have also changed or omitted identifying characteristics, such as the physical descriptions, occupations, and places of residence. Any resemblance between fictional names and descriptions and the names and descriptions of a real person is strictly coincidental

Original Artwork by: Ryan (author's son)
Photography by: Diane Schafer Photography
Cover Design by: Glen M. Edelstein
Interior Design by: Glen M. Edelstein
Stock Image Design by: Yuryy Bezrukov

For more information, please contact:
www.HOPEaddictionBook.com
Deni@DeniBSher.me

I dedicate this book to my son, to his wife, and to my grandson. May you live, grow, and prosper in a nurturing, love filled home, free of familial dysfunction. And, may you each awaken spiritually to all of your divine talents.

One evening an old Cherokee told his grandson about a battle that goes on inside all people. He said, "My son, the battle is between two 'wolves' inside us all.

One is Evil.

It is anger, envy, jealousy, sorrow, regret, greed, arrogance, self-pity, guilt, resentment, inferiority, lies, false pride, superiority, and ego.

The other is Good.

It is joy, peace, love, hope, serenity, humility, kindness, benevolence, empathy, generosity, truth, compassion and faith."

The grandson thought about it for a minute and then asked, "Which wolf wins?"

The grandfather simply replied, "The one you feed."

—AUTHOR UNKNOWN

CONTENTS

PART V: 2012 – 2014 MORE TRUTH

FOREWORD

By Paul Fletcher and Anne Salter, LCSW

I MET DENI IN 2007, WHEN she sat next to me during an eight-hour real estate seminar. Outwardly, we were both *cheerful* realtors seeking to improve our marketing skills. Internally, tucked safely inside both of us—we were *wounded* parents of addicted children, seeking to become whole. We did not meet by accident. It was divine intervention—a meeting of two souls.

After a few hours of intermittent, friendly conversation, Deni openly shared that her son was a recovering alcoholic and drug addict and that she had been writing a musical, inspired after doing tough love[1] on him, in 2002. I knew all about tough love, and the painful struggle parents endure.

I am the parent of two (now grown and in recovery), alcoholic children. I shared this with Deni. I also shared, that two of my siblings had overdosed from heroin and that I, too, was in recovery. When the meeting was over, we sat together for an additional two hours sharing our histories. We bonded that day.

Shortly thereafter, Deni sent me a copy of her writings from the past five years. I was the first person she entrusted with them. I stopped reading at the introduction. It was crystal clear to me that Deni had no idea of what really took place on the day she did tough love. As someone having years of experience with codependency, familial dys-

---

1. Tough love is an expression used when someone treats another person harshly or sternly with the intent to help them in the long run. From what I have read, Bill Milliken first used the term, when he wrote the book *Tough Love* in 1968, and has been used by numerous others since then as a psychological procedure. There must be some actual love or feeling of affection behind the harsh or stern treatment to be defined as tough love. Genuinely concerned parents refusing to support their drug-addicted child financially until he or she enters drug rehabilitation are practicing tough love.

function, enabling, addiction, alcoholism, and recovery, I felt moved to respond to six particular lines Deni wrote. Lines, that stopped me in my tracks. What Deni wrote is in *italics*. My response follows each of her statements.

Finally, the day I started to write this story, I did tough love.
I turned my back on my son.

Tough love is not turning your back. Tough love is staring your adversary in the face. Tough love is facing your demons. It is looking straight into their eyes and saying, "No, I will not continue to enable you!" That's when it begins. One of you was going to have to quit. One of you was going to have to begin healing. Someone has to start the process, but it is a joint venture. Your back was turned when you were in denial. Your back was turned to your son and to your participation in his addiction. When you started your recovery, you began to face yourself and your son's addictive behavior. That began the healing process. It is about saying no to the addiction; saying no to the drugs, alcohol and nicotine; saying yes to love, to loving the person, to hating the addiction, alcohol and nicotine. You can love the person, but you do not have to love what they are doing. You do not have to love the behavior, the acting out, or the self-destruction. Love your son. Hate the addiction. Love the person. Hate the drugs.

Oh, it was a horrible day!

In fact, it was a great day. A day of awakening!
It was the best of times, and it was the worst of times.

I finally did hit bottom when I was emotionally and financially
bled to death.

The bottom and the top are at the same point. The bottom is at point zero. It is from point zero that all things are possible. Each new development—each new awakening starts from realizing you can begin again. Erase the past, and start all over. You are the master of your fate, the captain of your ship. Go find your destiny.

I couldn't listen to another lie.

The lies were those you were telling yourself. Stopping the enabling was the truth.

Giving means we love them, doesn't it?

Giving means we have given up, when all we give are material things. We treat things as though they are an expression of love, when in actuality they are an expression of one's inability to give nurturing love. Anybody can give things. Love comes from within. Love is spiritual. Love takes a lifetime of giving. Love never ends, and it has no beginning. It just is.

Let your journey begin—your journey in the healing process.

We are all on this journey. Some of us are conscious of the part we are playing. Others are still in denial. But this whole society—this entire culture must first become aware and then become part of the healing process. Your story is one of a million, but one from which millions will learn. What you are doing is excellent. I am proud to participate and to share my thoughts. Thanks for asking. It is helping me to heal, as well. May we all be better parents, teachers, leaders, and human beings because of the heightened awareness. Your son's artwork is his expression and his way of communicating, to let us know what is going on inside. Thank you for listening to his creative expression. Thank you for sharing it with the world.

I knew Deni never expected this nature of feedback from me. When Deni read my response, she received valuable insight to open her mind further to the process of recovery she had begun, as an enabling, codependent parent. In doing tough love, Deni had not turned her back on her son. In fact, tough love represented the first step of her recovery. Until Deni began to face her own disease of codependency, her son could never face his. Her enabling had kept them both imprisoned.

The insights I received while reading her poetry and prose helped in my continuing growth and healing process. When I told Deni I was proud to be able to participate —I meant it. I believe Deni is the Shakespeare of the new millennium. I had told her this about two years before she completed her book. She truly had no full concept of her own talents. I have been gently nudging her to publish her writings for the past two years. This book's publication will begin the manifestation of the musical Deni envisioned for over ten years. It will also provide a needed beacon of light for others who suffer.

Deni's journey was an extremely personal and brave transition, which she began to save her son's life. Her path ultimately led her home. Home to her divine Higher *Self*— home to her soul's purpose on earth, and ultimately—home to a place inside, where she was able to release her son to the Universe while knowing all is as it should be.

Today, as I write this foreword, I feel extremely honored Deni asked me to do so. As a teacher in today's classrooms, I believe Deni's memoir could help to prevent adolescents from using drugs and alcohol, and possibly, to think twice before becoming involved in irresponsible sexual activities. Most of us do come from various forms of dysfunctional backgrounds. We can all benefit from her embracement of truth and from the intense labor of love she underwent to uncover and to work through unresolved wounds from her early relationship history. Change happens because of people like Deni.

Paul Fletcher
Parent, Teacher, Friend

I MET DENI IN 2007, in a New York City diner after we had both attended Broadway shows. In this people-packed diner, we began talking. I discovered that she was writing a musical about her son's addiction. She discovered that I was writing a book about family addiction, as an addictions specialist. After learning we lived only forty minutes apart in Florida, we decided to get together and explore how I could assist Deni as an expert in my field.

We eventually convened, and over time found I needed some technical editing (she has an English degree), and that Deni needed to understand the web of family addiction better, and particularly her own role as a "codependent" mother.

The outcome of our collaboration has resulted in the publication of my book, *Family Stew: Our Relationship Legacy*, and the publication of this book. (She decided to write a book before moving on to her musical, *which is sure to be a hit*.) Working together has resulted in what I know will be a lifetime friendship.

How One Parent Engaged Addiction, is not only a memoir of her painful and persistent determination, to help her son out of the despair of addiction, but also an honest sharing of the pitfalls of enabling behavior and of her own family history of alcoholism and dysfunction. Her constant obsession with her son's disease is a great example (evident in her book), of the codependent's own, emotional disease. She writes with raw honesty, chronicling her eleven-year, arduous journey to recover both her Self and her relationship with her son.

Her hope is that others will be able to see and overcome their enabling and denial in much less time, and realize that there must also be therapeutic, professional help before the addiction can be truly arrested. Again, she is clear in sharing so many of the enabling behaviors that come so "naturally" to those who love a family member in trouble.

Something else I admire, so much about Deni, is her willingness to learn more about both her own and her family's dysfunctional history, so that she can continue to grow. Her desire to help others is a hallmark of her personality and character. As someone who has worked thirty-seven years with addiction in families and the painful fallout on relationships, I highly recommend this book to anyone who struggles in their relationship with an addict or who feels trapped in codependent relationships.

I also cannot wait to see her musical about addiction—on stage!

Anne Salter, LCSW, Family and Addictions Specialist
Author of Family Stew: Our Relationship Legacy©2012
www.centerforselfdiscovery.com

PREFACE

SOME OF YOU, WHO HAVE PICKED UP THIS book, may be dealing with an addicted child, or other loved one. If so, most likely you are struggling to maintain your sanity. There is *hope*. Trust me, I walked in your shoes. My story, however, holds value for all codependents struggling with an obsession to control other's behavior. It is a journey into the letting go of one's ego in the quest to discover and to love one's true *Self*—from the inside out.

I am the mother of a child addicted to alcohol and to drugs.
I am not a psychologist, psychiatrist, or doctor.
I am a parent who feared her child was going to die.
I am an Adult Child of an Alcoholic father (ACoA).
I am a recovering codependent.

Fearfulness, pain, anger, sadness, guilt, shame, frustration, anxiety, and hitting rock bottom, as an enabling, codependent parent who had lived for years in denial, happened to be my qualifications to begin writing this book.

Fearlessness, surrender, acceptance, forgiveness, internal peace, understanding, wholeness, the joy of rediscovering my true *Self,* and the serenity found in being a healthy woman, wife and parent would overtime replace those dis-eased feelings, inspiring me to continue writing and to share my story with you.

To most friends and acquaintances in 2002, at age fifty-two, I seemed to be *thee* epitome of a successful baby boomer, who lived an ideal life in the upscale city of Weston, Florida, and the lucky lady soon to marry her 'knight in shining armor.' I was in perfect health, an avid tennis player, and had recently earned my BA in English. I had also just opened a marketing business, after having owned a computer company for fourteen years. Outwardly, I appeared as one of the happiest, successful and most fulfilled women around. Behind closed doors, however, I suffered emotional chaos.

What most people never knew, was that my only son Ryan (not his *real* name), at twenty-five years old, was a full-blown alcoholic and drug addict. That was my secret, and the one thing concerning my status I did not share with many people. It was such a secret; I had not yet told myself the truth. I couldn't. For you see, long ago and without realization, I had buried my psyche deep in denial. To admit to such a thing would mean I failed as a parent. I only had one child. *How could I face such failure?*

In the summer of 2002, I hit my bottom. I vividly remember facing the harsh reality that my '*beautiful boy*' was an alcoholic and a drug-addict. I had no idea of what to do, where to turn, with whom to speak, or how to handle the situation. This truth all but destroyed me. I walked a fine line between sanity and insanity. Without a doubt, it was the most devastating, helpless, and anguish-filled state-of-mind I'd ever experienced. Let's face it, *the fear our child may die* is the paramount fear keeping us imprisoned.

In desperation, I busted out by doing *tough love* with my son. I cried my heart out believing I had deserted and turned my back on him. *What kind of mother am I?*

Still standing, yet on my knees emotionally, I willfully and humbly surrendered to my Higher Power God for answers. Crying out loud, I asked:

How does a mother turn her back on her son,
When her son is lying in the gutter?

How does a mother turn her back on her son,
When she knows he truly has no one other?

The content of this book is my *HOW*.

INTRODUCTION

THIS MEMOIR CHRONICLES *HOW* I FACED the truth and *how* I engaged the diseases of alcoholism and drug addiction in a war only one of us could win. My pen became my sword as I painfully pulled my buried head out of denial, to do battle after battle with a cunning opponent threatening to kill my son.

I figuratively grabbed my sword, mounted my horse, and went to war—intending to be victorious. In my victory, I intended to pull Ryan out of the monsters' grips. I intended to save my son's life and to slay his demons.

What I did *not* intend to do was uncover my own dysfunctional behavior. It wasn't my son's monsters I needed to slay. Only Ryan could fight his battles. Only Ryan possessed the ability to slay his demons. I had my own monsters staring me in the face. My demons became as cunning for me as Ryan's were for him. I was knocked off my horse, and brought to my knees countless times before being able to recognize the diseases of codependency, enabling, and denial (hereafter termed codependency), as the symptoms of my diseased thinking.

In my codependency, I frustrated myself by a destructive form of helping known as enabling. Without realizing, I had enabled Ryan throughout his life by always rescuing and fixing everything for him. He became dependent and consumed with entitlement issues. My son deserved to be drug-free, healthy, productive, and independent. Being a parent is the only relationship in which the true mark of success is healthy separation. I had failed at the task.

As an enabling parent, I had a difficult time letting go. By not letting go, I deprived Ryan of recovery. I needed to hit bottom as a codependent. I needed help. I needed to recover. Intellectually, I understood why I shouldn't financially help my addicted son, yet out of a paralyzing fear of Ryan dying, I continued enabling his decadent lifestyle. In my helping, I kept him helpless.

I never allowed Ryan to suffer consequences for his actions. I never allowed him to hit bottom. He had never learned accountability. To recover or to die became the most critical choice that only my son could make. It was impossible for me to make that choice for him.

Enabling is a vicious cycle, destroying lives, and perpetuating addiction. I am here to say, the cycle can be broken. I did it. I broke the cycle!

It feels magnificent to put my head peacefully on the pillow every night without worrying the phone might ring with a voice on the other end saying, "Your son is dead. He overdosed." Those nights have gone. This doesn't mean my son will never overdose, but today, *I do not worry about what I cannot control. I have let go and let God.*

My Higher Power God answered my prayers and sent me on the greatest healing journey of my lifetime: a journey of letting go, a journey of acceptance, a journey of forgiveness, a journey toward truth, and a journey leading me to understand my soul and my soul's purpose here on earth. I used the power of prayer (focused thought), intention, possibility thinking, creative visualization, imagination, music, and writing to *create a new reality.*

Strange as it may seem, once I surrendered to my Higher Powers, opening myself to receive messages from the Universe, God, Spirit, Source, Buddha, or whatever name one wants to affix to higher frequency energy existing outside of man's five senses, I received inspirational messages in the form of songs and poems. When the Universe spoke—I wrote. I picked up a pen to write on whatever I found within arm's reach: napkins at tables, airsick bags on airplanes, inside covers of books, on pages of magazines, and when the timing was right, I typed on my computer keyboard.

I usually heard music along with the words, so I believed I was meant to write a musical. I started telling people I was writing a musical called, *Mom's Opera.* For seven years my intentions were focused only on writing an inspirational, staged musical production offering *hope* for other families battling against addiction, codependency and familial dysfunction. While working towards that goal, I wrote and recorded seven original songs with two, talented, composer lyricists.

Whatever internal struggles I endured, while processing our journeys, I found solace in writing. Essentially the poems and songs began writing me— if that makes sense. Over time, I put those writings into a linear sequence, which began unfolding the story of what had transpired. I saved every letter and email written or received over nine years and with the occasional help from Ryan, I was able to piece our story together. Before I knew, I had the basic storyline for a musical, or a book.

In 2011, after doing much soul searching and praying, I realized a book was a more attainable vehicle for telling my story and far easier to complete than an entire musical. With that realization, I began focusing on writing and publishing a memoir. My healing journey covers over eleven years and includes different stages of growth, therefore, I divided it into five parts.

Written between 2002 and 2007, I titled part 1: *My Five-Year Crusade of Insanity*. At fifty-two, I had absolutely no understanding of how deeply my unresolved wounds from early relationship history with my family-of-origin had affected my behavior, choices, relationships, and much more. As a result, I had dysfunctional parenting skills, which becomes apparent in letters written to Ryan, and in my codependent thinking and behavior while interacting with him. Should you happen to be the parent of an addict, I am positive you will relate to my insanity.

I was blessed to meet Anne Salter, an addictions therapist, while visiting New York City in 2007. Our meeting led to my helping Anne in the early editing and organizing of her therapeutic book, *Family Stew: Our Relationship Legacy*. In the course of a year's time of reading, analyzing and editing Anne's professional work, I inadvertently recognized my own dysfunctional behaviors, as a codependent, Adult Child of an Alcoholic father. Spirit works in mysterious ways and for that reason, I titled part 2: *There are No Accidents*.

In 2010, once ready to begin facing my dysfunctional childhood history, I put a time chart together of major life events that shaped my life, starting from my first memories of childhood until the present. Processing my past and writing about it was pain-filled and challenging to my heart, but at the same time, provided the ability for me to recover my *Self*, my soul, my truth, and in time to become whole as a woman, daughter, sister, wife, friend, and mother. I healed from the inside out. All of which led me to title part 3: *The Miracles of Deni & Ryan*.

Sometime between birth and adulthood many of us do lose our true *Self* to the demands and desires of what others want for our lives. We lose our unique, divine gifts and talents received at birth. I believe we are each a spiritual being, having a human being experience, but at some point, our ego *Self* takes over and we lose touch with our spiritual purpose on earth. We get sidetracked and off course. For sure, I did. Finding my way back, at age sixty, was nothing short of a miracle.

It was the law of Spirit working within my soul that inspired me to write, to grow, and to examine my past in search of true *Self.* Then, in 2012, I began reading books, which shed additional light on my transition. Part 4 is personal and meaningful to me. I chose to share my experiences, as they are important in understanding the person I am today, so I titled part 4: *Who Am I?*

Though my manuscript was near ready for publication by late 2012, there still remained fear-based roadblocks I needed to overcome before publishing. *Did I really want to publish this open, honest book that will expose the many dysfunctional parts of my life? How would my son react to my side of our story? Would he hate me for being so open with our past lives? Everybody has a story. What makes mine unique? Maybe I should forget the book and only write the musical. Did I need to expose my Self, my poor choices, and my deficient mothering skills for others to judge?* I found hundreds of excuses not to publish. Inner strength was not coming easy for me. Fear of my own vulnerability had me stuck in a rut.

Without a doubt, the Universe picked up on those fears by putting meaningful books and television programs into my life, providing the motivation and inspiration I needed. Truths were coming at me from many directions, which I include in part 5. Oprah's *Super Soul Sunday* conversations blew my mind. I especially can't wait for you to read about her interview with Brene' Brown, Ph.D., on May 5, 2013, regarding Brene's book, *Daring Greatly.* This particular interview freed me to move forward with publishing. When I finished writing, I titled Part 5: *More Truth.*

My memoir ends with written snapshots of what was happening in Ryan's and my life, up to the last moments before sending off the final manuscript. My wish is for my journey to be received as a gift of *hope* for others, who like myself, struggle with codependency, denial, and enabling issues; and also as a gift of *hope*, for those feeling frustrated by being powerless to change the behaviors of those we love.

Within this book are fourteen, full-color pieces of artwork Ryan painted in 2003, when he first attempted to quit drinking and using drugs. You will also find two additional full-color paintings. Ryan spray-painted one of them in 1999 while at the peak of his partying with drugs and alcohol, and the other he painted in 2010, after getting out of rehab. For those who purchased an eBook, and if your device performs in color, you will view Ryan's artwork in full color. Ryan's artwork can also be seen on my website: www.HOPEaddictionBook.com

I have combined poetry with prose in my book. I realize everyone is not comfortable reading poetry, so I would like to make a suggestion. When you come to one of my inspired poems or songs, take a deep breath, slow down in your reading, and become one with me. Step into my shoes. Try becoming me in each particular moment of my life. Feel what I felt. Go where I went. See what I saw. I was projecting. I was envisioning. I was creating new possibilities for both myself and for my son.

Much of what I wrote as poetry or scripted dialogues was fantasized conversations, written in poetic form. (Also known as creative visualization and possibility thinking.) The most exciting part is that overtime, my visions materialized, my fantasies were fulfilled, and my possibilities became reality! All of which, is why, I wrote this inspirational book to share our success story.

I think the possibility exists for you to do the same in your own life, in your own time, and in your own process of healing. Recovery requires the changing of one's thinking. Diseased thinking creates disease. Healthy thinking creates health. It's actually almost that simple, although it requires much internal healing work.

Our personal stories are all different, because our lives are all different, but our pain is universal. My story is filled with *believable hope* for that pain. Today, I believe in miracles. I witnessed many over the past eleven and a half years. Miracles can also happen for you. If my poetry and prose radiates light into your life and fosters positive change, then my mission will be fulfilled.

Welcome to my world—to my courageous, spiritual, and healing journey of *surrender and recovery—from darkness into light.*

Deni Boehm Sher
Weston, Florida
July 2014

PART I

2002 – 2007

*My Five-Year
Crusade of Insanity*

I

Insanity

Doing the same thing over and over again...
and expecting different results.
—*Albert Einstein*
(adopted by Al-Anon as an ongoing mantra)

AT TWENTY-SIX, I GAVE BIRTH to my beautiful, healthy, and perfect son on September 10, 1976. We named him Ryan Michael. The pain of natural childbirth quickly vanished while gazing into Ryan's eyes and seeing the miracle of his life reflecting back. During the following thirteen months of breastfeeding, eye gazing, and maternal nurturing, Ryan and I created a bond I knew would never be broken.

At that time, however, there was no way of foreseeing a future where the monster-like diseases of alcoholism and addiction, would consume Ryan's body over many years until possessing him both mentally and physically. Regrettably, that future was only fourteen short years away from its first stage.

At fourteen, Ryan was as cute as any fourteen-year old could have been. He had straight blonde hair, worn long, and covering his dark brown eyes. Like most surfers in Florida, his skin was golden tan from days in the sun, and his dimpled smile full of healthy white teeth. When he wasn't surfing, his lean, muscular and flexible body was on a skateboard. Physically, he was the perfect specimen of a teenage boy. Emotionally, though, my son suffered. He was full of anger and rebellion but couldn't discern why. I would say lightheartedly to him, "Ryan you are a rebel without a cause."

I know, Mom," Ryan would answer. "I just am. I have no idea why."

And sadly, neither one of us understood then, how much of Ryan's anger and rebelliousness resulted from being born into a family filled with dysfunction. Dysfunction led to divorce as Ryan turned four. Dysfunction fostered repressed pain inside our young son. Ryan's pain festered over time, breeding low self-esteem, anxiety, despair, shame, and depression.

In his teenage innocence, Ryan discovered that alcohol took those painful feelings away and made him feel happy and silly. He also found marijuana relaxing while changing and enhancing his reality, after only a few tokes. Ryan didn't need to deal with his negative, uncomfortable emotions any longer. Over the next ten years, nicotine, alcohol and pot led to cocaine, and various other "feel good" pills like ecstasy, LSD, and other amphetamines to provide and maintain Ryan's means of escape.

Fast forward.

When Ryan turned twenty-three, he met a girl his age while partying in South Beach. Sandra was tall, thin, dark complexioned, very sexy, and with an Iranian and German heritage. She was quite exotic. Ryan and Sandra fell in love. They moved into Sandra's South Beach apartment, and lived there until both ran out of money. At that point, I allowed them to live in an unfinished, storage loft above my computer company's warehouse. Not only did I let them live there, but employed both in my computer business. Essentially, I liked Sandra. She seemed very intelligent and extremely polite. Evidently, I was a poor judge of character. I learned over time that she too was recklessly using drugs and possibly had a more dysfunctional family than Ryan (if that was conceivable).

Meanwhile, the two of them legalized their love through marriage. I encouraged their marriage. I think I felt relieved that there was someone else to take care of Ryan and his reckless lifestyle. (That was extremely irresponsible thinking on my part, but it's the truth.)

They soon made plans to move to Munich, Germany, where Sandra and her family had once lived, after fleeing Iran in 1979. While their plans to move were in the making, Ryan pushed me to my limits with his out of control, drug-induced behaviors of lying and stealing.

At twenty-four, Ryan received the following letter I wrote to him on June 6, 2001:

> To: Ryan
> You are an addict.
> Until you accept this and deal with your reality, there is absolutely nothing else I can do for you or with you.

I know you took my computer monitor. I don't know if you sold it or bartered it, but I know you took it. Then you lied about it, to me. Yesterday, you stole rubber trim from someone's car. I threw it away.

You are a thief and a liar. You are an addict. You drink, and now you are most likely doing drugs again.

I will be back in my office on Tuesday. I expect you to have a passport by then. Once you have a passport in hand, I will buy your ticket to Germany. It will be a one-way ticket only. I do not want you to come back to live here in my warehouse or to be in my life any longer. You have no respect for me or for anyone else. You have no respect for yourself.

One day when you are clean, and responsible, then and only then, do I want to hear from you! If you choose to never contact me again, after going to Germany that is fine too. That is your choice. You have done nothing but disappoint me time after time after time. I had enough last summer and then let you back in my life again. This time is it. I tried to help you, but you don't help yourself. The best thing for you to do is to commit yourself to a rehab facility somewhere to get the counseling help you so desperately need. Mom

I didn't even sign it *Love, Mom*. Where did my love go? I even wrote, *To: Ryan*, and not, *Dear Ryan*. How could I be so angry with my son, that I told him never to contact me again? I had heard so many lies from him, spent fortunes on him, continued to trust in him, and time after time he'd disappoint me. How many lies did I have to listen to before I accepted the truth? My son was out of control. I was done. I had hit my bottom (for the first time).

Shortly after giving him the letter, I purchased Ryan's one-way ticket to Germany. Within days a huge pond, called the Atlantic Ocean, separated us. Time and distance, however, do tend to make one's heart grow fonder. So after five months, I flew to Munich to visit Ryan and Sandra.

The three of us actually had a great time together, and Ryan and I were even able to laugh over some of his childhood memories. Ryan never let on that he had any problems with alcohol, drugs, or with his marriage. He was working in a coffee house and projected a happy and healthy personality. Getting married and moving to Germany appeared to help turn Ryan's life around. I was thrilled.

Seven months later, after being in Germany for one year, Ryan phoned me. "Hi Mom!" he yelled into the phone with his voice cheerful and full of excitement.

"Hi Ryan," I cheerfully yelled back. "What a surprise to hear from you. Is everything okay?" I asked, knowing in the past that phone calls from Ryan usually meant I would be asked for money or for some kind of help.

"Everything is great—sort of," Ryan responded, in a melodic, unhappy tone.

"What do you mean by sort of?" I asked, half fearful that I might hear they were pregnant with a baby they couldn't afford, or that one of them is injured or in trouble.

"Mom, I want to go back home," Ryan blurted. I said nothing. I prepared myself for his follow-up appeal for my approval. "Sandra and I want to divorce. I can't get a good job here because I don't speak German. I don't do drugs anymore. I don't even drink. I promise I will turn my life around if you pay my airfare home," Ryan pleaded.

"Wow! I didn't expect that Ryan," was all I could respond. Meanwhile, my heart pulled in two directions. The past year without Ryan tormenting my life with his irresponsible and irrational behaviors had been wonderful. My life felt almost *normal* without the seesaw effects of my son's chaotic lifestyle. And yet my maternal instincts began jumping for joy!

"Are you telling me the truth?" I asked. "Are you honestly not drinking and drugging, or are you telling me only what I want to hear?"

"I swear, I am not drinking, and I am not doing drugs. Mom, I am tired of wasting my life. I am so unhappy here. I miss you. It's weird being in Germany and fighting with Sandra all the time. I want to go home. Please Mom, let me come home," Ryan begged, pushing my maternal buttons like a champ.

Though I didn't miss the chaos, I did miss my son. I missed the Ryan I knew he could be, when sober. *Please God; tell me I'm not crazy.* "Of course I will pay your airfare home," I said. The forever hopeful and forgiving (codependent) mother won out, over the angered and hopeless mother, who had given up on him just one-year prior. *Maybe there still is hope.* Since learning of Sandra's history of drug abuse, I was actually pleased they were separating.

I agreed to purchase his one-way ticket home, for a date in the near future, and then we affectionately ended the conversation. "I love you Mom. You'll see a new me. I promise," Ryan cheerfully screamed into the phone, as if he had won the lottery. He sounded totally relieved.

"I love you too Ryan, and I can't wait to see you again!" Once making the agreement, I hung up the phone excited about all the possibilities for my son's life. I joyfully paid the thousand dollars to fly him home.

At this point, I lived with my fiancé, Arthur, in a comfortable home he purchased for us in Weston, Florida. We planned to marry sometime in 2003. Because of my son's history of lying and stealing from me over the years, Arthur was adamant when he told me Ryan was not welcome to live in our home for any extended length of time. As Ryan's codependent mother, it was easy for me to trust him again, but as an outsider looking in, and, as someone who loved and wanted to protect me, Arthur had a different perspective on the situation. Since I trusted and respected Arthur, I agreed.

Arthur also warned me not to get overly enthused about Ryan because inevitably, in the past, he would tell me good things about his life, only to disappoint me. How does a mother not get overwhelmed with joy, hearing that her child is clean, after ten years of drug abuse? And to have him back in the States—I was ecstatic.

I knew his coming home meant I would be dipping into my savings (once again), to set him up in a comfortable lifestyle. I was so thrilled hearing he was clean and sober that I would have done anything for him! After all, he was my only child. (And, after all, I was his enabling, sick mother.)

When Ryan arrived in Florida, we were both excited and looked forward to a bright future. He appeared so much older than when I had last seen him, and he had put on a few pounds since my visit. *Hopefully, it was not from beer!* After we shared hugs in a tearful reunion, we made our way to my car with his luggage, which included a mountain bike.

Since I had always been an eternal optimist with respect to most situations in my life, I wanted to share my positive feelings with Ryan.

So I did, breaking the uncomfortable, deafening silence in the car.

"As far as I'm concerned, Ryan, the past dark years of your life are over. They are history," I declared. "Today is the first day of the rest of your life!" I softly shouted in celebration of his return, and to his being sober. "In a few days we'll find an apartment, so you can be independent, and move on with your life."

"Thanks Mom. I really appreciate all that you have done for me in the past, and everything you are doing now. I admit I've been a real shit, but I'm ready to turn my life around. I promise you'll be proud of me."

"Ryan, all I have ever wanted is for you to find inner peace and happiness. You certainly can't do that, when you are drinking and drugging. You told me you are clean and want to change, and that is why I am helping you again. I believe you and I trust in you."

With that being said, Ryan and I both settled into our short drive home and into our private thoughts. It felt so good to have my sober son home. Inside my heart, I allowed myself to feel the first ray of hope—again. Though Arthur was usually right concerning most things, I was praying he would be wrong about Ryan.

Ryan stayed with us a few days while we discussed his options, and came up with an overall game plan. We drove to Deerfield Beach, where he was raised most of his life, and found the perfect apartment. It was a fully furnished townhouse. The owner was looking for a short-term lease of six months and asking only $500 per month. That was perfect. We figured, in six months, Ryan would know where he'd settle long term, and most likely, it would be based upon where he was working.

"I don't want the lease to be in my name," I told the landlady. "My son is twenty-five, and it's time for him to be responsible. I am more than happy to help him get started, but I would really like to keep my name off the lease." The landlady, also a parent of grown children, understood and respected my feelings. Graciously, the lease was put only in Ryan's name.

"This lease represents a new lease on my life, Mom," Ryan said while signing the paperwork. We laughed together while I silently prayed: *from his mouth to God's ears.*

"This is the last time I am going to pay for your lifestyle," I reminded Ryan as we settled into the car. "I will pay the first month's rent, then you are responsible."

"Not to worry, Mom. I'll get a job, and you'll see a new me," Ryan promised.

"Since I don't want you to starve to death, I'll fill your refrigerator and cabinets with food and basic supplies to get you started," I offered, not wanting Ryan to go hungry while looking for work.

The next day we drove over to my good friend's auto shop. Don always had used cars in and out, so I knew we'd find an affordable and decent car for Ryan.

"Are you nuts?" Don asked. "Why are you buying Ryan another car? Don't you remember what he did to the other ones you purchased from me?" Don scoffed.

I quickly made one of my, *don't look at me that way* faces at Don and ignored his candid, yet well meaning remarks. Of course, I remembered, but I wanted to forget (unknowingly, blinded by denial). In the past, Ryan was very irresponsible with every single one of the cars I had bought him.

One time, when he was in the depths of cocaine use, he parked his car on a street in South Beach and just left it to gather parking tickets. Who do you think paid those tickets? Of course, I did. I didn't want Ryan to lose his license over $500 worth of tickets. What's $500, when it comes to helping your son? So I paid the tickets, and then admonished him never to do that again. Ryan promised (as always) to change his ways.

Another time, Ryan actually destroyed his car. He parked it on the street and accidentally locked his keys inside. He recklessly broke one of the windows to gain entrance, and then irresponsibly left the car parked with an open window. Over time, rain flooded the car, ruining its interior so that it had to be towed to a dump. I can't recall what happened to the other used car I bought him, but I'm sure it's in a junkyard where it sold for pennies on the dollar.

There I was again, buying Ryan another car from Don while Ryan promised not to be irresponsible. As I handed Don my check for $3,500, his face read like a book. "Please don't say a word, Don. I know what you're thinking," I said, pathetically.

"If you know what I'm thinking, then take the money back, and let him ride a bike," Don begged while trying to push the check back into my hand.

The car was registered in Ryan's name. I insured it for one year, and gave both Ryan and his car my blessings. All I wanted for Ryan was to be happy, to be healthy and to prosper in life. When he drove off in his car that was the path I hoped he would follow. I was a pro at setting myself up for disappointment!

Our next purchase was a cell phone. "Mom, just get me any phone that works. I don't need anything fancy. I just need one for finding a job," Ryan kindly said.

Was that my son speaking? Since when did he ever not want the best? "Pick out the one you want and get one of the basic plans," I replied. "Be sure you get enough minutes; otherwise you'll end up paying overage. Remember this time, you're responsible for the bills," I reminded him.

We put the phone in Ryan's name. All he needed to do was make his monthly payments. "I can't believe I finally have my own cell phone!" Ryan said cheerfully. "Do you realize this is the first time, Mom?"

No, I hadn't realized. How could I? I was buying the phone. I did realize this was significant for him, so I happily said, "Congratulations Ryan. Use it well and don't forget to call me when you get your first job!" We smiled and moved on to our next task.

I took Ryan to buy a new wardrobe. Naturally I couldn't expect him to find a job unless he was well dressed. We outfitted him to look very neat, clean, and preppie. Ryan had never been preppie in his entire life, but if I were willing to spend the money on clothes, he was willing to wear them. He agreed he looked great. With his new look, Ryan felt confident that he would find employment.

I promised myself that this was the last time I would bail my son out in an effort to *save* him. On June 7, 2002, almost one year to the day from writing my anger filled letter to Ryan, I wrote the following letter to myself:

ON HELPING MY SON.

My son returned to the States recently after I sent him $1000 to tie up his life in Germany and to fly home. I previously sent him $600 to use in Germany while he was trying to survive. When Ryan returned, we had many conversations regarding his current life and his past life. Ryan has matured considerably. He has finally decided it's time to grow up, get serious about life, set goals, and eventually pursue an education. I believe him. Others do not. I choose to believe him. Others choose not to.

I have seen Ryan's changes since quitting drugs. He is sober and sound. He is talented, and he deserves one more chance to be treated with dignity and respect. Until he respected himself, there was no way he could have benefitted from my good deeds in the past. I trust that Ryan has made a life-altering decision, and I believe he is capable of turning his life around from this point forward. I am leaving whatever happened in the past, where it belongs: in the past. No grudges. No guilt. We all have our paths to follow. Some are more challenging and difficult than others.

I have assisted him for the final time. I chose to believe him and in him, and in doing so, I invested a total of $7,282.00. A drop in the bucket to rebirth my child. Ryan has a clean start with a job as a waiter. Now, it's all up to him. I am not responsible for any of the liabilities he may create. Will I ever give him more money? Yes, but only if he is independent and has progressed in his life. If I find he has continued to party in any way, I will never aid him again. Ryan knows what I expect. I have chosen to have faith in Ryan. He is the only one who can destroy that faith. Time will tell.

This is my commitment to myself, and to the world, that should Ryan fail this time and fall back into his old habits that I will never help him again. Ryan needs to know I am serious; therefore, I intend to send him a copy of this letter. So Ryan, when you are finished reading this letter, please understand that I am very serious. I will always love you whether or not I hand you money again, but it's time for you to be a man.

With love always, Mom

Finding employment was easy. Staying employed was another story. Ryan just couldn't hold a job. He definitely lacked discipline. He either didn't show up for work at all, or he would show up late. By August, he had lost both his first and second jobs. Of course, I paid another $500 for his second month's rent. I kept telling him not to give up. I justified his irresponsible behavior, by using his maladjusted body clock as an excuse, after living in Germany. (I was very good at rationalization.)

It was mid-August when Michelle (Ryan's childhood sweetheart from Virginia) couldn't reach Ryan by phone, so she called me. "Hi Deni. It's Michelle," she said, in her soft, sweet, Southern accent.

"Michelle, what a pleasant surprise," I replied, quite surprised. I hadn't heard from Michelle in over four years. I had never told her Ryan married and moved to Germany. I had never wanted to break her heart. I knew she had a tender spot for Ryan. "How the heck are you?" I asked.

"I'm doing fine, but it's Ryan I'm worried about," Michelle said in a serious tone.

"What do you mean?" I asked in shock. "Are you here in Florida?"

"No, but I was. I visited him for a week recently, in his new town-house. I have been calling and calling, but he doesn't answer his phone, so I'm a bit concerned."

"For how many days has he not answered?" I asked calmly, think-ing perhaps he was working full-time, and had turned off his phone while sleeping.

"Today is the third day. That doesn't seem normal to me. I don't want to worry you, but I think you need to know he's drinking again. He's very depressed. It's his depression that has me concerned. I hope he doesn't do anything stupid if you know what I mean."

"I do know what you mean, Michelle, and I hope he doesn't either. He told me he stopped drinking and using drugs, and that's the *only* reason I helped him again. I am shocked!" I certainly did not expect to hear all of this from Michelle. Talk about being disappointed. How could I have believed he changed? Arthur was right. Ryan always disap-points me.

"Deni, please don't tell him I called you. He'll hate me," Michelle begged. "I think a huge part of his depression is because he knows he really screwed up again."

"Yes, he certainly has. If he's still alive, I'm going to kill him! I ap-preciate your concern for Ryan. I'll drive up there today to see how he's doing. If he's depressed, then he's probably sleeping a lot. I am very disappointed. It makes me extremely sad, Michelle."

"It makes me sad too," Michelle concurred. "I know deep inside that he truly is a good guy. It just sucks that he can't control his drinking. Would you call me after you see him, so I know he's all right?" Michelle asked.

"Absolutely I will. Thanks for the heads up, Michele. I'm sure it wasn't easy for you to call me. Please take care of yourself." Michelle agreed to take care of herself, gave me her phone number and then we hung up. I was so upset I wanted to scream. I wanted to strangle him with my own hands and shake some sense into him! How could he do this to me? (Of course, as his codependent mother, I immediately felt he did this to me. This is how the family disease affects us.)

I couldn't get dressed and into my car fast enough. Once on the road to Ryan's, I phoned one of my best girlfriends, Kat, who has an addicted brother. I told her what was happening with Ryan. She spent the next half hour in my ear, telling me how much money her brother drained from her parents, how they continuously enabled him, and how he never got off drugs because her parents kept giving him money. She went on and on lecturing me about my enabling, and how I had to cut him off before I did the same thing with Ryan. Her brother, now in his fifties, is still dependent on his parent's money and still using drugs. By the time I pulled up to my son's house, she had primed me like a pump!

I knocked. I impatiently waited a few seconds that felt like minutes, and because I had a key to his apartment I aggressively entered. "Hello?" I yelled into the darkness. No answer. "Ryan?" There was still no answer. I closed the door behind me. *God, please let Ryan be alive,* I silently prayed, while flicking on the lights. *Breathe, Deni breathe.*

I was utterly shocked. The home was totally trashed. Had I not seen it before, I would never have known it was the same place. Various brands of empty beer bottles littered the downstairs. There was almost no food left in the house. The kitchen sink had every dish piled inside. Food was crusted on plates while every glass had mold growing inside. The small downstairs bathroom reeked. Ashtrays filled with smelly cigarette butts were overflowing with ashes and stench. A bum wouldn't have lived there. I am not exaggerating. I was disgusted.

Slowly and silently I walked upstairs, afraid of what I might find.

I found Ryan in bed—breathing. He was fast asleep. More of the same repugnant mess surrounded him, and his room stank from the odor of beer. Now, I was even more disgusted. I kicked the bed to startle him awake. He was lucky I didn't kick him. "Ryan! Ryan, wake-up!" I screeched.

"What are you doing here?" Ryan demanded to know in a voice filled with contempt as if I were an unknown intruder.

Wanting to yell my head off at him, I dug deep to find restraint and then calmly said, "I came to check on you out of concern, but now that I know you're still alive, I want an explanation. You told me you stopped drinking."

"You have no right being in my home! I did not let you in! You need to leave, Mom!" He fired back at me with both barrels loaded.

"I need to leave? Excuse me! Who in the hell do you think you're speaking to?" I shot back in total disbelief. I felt like a ticking bomb ready to explode. The audacity of my son made my blood pressure escalate to points it had never seen. "What's going on with you?" I asked as calmly as I could speak. "Talk to me," I begged while trying desperately to control my anxiety.

"I'm depressed," Ryan moaned.

"You're depressed? How do you think I'm feeling right now?" I remarked sarcastically.

"I'm sorry Mom. I fucked up." His eyes never looked into mine, as he hugged his pillow to his scruffy, unshaven face.

"Sorry does not work anymore, Ryan. You can put the fucking pillow over your face, but you can't hide from the truth." I left his bedside in disgust. My brain was racing. I walked downstairs to think and to pace.

Anything of his, of any value, I noticed gone. "Where is your bike?" I screamed up the stairs in a burst of anger.

"I pawned it." Ryan yelled back also in anger. "I took it where you bought those gold earrings."

"You pawned it! Why doesn't that surprise me? Well, I'm going to go get your bike. Consider it mine," I shouted like a crazed person.

Of course, this wasn't the first time he pawned his possessions. When he studied graphic design in South Beach (while high on cocaine), he pawned every piece, of computer and photography equipment I had bought for him. Ryan even sold his candy-apple-red Gibson, collector's electric guitar, that he "just had to have," and that I "just had to buy" to keep him happy.

In frustration and anger, I stormed out of Ryan's apartment. I headed directly to the pawnshop intending to take possession of the $1000 bike, as a way to recoup part of the money I had apparently wasted. Ryan pulled himself out of bed, followed me in his car, and then went into a fit of rage when I again told him I wanted his bike.

"There is no way I am going to give you the bike. It's mine, and I need the money," he shouted.

"Ryan, I have given you over $7,000, and I want the bike to cover part of my losses."

"I don't care what you want. It's my bike, and I'm pawning it," Ryan defiantly said with such disrespect that I went into a state of shock. I was literally shaking.

We continued in a verbal sword fight, outside the pawnshop as if we were two maniacs. Anyone who might have seen us would have thought we were nuts. I suppose, in retrospect, I was nuts at the time. My son finally had pushed me to the brink of losing my sanity.

(As an aside: Today, I understand that I allowed my son to push me to the brink of losing my sanity. I was a major participant in our craziness, as the codependent mother.)

"No, you are not pawning it." I screamed back at him. My body was so filled with tension I was ready to explode. I headed into the store like a bull, only to be told that unless my son released the bike to me that it was his and not mine. Stunned, I went back outside to do further battle. "Sign the bike over to me now, Ryan!" I demanded.

"I told you the bike is mine. You're a horrible mother, and I hate you!" Ryan screamed at the top of his lungs while drooling and with spit coming out of his mouth like a rabid dog.

His using the, I hate you card, was not going to work this time. Though shaking, I stood my ground. "I love you, but I hate your behavior at the same time," I yelled back. "I hate the person you have become. I don't even know you anymore. I am not going to continue paying your rent while you drink and drug. I want you out of the apartment. You have two weeks to move out. The son I remember is gone. You need to be on anti-depressants." *Oh my God, did I really just say all that?* I was hyperventilating. Now, I too had spit flying out of my mouth.

"Great Mom, you tell a drug addict to take drugs. That's real smart," Ryan retaliated sarcastically.

"I did not tell you to take drugs. You need professional help. I can not help you any longer," I angrily said in my defense.

"You'll be sorry Mom. I'll never speak to you again," he snarled. Then, he turned his back and walked away from me, as if, he was the parent and I was the child.

"Call your old girlfriend, Michelle, maybe you can go live with her. You need to get out of Florida and away from all your loser friends. I'm done!" I yelled to him, in my last desperate attempt to help. I opened my car door while falling into the seat and then slammed the door shut in an effort to find refuge.

We parted in such anger. Anger that ran so deep into my guts I was shaking. As soon as I drove away from the pawnshop's parking lot, I pulled off to the side of the road, where I thought Ryan could not see my car. And, when I tell you I cried my heart out, I literally cried my heart out. In my heart and soul I knew I lost my son. I felt as if I gave my son a death sentence. I was bleeding internally. I had just turned my back on Ryan. In the pit of my stomach, I feared he would die without my help. I had just walked away from my only child and left him to his own devices. I cried and cried and cried and cried until I had no fluid inside my body. I was cried out and mentally exhausted.

After an hour of blowing my nose (wondering how I had so many mucus stored in my head), I took a few deep breaths and pulled myself together enough to drive forty minutes home. That was the longest and hardest drive of my life. I felt anguished, depressed, guilty, hopeless and defeated, believing my son was going to die. How can I bare this pain? In a daze, I staggered into our home, dropping my purse to the floor. I then stood in the family room with its ceiling-high picture windows, faced upward to the Universe's blue sky and began speaking out loud to my Higher Power God. With tears pouring from my eyes, sobbing like an animal run over and left dying on the side of a road, I cried out, asking:

How does a mother turn her back on her son,
When her son is lying in the gutter?

How does a mother turn her back on her son,
When she knows, he truly has no one other?

2
Mom's Opera

FROM THE FAMILY ROOM, I RAN into my office. The words I had just spoken resonated inside of me. I sat at my computer keyboard where I rapidly typed what I had just asked of my God. And then, as if my Higher Power spoke right into my ear, I heard answers. I heard them as songs. Then, as answers were poetically whispered in my ear, I wrote. I wrote for four hours. I cried. I wrote. I cried. I wrote. Sometimes I could not type fast enough. While other times I couldn't even see through my tears enough to type. I found solace in writing. My fingers flew across the keyboard the day I began practicing tough love as I wrote:

Mother
How does a mother turn her back on her son,
When her son is lying in the gutter?
How does a mother turn her back on her son,
When she knows he truly has no one other?
I can't.
But, I know that I must.
Though my heart is ready to bust.
Voice
I'll tell you how she does.
She looks in his eyes, and she sees all his lies,
And, she says, I don't deserve this.
But, he says...
Son
Don't you see—it's all about me?
Can't you see the pain that I'm in?
Can't you see I'm dying inside?

Mom
Then, die if you must, 'cause it's killing us,
And I can't go on seeing you as you are.
Who are you today? I do not know.
Where did the perfect baby I birthed go?
What roads did you take?
How did your heart break?
Which paths have you known that brought you to your knees?
Please, tell me my son, so you can stop running away.
Son
Mother dear, my Mother dear, dear Mother I do not know.
When I was young, I heard the songs that you sung,
They were loud, beautiful and clear.
But, Mother dear,
As time passed by and seasons changed,
Life went on, and we grew apart.
The paths I took were mine alone,
And, as I walked I changed my talk,
I changed my point of view.
I thought of me and only me,
And Mother dear, I didn't think of you.

And, now I must pay the tolls on this road,
For this road comes at a high cost.
It cost the loss of those, who truly loved me.
It cost my self-esteem.
It cost my will to live.
It cost my sense of *Self.*

I spent my youth planting seeds,
That grew like weeds to smother me.
They smothered me.
I barely see.
I barely feel.
I barely know from day to day,
How I will live.

I have no air,
I have no sunshine in my world,
I have no friends.

I have my art.
I have my paintbrushes.
I have my paint.
I have my canvas.

I stopped writing at this point. I remembered somewhere in our home was a painting Ryan did back in 1999 while living in the loft above my computer company. This painting was done during the time he was partying hard in South Beach, drinking, snorting, and dropping ecstasy and other pills. He had taped a large sheet of brown paper to the loft wall and like a graffiti artist, used spray paint to do the painting.

All I wanted to do, at that exact moment, was to see his painting. I needed to find it. I had no idea where it was hiding in our home, but that one painting represented my son's voice. That one painting was all I had left of him. I felt as if I would be holding Ryan while holding his painting. My fear and loss of control was driving me crazy, beyond all reasonable and emotional sanity.

I got up from my desk, running around the house like a crazed animal pulling things off shelves, rummaging through closets, and attacking every possible spot where I might have stored this one painting. I finally found it, rolled up in the corner of my closet, buried behind my clothing. With tears pouring from my eyes, I unrolled it. I sat trembling and cried my heart out again. Seeing my son's pain in his painting was overwhelming. *How could I not have seen his pain three years ago? Where had I been?*

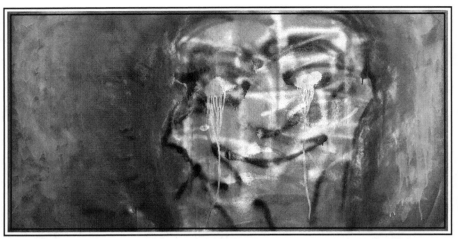

Once I regained my composure, I sat again at my computer. Instantly, I heard music once more and pounded out the rest of the song. It felt as if my computer keyboard was a piano keyboard, though I had never played piano in my life. I will say while typing, I felt a connection through my Higher Power to what a maestro feels while composing. I truly was a vehicle for divine inspiration, as I continued:

Son
When I am alone,
Which is most of the time,
I pick up a brush as I feel the hush of my pain,
I hear the hush of my pain,
It gushes to my veins,
It gushes to my heart—it gushes to my heart,
And, that is how I do my art.

I paint. I paint. I paint until I faint.
I paint. I paint. I paint just like a saint.
I dip my brush.
I dip my brush.
And, in the hush of my pain,
I stroke. I stroke.
I stroke upon the canvas.
I stroke upon the canvas.

I spread my pain all around in colors bright and red,
And, sometimes while I paint,
I wish I were dead, instead.
But, I still stroke. I stroke. I keep myself alive.
I strive. I strive. I strive to stay alive.

So I paint. I paint. I paint. I stroke. I strive.
For Mother dear,
Oh, Mother dear,
I'm your child.
I want to stay alive.
I want to stay alive.
Mother
Strip yourself to your soul child,
Strip yourself and be bold.
Deal with your fears,
Stop holding in tears,
Drain yourself of your pain.

Strip yourself to your heart child.
Strip yourself and be smart.
What you feel is real,
It's the real deal,
Drain yourself of your pain.
Son
I don't know where to start.
Mother
May I suggest your heart?
Son
I don't know what to do.
Mother
I'll walk along with you.
The road may be winding,
The road may be long,
But, it is worth the trip.
If you stay steady,
If you stay strong,

Your life will be in your grip.

It may take years.
You'll change some gears,
First you'll go fast then slow.
But, in the end,
Your best friend,
Will be your *Self* to know.

You'll say, Hello!
Hello to your *Self.*
Self, how do you do?
I'm so glad that we've met,
Together we'll see life through.
Together.
Together.
Together.
You'll be together, as in whole.

Son
Mom, you really think I can find out—who I am?
Mother
Absolutely.
Son
Do you really think one day, I'll be able to stay centered?
Go back to school, get a degree, find out who I'm meant to be?
Mother
Absolutely.
Son
But, I'm near twenty-six, and I just know tricks.
Do you really think I can stop the illusions?
Mother
Absolutely.
Absolutely, absolutely, absolutely, absolutely,
But remember, there are no absolutes.
Absolutely, absolutely, absolutely, absolutely,
Just remember, there are no substitutes.

Son
Substitutes?
Mother
Yes, substitutes.
The substitute for right's NOT wrong!
The substitute for good's NOT bad!
When faced with a choice,
Listen to your inner voice.
Son
The devil?
Mother
No, there's an angel inside.
Let it be your guide.
Make the right choice,
Then, rejoice in your power.
Son
My power?
Mother
Your power!
You have the power to be.
You have the power to see.
You have the power to live as you choose.
Use that power my son.
It's a powerful gun.
Shoot yourself to the moon!
There isn't anything you cannot do.
Your mind will carry you through.
Believe in your *Self.*
Discover your wealth.
Once you know who you are—you'll go far!
Son
But,
I used to snort,
I used to sniff,
I even inhaled glue.
I used to drink,
I used to smoke,

I dropped ecstasy, too.
Was a child running scared, felt nobody cared,
Felt nobody understood me.
Was a child running—free,
Wanted no holds on me.

I was always rebelling, but didn't know why.
I was always going against the flow.
If you said, yes—
I'd say, no.
If you said, go fast—
I'd go, slow.
I was always rebelling,
At the same time selling,
My *Self* to the devil below,
It was always so easy,
To do what was sleazy,
I had no conscience to tell me, no.

Mother
Where did your conscience go?

Son
I don't know.

Mother
Where did your feelings hide?

Son
I don't know.

Mother
Did you have any pride?

Son
No.

Mother
Did it bother you to lie?

Son
No.

Mother
Did it bother you to steal?

Son
No.
Mother
So, you really didn't feel?
Son
No.
No, no, no, no, no.
And, neither did my friends.
It hurt too much to feel.
Our pain was very real.

I came from a broken home.
My friend's homes were broken, too.
This turned our red hearts blue.
This tore our hearts in two.
One piece went with our fathers.
The other stayed with our mothers.
This turned our psyches,
So, we picked bad sidekicks.
Sidekicks
Traumatized at the age of 2.
I was 3.
I was 6.
I was 9—turning tricks.
I was 13— going on 20.
So, you see our problems many.

Who do we live with?
Where do we stay?
With, Mother by night.
And, Father by day.
This weekend's Mom's.
Next weekend's Dad's.
Mom has no support money,
So, this makes Dad bad.
And, this makes me sad.
I didn't want a bad dad.

So, Mom takes a night job,
To make ends meet.
We're now home alone,
Trouble's waiting on the street!

When I finished, I went back to the top and without any hesitation, titled it, *Mom's Opera*.

I don't know about you, but the few times I have gone to watch an opera it just seemed like the singers poured their hearts and souls out in clear and emphatic Italian lyrics. Though I had no idea what they were saying, the emotions emitted through both music and lyric penetrated deep into my being. I felt their pain, sorrow, and ecstasy. For me, what I had just written was my personal opera.

When I stood up to stretch, I felt counseled. I knew at that moment what I had just written and the emotions just voiced were therapeutic. My Higher Power had answered my questions of *how* and held my heart while guiding my hands. If not for the divinely inspired universal knowledge I received, I now believe I could have lost my sanity that day. At that precise moment I knew, beyond a shadow of a doubt, I had done the right thing in my act of *tough love* with Ryan.

Applying tough love meant Ryan needed to start being responsible for the choices he made. I no longer could continue rescuing him by financing his deteriorating lifestyle. Tough love also meant I had to be willing to let Ryan kill himself with his drinking and drugging if that's what he chose to do. Only Ryan could change his life. I was powerless. That is why tough love is so challenging and painful for parents and other loved ones.

Tough love takes discipline because it is extremely difficult. Letting go of our children when they are in the grips of addiction goes against everything we are accustomed to doing. Our role as parents has been to love our children, to protect them and to catch them when they fall. These roles alter when our child becomes addicted. We must learn to live and to play by new rules because the old rules no longer apply. These new rules take practice. And, like most achievements in life, one must practice, practice, practice, to succeed. Just like our addicted children we relapse. With each relapse, we become stronger and stronger until; ultimately, we hit our rock bottoms! Then, just like our addicts, our way out, is up.

I had threatened Ryan hundreds of times, telling him I was going to monetarily cut him off and not pad his life if he didn't change. But I never did what I said until I hit my rock bottom, came out of denial, and honestly did not recognize my own son. A monster, called addiction (a disease as defined by the American Medical Association), had control of Ryan. Until Ryan was ready to free himself of that monster, I was helpless. The day I did tough love, it felt as if I had literally turned my back on Ryan.

We wouldn't speak for nearly seven months. That was tough.

3
Michelle to the Rescue

FORTUNATELY, RYAN HAD ENOUGH SENSE TO realize I meant business this time when I told him to move out. This led him to return Michelle's calls and to ask her for help.

Michelle was a very levelheaded and successful young woman. She graduated college as a math major, still lived in her hometown, was gainfully employed, had her own apartment, and taking postgraduate courses when Ryan reached out to her. Since dating Ryan, at fifteen, she'd been involved in two other, unsuccessful love affairs. Being a positive person, however, Michelle believed the apple cart still held a good apple for her. She anticipated that apple was Ryan.

As a young boy, Ryan had been a good apple for Michelle and he remained special to her over the years. They spent many childhood days laughing together and having fun. It was those memories Michelle held onto, endearing Ryan to her. She clearly remembered the adorable, pre-drug and alcohol Ryan. He smoked cigarettes while in military school as I had given him permission, thinking cigarettes were better than pot. Plus, if he had been caught smoking cigarettes without my permission, he would have received demerits and punishment. He didn't have any problems with amphetamines or cocaine at fifteen, but Michelle knew he had experimented with pot and alcohol.

When Ryan called Michelle for help, I imagine, he told her everything she wanted to hear (knowing him), because before I even knew what was happening, she flew to Florida with the intentions to drive back to Virginia in Ryan's car. It was the beginning of September and less than two weeks from our blowout. Ryan and I were still not speaking, so I didn't get to say good-bye, I didn't give him a hug, and I didn't get to participate in his departure.

All I got was a filthy townhouse to clean, and three more months of rent to pay. Three years prior I cleaned another apartment Ryan destroyed in South Beach. I experienced déjà vu. These "clean up duties" were what I did in my diseased codependency, so I could get my security deposits back and maintain my integrity as a responsible parent.

Ryan hated me at this point. I was the bad mother, and he planned to punish me. He intended to make my life miserable by not speaking with me and by my not knowing where he went or whether he was dead or alive. He ultimately expected me to apologize to him for doing tough love. (That's the mental disease of addiction—a totally altered thought process.)

I knew from Michelle that Ryan moved into her apartment. She told Ryan she did not expect anything from him financially and that she only wanted to be his friend. She understood he was depressed and moneyless, so she didn't expect him to contribute until he found employment. Michelle became Ryan's harbor in the storm. (Unfortunately, what she became was his mother substitute, and his next codependent enabler.)

Michelle had more patience than imaginable. Later she would tell me, she believed she was the only person in Ryan's life, who intimately knew him deep inside, under all his pain. She truly felt, in her heart, that she could help Ryan out of his drug and alcohol addictions. She didn't focus on the dysfunctional Ryan. She saw the sweet, innocent Ryan from by gone days. It was *that* Ryan she yearned to rekindle through her kindness and love.

Michelle had no idea what she was in for when she took Ryan back into her life. Rescuing Ryan became more than her two shoulders were capable of handling alone. Michelle had barely left Virginia most of her life. Michelle didn't lie. Michelle didn't steal. She got up every day and went to a responsible position in a large corporate environment. She didn't party. She didn't smoke. She never ever used drugs. She hardly even drank alcohol. But, she cared about Ryan. Michelle loved Ryan. She didn't expect anything in return. She only wanted to see Ryan happy and healthy, and to rediscover the qualities he possessed when they first met ten years earlier. Michelle knew they were locked inside of Ryan. She wouldn't give up. She just needed to find the key.

Michelle became an expert enabler. Just like Mom. This only served to postpone Ryan's agony and recovery. There are no shortcuts in recovery for the codependent or for the addict. Eventually, however, my phone rang. Michelle was on the other end in total frustration.

"Deni, I need your help," she cried.

"What's going on Michelle?" I asked, praying I could provide the wisdom she needed. It was through Michelle's phone calls that I was able to know what was happening with Ryan.

"Ryan is just so depressed and lazy. I can't get him to function most of the time. He just wants to sleep and hasn't even looked for a job. I'm getting frustrated. I don't know what to say or do to help him without causing an argument," she cried.

I knew how draining Ryan had been on my life, as an addict. I certainly didn't want him to drain Michelle. "Michelle, Ryan is an alcoholic and a drug addict. Until he wants to quit drinking and drugging, he isn't going to change his behavior. Do you know if he's still drinking or using drugs?" I asked.

"I know he still drinks beer, but he promised me he wasn't using drugs. Besides, he has no money for drugs. I buy the beer for him. If I don't, he gets mad, and I can't deal with his anger."

"By buying his beer you are enabling him to continue to live as an alcoholic. You are not responsible for Ryan's life. He is responsible for his own life. You need to know, if at any time, it becomes too difficult for you, you need to tell him to move out. Ryan sucked my blood for years, Michelle, and I do not want him to suck yours."

"I know Deni, but if I kick him out he has no place to go. He doesn't know anyone here. I am just afraid for his life. I am so frustrated, that I want to kick him, yell at him, and tell him how stupid he is, but I don't like fighting, so I keep my mouth shut."

"He needs to know how you feel Michelle. You love him as much as I do, or you wouldn't be putting up with him. When he's not drinking, tell him how you feel. Let him know you won't tolerate his laziness, and that you'll only carry him financially for a limited time. Give him a deadline. He needs to know you won't tolerate his irresponsibility and his drinking forever," I lectured.

"Thank you Deni. It helps me to speak with you. And, I do love your son."

"I know you do. And, I love him too, but sometimes tough love is what he needs and I don't think you are capable of doing that yet."

"No, I'm not. I'm still hoping he'll open up to me through my patience and kindness. I just need to give him more time," Michelle said sweetly.

"I understand Michelle. And, I'm always here for you whenever you need to talk." I hung up praying for Michelle and Ryan. It had taken ten years before I was able to do tough love with my son. I prayed it wouldn't take Michelle that long to see the light.

I don't know when their relationship went from friends to lovers, but eventually it did. As a symbol of their love for one another, they adopted a four-legged child from the local humane society and named her London. London was a longhaired, short legged, multi-colored mixture of a mutt who would eventually play a key role in Ryan's recovery process.

4
Mellow Yellow

RYAN CONTINUED DRINKING until the first part of November, when his skin started turning yellow. Ryan and Michelle went to see a doctor. The results of the lab work showed that Ryan had contracted Hepatitis.

Did that ever scare him! Ryan had never been sick as a child. He had perfect health. At twenty-six, Ryan had not even a cavity. Now he learns he has hepatitis. In my opinion, Ryan's hepatitis couldn't have come at a better time!

The doctor told Ryan if he didn't stop drinking he would destroy his liver and die. At this young age, he didn't want to die of cirrhosis. I'm sure the doctor may have exaggerated the diagnosis to make his point. But, whatever he said, it worked. Ryan stopped drinking that day.

After being sober for a while, Ryan was able to find employment as a waiter. He worked part time, started making a modest income, and was able to contribute to Michelle's living expenses. Because of Ryan's inability to manage money, he agreed to give all his earnings to Michelle with the understanding that she would manage their funds. Michelle feared that if Ryan kept pocket money he might be tempted to buy drugs.

While recovering from hepatitis, Ryan became "Mr. Clean." He became an angel. After all, he was *scared to death*. As months passed, however, and Ryan recovered his healthy skin tone and felt better, sadly, his angelic *Self* disappeared, and his addict, diseased mind started to return.

Ryan assured Michelle he wasn't drinking or using any drugs. He told Michelle the only thing he was using was nicotine. She believed him and accepted his smoking. After all, Michelle knew Ryan was human. But Michelle insisted Ryan smoked outside and not in the house, and that he was never to bring illegal drugs into her home. She adamantly told him, if she ever found drugs in her home he'd be kicked out.

Well, on one of Ryan's cigarette smoking jaunts outside with London, he met a cute, young, neighbor girl, who thought he was cool. Evidently, the two of them fooled with drugs together, and she hooked Ryan up with her friends, who were also into drugs. Ryan now had a *source*.

Through his source, Ryan started buying small amounts of cocaine with money he was withholding from Michelle. He concealed the coke within his clothing, inside his closet. Then one day by mere accident, Michelle discovered Ryan's *stash* and freaked out. My phone rang.

"Deni, it's Michelle. I don't know what to do!" she cried, in a voice tone I had never heard coming from her lips. Gone was her southern drawl and sweetness. Michelle was in full panic.

"What happened? Tell me," I responded, half with the dread of knowing.

"Ryan's lying to me, withholding money from me, and I just found cocaine inside his pant pocket while I was looking for loose change. I am so pissed off at him I could kill him. I told him never to bring drugs into my home. And now I know he's been lying to me about not doing drugs. Shit. I am so pissed off, Deni. I don't know what to do!"

"You should be pissed off, Michelle. Confront him. Tell him you know about his cocaine; that you want him to move out and that he broke your rules." Michelle was taking my place in Ryan's life, and I didn't want to see that happen. I was as angry, and as disappointed as she was.

"I will confront him. I do want him to move out. I am not going to have my life ruined by having drugs in my home. I'm sorry Deni, but this time I'm done."

"Don't be sorry Michelle. You have relentlessly tried to help Ryan. Addicts think only about themselves and about getting their drugs. You need to stand up for yourself."

"I will Deni. When he comes home tonight, I am going to confront him. I can't do this anymore."

"Okay, well let me know how it goes. I'm here for you," I replied in kindness. When we hung up, I prayed for Michelle to be strong. And, at the same time, I worried about what was becoming of my beloved son. Was he going to drink and drug himself to death?

Michelle confronted him that night. In typical Ryan fashion, he tried turning the tables on her by getting mad. He became verbally aggressive and abusive with her for going into his closet and pockets, telling told her she violated his privacy.

When his aggressive approach didn't work, he did what he was very good at doing. He proceeded to sweet talk his way out of the mess and back into Michelle's heart by admitting to being a "bad" boy and by again promising to stop his drug use. These were the same techniques he used on me for most of his life. He was a professional at saying what others wanted to hear.

Ryan and Michelle were lovers at this point, so I'm sure it was more difficult for Michelle to stay firm and easier to soften and to be vulnerable to his pleas for forgiveness, than when they were just roommates. When we love someone, we don't want to give up. In a loving relationship, we commit to one another and try to work through issues. We try to trust our partners and to believe in them. Michelle was no different.

Michelle wanted to believe Ryan, just as I had wanted to for so many years. It's normal. Michelle pumps the same kind of blood we all do. So, her heart won out over her head. Ryan continued living with her while promising never to do any more drugs, never to lie, and never to withhold money again. He truly meant every word he said.

Ryan stayed clean for the next five months, or so, and Michelle kept me in the loop either by phone or by email. There were nights, though, when he left the house and drove off while Michelle was sleeping. Michelle had no idea where he went or what he did. She told me she didn't want to become his "mother." She felt if he needed to go out, then she needed to trust him. During these times, Michelle took deep breaths, tossed and turned, and eventually went back to sleep, praying he would be okay. Fortunately, her prayers were being answered.

In time, once Ryan started dealing with his anger issues and was willing to listen to Michelle's logical explanations of how much I loved him, and how hard I had tried to help him, Ryan started owning his part in our deteriorated, dysfunctional relationship. Once he was not using drugs and alcohol, and when his mind had time to clear, Ryan understood how much I did love him. He realized that his past actions were very irresponsible and had warranted my actions of tough love.

Once he reached this point of understanding, we were able to speak again. Unexpectedly, one day in early April 2003, my phone rang.

"Hi Mom, it's Ryan."

I only could imagine how hard it was for him to call me after going so long without speaking. So, I was extremely careful with my words. "Hi there. What a pleasant surprise to hear your voice! How are you doing?" I sweetly asked. Of course, I knew how he was doing by way of Michelle, but wanted to give him the chance to tell me.

"I'm actually doing great right now. I haven't had a drink or drugs for five months," Ryan said with pride.

"Wow, that's wonderful, Ryan! I'm so proud of you!"

"Thanks, Mom. I drank so much beer, that I contracted hepatitis last November. The doctor recommended quitting, before it killed me. So, I *had* to quit drinking.

"Well, I'm glad you took the doctor's advice, Ryan. You must be doing much better now that you can think straight."

"Yep, I really am. I have a job as a waiter, so I'm finally making money. Michelle and I are doing well. How are you doing, Mom?"

"I'm happy, Ryan. I miss you, but I'm very happy with my life. I'm planning to get married this May. Would you and Michelle like to come to our wedding?"

"Sure. Where is it going to be and when is it?" Ryan asked with such joy in his voice.

"It's going to be here in Fort Lauderdale on a big party boat we've rented. It's at sunset on May 24. It should be very nice. Now that I know you're sober, I'll put an invitation in the mail for you and Michelle. I'm so excited that you'll be able to attend."

"Me too, Mom. I'm really happy for you and Arthur. You deserve to have a good life."

"So do you, Ryan. All of us deserve to be happy. I'm glad you're getting your life together. That alone, is the best wedding gift I could receive."

"Would you like to come up and visit us?" Ryan asked.

I was shocked that he wanted me to visit. "Yes, of course I would. I'd love to see you again. I miss you. I love you so much." I was glowing. I was beaming with pure joy.

"I miss you also, Mom. And, I love you too," Ryan said sweetly.

"I know you do, Ryan. We'll never stop loving each other. We just need to work through our issues, that's all. And it sounds as if you're on the right path. I'm very happy for you, Ryan. I'm glad things have worked out with you and Michelle."

"Thanks, Mom. I'm happy for me too."

We ended our conversation with love oozing out of us. I immediately made plans to visit a few weeks later, as I became ecstatic with the idea of seeing my son sober and alive!

5
Ryan's Artwork

WHEN I ARRIVED FOR MY FIRST visit, I was totally unprepared for the many impassioned, powerful and emotionally moving pieces of artwork Ryan painted while coming off drugs and alcohol. I knew in the past Ryan liked to draw and paint to express his feelings, but never had I seen paintings that spoke so loud and clear of Ryan's pain. My heart cried in sadness by what I saw in Ryan's artwork.

I was witnessing the misery, agony, and suffering of my son's tormented soul. It was all being displayed in front of me, like an injured animal with its guts pouring out. I bled inside for my son. I felt his pain. Each painting held its own, unique distortion of the human face. Sadly, they were all faces of a tortured Ryan.

One particular self-portrait (Painting 1) overwhelmed me. If you recall, in *Mom's Opera*, I had written about the pull of *good* and *evil* the day I did tough love, saying to Ryan:

Mother
Yes, substitutes.
The substitute for right's NOT wrong!
The substitute for good's NOT bad!
When faced with a choice,
Listen to your inner voice.
Son
The devil?
Mother
No, there's an angel inside.
Let it be your guide.
Make the right choice,
Then, rejoice in your power.

Son
My power?
Mother
Your power!

Now there I was standing in front of this near life-size self-portrait of Ryan, where he painted himself standing with the lower half of his body in the orange, red and yellow flames of hell and with his upper body in the blue skies of heaven. He painted both the halo of an angel and the horns of the devil on his head.

It seemed apparent to me, seeing both hands painted inside his pant pockets that he was contemplating whether to listen to his internal demons (symptoms of the disease of addiction), or the angel inside (the innocent child, born perfect). I believe the painting captures him at the exact moment in time when Ryan makes his decision, and yet, one cannot discern his choice. He gives nothing away. For me, it was an extremely thought provoking painting.

Upon seeing this painting, I realized we had both acknowledged the same pull of opposing forces at work within Ryan's life, and had both expressed it through art. It was as if Ryan had tapped into the same vibrational energy I felt while writing Mom's Opera. We were on the same wavelength, connected by universal mind energy. I wrote. Ryan painted. We both voiced. We both vented.

Painting 1

Painting 2

Painting 3

Painting 4

Painting 5

Painting 6

Painting 7

Painting 8

Painting 9

Painting 10

Painting 11

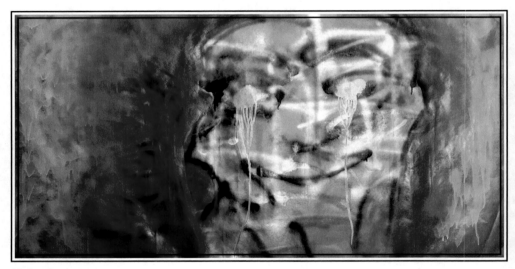

Painting 12

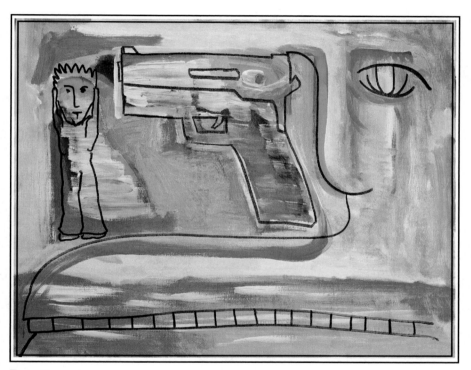

Painting 13

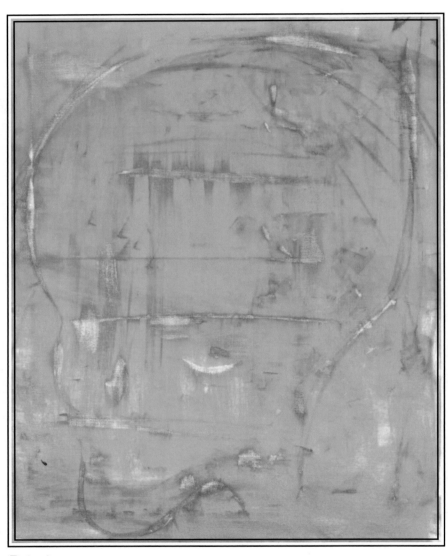

Painting 14

Painting 15

Painting 16   Painted 2010 (*after rehab*)

It's difficult to describe artwork when artwork is so personal and speaks differently to everyone. Seeing the pain Ryan painted into his art, I have to believe, just like writing was the vehicle I used to maintain my sanity, painting provided the vehicle for Ryan to maintain his sanity while coming off drugs and alcohol. I wrote an entire song in *Mom's Opera* that had described my son painting to keep himself alive. You can imagine how I felt, as his mother, seeing these paintings. Paintings that I know kept Ryan alive!

The lyrics I wrote in *Mom's Opera* kept resonating in my head:

I stroke upon the canvas.
I stroke upon the canvas.
I spread my pain all around in colors bright and red,
And, sometimes while I paint,
I wish I were dead, instead.
But, I still stroke. I stroke. I keep myself alive.
I strive. I strive. I strive to stay alive.

So I paint. I paint. I paint. I stroke. I strive.
For Mother dear,
Oh, Mother dear,
I'm your child.
I want to stay alive.
I want to stay alive.

See Ryan's artwork at: *www.HOPEaddictionBook.com*

6

Blame

WHEN I FINALLY WENT TO BED THE first night of my visit, Ryan's paintings haunted me. I felt so sad for my son. It depressed me that my young son had suffered so much in his life. Saddened and exhausted emotionally by what I had seen, I cried myself to sleep.

The next morning I tried putting my feelings of sadness behind me while looking instead at how wonderful my son was now. The two of us went out for breakfast looking forward to a day of reconnecting. Naturally, I fell head first into my enabling behaviors, buying Ryan new clothes and providing things for him he couldn't yet afford. Much of our day together was enjoyable, but at times there was tension and stress between us. Ryan's anger toward me would flare, and he would abuse me verbally. It became hard for the two of us to be together. It felt like I was walking on egg shells most of the day. The anxiety I felt was horrible.

That night, within the shelter of my bedroom, I went to bed with horrible feelings of guilt and sorrow. Tossing and turning I tried finding escape in sleep. I wanted so badly to take away Ryan's anger and pain. Feelings of sadness led me to write the following lyrics on blame and forgiveness that started playing in my head:

"For Many Years"

Mom
For many years, I always blamed me.
For many years, I just couldn't see.
No matter what I did, it wasn't enough.
The more I loved him—he'd grow tough.

Son
For many years, I always blamed Mom.
For many years, I just couldn't see.
No matter what she did, it wasn't enough.
The more she loved me—I'd grow tough.
Both Together
Our heads were always bashing.
Our anger made us blind.
Son
My hurts had turned to anger.
Anger led to rebellion.
Mom
Anger led to frustration.
Both Together
Our blindness led nowhere.
But, today—today we know,
Blame, is the wrong way to go.
Blame, does no one any good.
It's only through forgiveness,
That—we'll both be understood.

I then started thinking about how Ryan just needed to 'fess up to whatever he had done in his past. Once he 'fessed up he could move on with his life, feel free and find forgiveness of *Self* and others.

When I began hearing the following lyrics, I wholeheartedly thought I was projecting Ryan's feelings about fessin' up and that the lyrics had nothing at all to do with me. Then, as I continued writing, I began uncontrollably crying in horrible pain as the lyrics grew into being mine—my song. After the first twenty lines or so, I changed Ryan's name to Mom. *I realized then* that I was the one needing to 'fess up. By the time I finished writing this song, I was an emotional wreck:

"Fessin' Up"

Mom
I'm fessin' up,
Fessin' up to my crimes,

I want to make—make my life rhyme,
I want to put—put my steps in line.

I'm fessin' up,
Fessin' up to the truth,
Lookin' my *Self* in the eyes,
Dealin'— yes, dealin'—with problems, of my own youth.

Fessin' up,
Fessin' up, it's causin' some pain.
Yes, my fessin' up makes me hold tight to my reins.
Don't want to fall off,
Don't want to fall,
Don't want to fall off my horse again.
This fessin' up,
It sure ain't easy—it sure ain't easy.
But, this fessin' up—is what I must do,
If I want to be true,
And I do, I want to be true.
That's why I'm fessin',
Fessin',
Fessin' up.
Son
Mom,
Is that you?
Mom,
Is that true?
Are you saying?
Are you saying?
That the pain that I feel, is the pain that you feel, too?
Mom
Yes, it's true.
Son
Are you saying?
Did I hear?
You're fessin' up to crimes.
But, what crimes did you do?

Mom
My crimes were in not knowing,
How I was bestowing,
Hurts from my own life onto you.
It seems—it seems to me,
That life is perpetual motion.
Life is perpetual and we perpetuate,
Our painful lives onto the next generation.
And, you were the next generation for me.

I just didn't see—I just couldn't see,
Your life was left to me.
You were in my hands,
To raise alone,
I was unprepared,
To say the least,
I did the best,
That I could do,
But it seems I so failed you.
Son
Mom, you did your best,
Now the rest is left to me.
I realize, accepting the truth will set us free.
Both
Keep fessin' up,
Keep fessin' up,
I'll start fessin' up too.
If we both 'fess up,
And we both give up,
We will both grow, you'll see.
We can both begin,
To forgive our sins,
And love will begin to show.
Son
I was your little boy.
Mom
I was your young mother.

Son
You still are my young mother.
Mom
You're lying!
Son
No, I'm trying to tell you that—I love you.
You're my mother,
My young mother who did her best,
Although I failed,
My failure came, through years of blame.
But you really tried to be my guide.
Mom
I did my best.
Son
I know you did.
Mom
I didn't know how we would live.
There were bills to pay.
I struggled so.
Son
I didn't know.
Mom
Of course, you didn't.
I hid the truth.
We had no money,
To pay the bills,
But still we'd laugh,
And still we'd play,
When you were sleeping in bed I'd pray,
Oh help me God, lead me to light,
Give me the strength, to do what's right.
Both
So now we're fessin' up,
Both are fessin' up,
We're fessin' up, to truth.
Neither of us had perfect youths.
We're fessin' up,

Fessin' up,
Fessin' up to the truth.

Knowing that one needs to 'fess up and actually fessin' up are two entirely different things. It hit me like a ton of bricks. At the end of writing I asked my Higher Power God to help me and lead me to truth. Miracles take time. It would be another seven years before I would be emotionally able to process my repressed pains from my own childhood and 'fess up to my truths (which I do in chapter 48).

I'm quite sure my lyrics were right on target because we continued bashing heads during my visit. I felt blame was at the center of our issues. I believed there should be no blame. At this point in my journey, I felt it didn't matter, who did what to whom. What mattered to me was only forgiveness. I just wanted Ryan to forgive and to forget, so we could move on and be friends in our relationship as mother and son. Then over time, I believed, we could both heal.

(In hindsight: Because of my own denial, I had no idea how deep Ryan's wounds were; nor did I realize the tremendous amount of work involved in the recovery process. Because my finger was only pointing at Ryan, I ignored my own emotions that surfaced. I pushed them back down where they had laid buried for so many years.)

I focused on the good in Ryan's life. Overall, Ryan was doing great with not using drugs and alcohol. He had recovered from hepatitis and was staying out of trouble. Though he obviously had not dealt with any of his issues, or the triggers for his anger, he at least was staying clean and sober. I knew nothing about relapse, so I had no idea what the future held. At this point, I had never attended any of The Twelve Step programs for codependency, nor had I read any books on addiction or recovery. Thus far, writing was my only program.

In my own ignorance, I never thought Ryan would use drugs or alcohol again, and especially after having hepatitis. I thought he was smart enough to know better. I did not know being smart couldn't block the disease of addiction. I was still operating under the etheric disease of codependency, believing my son was over his addictions.

I had such mixed emotions. My son didn't die! My son was sober! I was walking on clouds. My son was clean! My son and I were talking again! It was thrilling. Yes, Ryan painted artwork during his battle with his monsters and the tortured soul of my son was blatantly evident (which freaked me out), but in my mind, I told myself those paintings represented his past. In my mind, I believed he had left all his pain on the canvas. I believed he had moved on, out of pain, and out of the monster's grip. I believed that he was the victor!

(In hindsight: I needed to think this way in my disease of codependency. A disease I didn't even know I had.)

I was on my own natural high. I had mounted my horse, gone into battle and felt victorious! My pen had kept me sane thus far. So my sword was working. I was writing my way through each battle. For the first time in years, I felt relief. Pressure was off. I could breathe. I was projecting my son's full recovery into the future and seeing him living happily ever after—just like me!

7

I Do I Do — I Am I Am

WHEN MY WEDDING DAY ARRIVED, ON May 24, 2003, my life couldn't have been any more perfect. Ryan was still sober and attended our wedding with Michelle. My ninety-one year old father gave me away... again while my ninety-year old mother danced and sang her heart out with pure joy at seeing her daughter genuinely happy and finally giving her heart to a wonderful man. The entire event was nothing short of spectacular. Arthur's son, who was his best man, made a most touching and heartfelt speech, toasting our marriage. Then Arthur and I went for a romantic honeymoon cruise.

Life was so good when we returned that I almost thought I had died and gone to heaven! I decided I needed additional inspiration for my musical. I hadn't seen a Broadway show in years, so I made plans to visit New York City. Since I was walking around telling others I was writing a musical that one day might become a Broadway show, it just seemed fitting! My dear husband (who half the time must have thought it was I who was on drugs) told me to go and to enjoy myself, if that's what I needed. So I did!

I purchased a little black book to use as my journal for when inspiration hit. There I was, in The Big Apple, writing. It was June 28, 2003:

> I begin this journal of thoughts while sitting at a window, overlooking 54th Street, inside the Iguana Restaurant. I am on a journey that took me to New York City, where I am finding all the inspiration, not just to follow my dreams and aspirations, but also to fulfill them. After seeing Gypsy last night starring Bernadette Peters, and then spending hours in Don't Tell Mamma's Piano Bar, I have had a great start! Later today I will

see Cabaret for the second time. Life is a Cabaret my friends…
and welcome to mine!!

As I bit into my Macintosh apple while walking around the
streets of NYC, it dawned on me that people either get eaten-
up by the Big Apple or they eat it up! I was eating it up! Juices
were flowing and not just in my mouth. My creative juices
have kicked in again. It's time. The time is now. This is my
commitment to *Self* and to others that I will write, publish and
produce a book, movie, or musical before I reach age fifty-five.
I'll be fifty-three in four days. (As an aside: I was ten years off.
I'll be sixty-three when this book gets published.)

While I was growing up and then continuing throughout
my life, all I ever heard was behind every successful man was a
woman. Well—I must say, behind me is a successful man, giving me the freedom to be Deni B. When I succeed at reaching
my goals, it will be because of the man behind me, my darling
husband, Arthur.

Things to do:
- Find a mentor for music.
- Start going to as many musicals with Arthur as possible.
- Clean garage.
- Organize my new office and set up computer.
- Discipline *Self* to work 5 hours per day toward earning
  money.
- Write two hours per day minimum on *Mom's Opera*.
- Work with Karen on music once per week.
- I'm also thinking I should put a comedy routine to-
  gether for Uncle Funnies and test the waters for my
  humor. Stand up truly makes me glow and feel alive.

My son just called from Virginia, and I find it amusing
that the tables have turned for us. I am unemployed while he
is working. This is a first in twenty-six years. The other funny
thing is, I was twenty-six when he was born, and he is twenty-
six now. Maybe twenty-six is the magical age for us both. I really like being the age I am—no matter what the age! It's a good

feeling, especially since we don't have a choice.

A nice thing for me is that although I am nearly fifty-three, I do have the choice to act my age or any age I desire. I absolutely love feeling twelve! I was twenty-one recently while putting my wedding together and felt twenty-one the day I married. I had all the emotions of a young bride, marrying for the first time. How many times have I been married? I plead the fifth!

With my creative juices flowing in NYC, I was feeling very good about both my life and my son's. On June 29, 2003, I wrote the following song:

"I'm Back"

I'm back.
I'm back.
Back, in the saddle again.
Riding life to the fullest,
Holding my reins very near,
Put my name on the "A" list,
I've come full circle, it's clear.
For, I'm back.
I'm back.
Back in the saddle again,
Pounding my heart as I ride,
Knowing life's an adventure,
Using my heart as my guide,
While tempered by knowledge for sure.
All can fall off our horses.
All can go off our courses.
But, we pick ourselves up, and we brush ourselves off,
As we say...
I'm back.
I'm back.
Back, in the saddle again.
This time I've learned from my actions.

This time they'll be no distractions.
But, there's no guarantee, no there's no guarantee,
You won't fall on your knees again.
But, if you do,
Just see *Self* through,
Feel the pains,
Grab your reins,
And climb back in the saddle again.
And say,
I'm back.
I'm back.
Back, in the saddle again!

I honestly did feel back in the saddle again. I felt my son was successfully on his road of sobriety. Overall things were going quite well. The initial fear I had when I did tough love, where Ryan might die, had passed. Little did I know that eventually Ryan would fall off the saddle, and little did I know how wonderfully he would pick himself up again and again and again, so perhaps the song had been a premonition!

While in New York City, I continued feeling positive. I thought about the friends I had in my life and how important one's friends are. Inspired to write the following poem, I drew an analogy between jewelry and friends:

"Friends Are Just Like Jewelry"

Friends are just like jewelry,
Some are silver, and some are gold.
Friends are just like jewelry,
Some are new, and some are old.
Friends, we put them on,
Some of us wear them well.
Friends, we put them on,
Some of them smell like hell.
But, the friends we choose,
Are ours to choose,
So, I suggest you choose well.
Take your time to dress,

Pick out your very best,
Match your personality, too.
For they're the reflection of,
The one you love,
When the one you love is you!

Along my journey, I realized more than ever, the importance of the friends we have in our life. I realized friends could make me a more beautiful person and enhance my appearance ever so more than jewelry. Jewelry, we put it on, and it's so easy to take off. Friends, however, enhance or detract from us for a very long time and influence our lives for as long as we allow. Allow is the key word. We all have a choice as to whom we choose to keep in our life's garden. I began seeing friends and acquaintances as flowers or weeds.

Weeds wrap themselves around, destroy, and ultimately kill. Flowers bring more beauty into one's garden of life. Why should I want weeds in my garden? That is one of the lessons I wanted Ryan to learn. Part of successful recovery is surrounding oneself with healthy people and not hanging around with old drinking and drugging buddies. That is one lesson I think everyone needs to learn. Choose your friends carefully. Stay away from weeds and seek out flowers!

(I would realize eventually that part of the codependent's disease includes allowing our children and others to take advantage of us because we have no boundaries. We allow weeds to choke us. We allow others to leave us feeling powerless. The book, *Emotional Vampires*, was published in 2012, focusing on the many types of people who drain others of their energy. My *weeds* are called vampires by its author, Albert J. Bernstein, Ph.D. I think it's a book worth reading.)

Though thrilled to be walking through the streets of New York City, taking in the sights, sounds, and smells, I couldn't stop reflecting on one of Ryan's paintings I'd seen when I visited him in May. A painting that had not only shocked me, but had made me cry. This painting affected me at my gut level. A level, that both tormented and empowered me at the same time. I did not want my son or any child, or any adult for that matter, to be in a position where they feel such horrible pressure. Pressure, as if there's a gun pointing to their head. Life should not be that painful. It empowered me to keep writing.

In my heart, I believed and told myself that both Ryan and I were on the other side of pain. As a naive parent, whose psyche was buried deeply in denial, I told myself the negative and painful feelings Ryan had when he painted the above painting were gone. I started positively *projecting* and creatively *visualizing* into the future; totally believing that one-day our lives (and eventually the story within the musical) would have a happy ending. That was when this song exploded inside of me. Ryan's painting was my inspiration:

"On The Other Side of Pain"

Ryan
I'm on the other side of pain,
I'm in control of my life again,
I've dug deep into my heart and soul.
I've seen the blackest black,
The wall has been at my back,
The gun has been pointed to my head,
I reached for life instead.

Like a baby starting to crawl,

Like a toddler wobbling to walk,
Like a newborn crying,
I started trying.

Today,
Today, I'm clean.
Today, I'm on my way.

I'm taking my parents,
Not letting the past stop my recovery.
One day at a time is my motto.
One day at a time is all I need.
One day at a time brings tomorrow.
One day, one step, at a time.
Mother and Father
I'm on the other side of pain,
We have our son in both our lives again,
We've dug deep into our hearts and souls.
We've seen the blackest black,
The wall has been at our back,
The gun has been pointed to our heads,
We reached for life instead.

Like a baby starting to crawl,
Like a toddler wobbling to walk,
Like a newborn crying,
I started trying to understand,
How I got to where I am.
Today,
Today, I'm clear.
Today, I'm on my way.
We're taking our son.
Ryan
I'm taking my parents.
All
Not letting the past, stop our recoveries.

That particular painting continued affecting me throughout Ryan's entire road toward recovering. After seeing it, I had so much more respect for the mental power and strength Ryan had used to stay clean, and I acquired more compassion for the emotional distress he had endured. I was ecstatic to have him back in my life—alive and sober. Yes, my son did reach for life instead!

8
Causes of Addiction

AFTER RETURNING FROM NEW YORK CITY, I started thinking about the various causes of addiction and all the children and adults around the world addicted to drugs and alcohol. I thought about how so many never get clean and stay addicted their entire lives, and how so many loved ones overdose. I started focusing my thoughts on the reasons a person might escape into drugs. Perhaps these characters will become Ryan's cohorts in the musical.

Once I began to write, my words kept flowing from one person to another and another, and I went off on different issues. But that's the way my brain worked. I pulled some of the personality traits from feelings I've felt throughout challenging times in my own life while others were those I just conjured up in my mind when I stopped to think why anyone would turn to drugs and alcohol, as a means of escape:

"Reasons We Become Addicted"

I came from a broken home,
This tore my heart in two.
One piece went with my mother,
The other with my dad,
This turned my red heart, blue.

My parents never parted,
Stayed married 'til they died.
Fought their entire marriage,
Happy family was a lie.
Always smiling in public,
Always the perfect pair,

Behind closed doors were monsters,
Just didn't seem real fair.
Stuck my fingers in my ears,
Led me to drinking beers,
Led me to men so wrong,
Who'd bed me once,
Then next day,
They were gone.

I, on the other hand,
Came from a family most grand.
Had everything you'd ever want,
Dining in five star restaurants,
Traveling first class around the world,
Wearing designer everything,
My jewelry was fit for kings.
But, the only thing I never, ever had,
Was the one thing I most needed, as a lad.
I needed to hear—just once in my life,
The words, I love you.
Never the words,
I love you.

I really had no excuse.
Had no trauma or child abuse.
Had no neglect.
Had tons of love.
Played lots of sports.
Got great grades.
Mom and Dad were there for me.
Went to college for my degree.
Lived with others in a dorm.
Started experimenting with other forms…of recreation.
First, it was a drink of only beer.
With a cigarette in my hand,
Due to pressure from my peer.
Beer turned to wine, then wine to liquor.

I was able to relax so much quicker.
Sex popped out of a zipper.
Started to feel a slight bit sleazy.
Someone suggested trying some pot.
So, I simply said, why not?
Pot worked for a while,
Made me laugh,
Made me smile,
Gave me munchies,
I grew like wild.
Gained some weight,
Was getting fat.
Didn't like being a fat girl,
So, I took diet pills for a cure.
Diet pills worked lickety-split.
Lost my weight, but could not sleep.
So, I took sleeping pills to help adjust.
Sleeping pills worked—were a definite must.
But, felt so groggy, when I tried to awake,
So, I took more diet pills for my own sake.
And, eventually to my surprise,
At the end of the day needed pills to close my eyes.
I needed, needed, needed my pills.
I became addicted—addicted to pills.

I feel funny.
Oh, so funny.
No, funny isn't really how I feel.
It's really funny.
No, it's not funny.
No, it's dirty, disgusting, and unreal.
For, I was a child of sexual abuse.
I say it laughing to cover my pain.
Yes, I say it laughing to cover my pain.
Do you know how it feels to have your childhood stolen,
By your father, brother, uncle, or a priest?
It stinks.

It smells.
It actually feels like hell.
The pain,
The scars run deep.
To ease the pain, I sleep.
To ease the pain, I drink and drug.
To push the pain, under a rug.

But, it's not easy.
No, it's not easy.
We all have our reasons.
We all have our pasts.
But, all our roads led us,
To the same destinations,
To the same desperations,
To the same solutions,
To the same illusions,
To the same destitutions,
To the same situations,
Just to different medications.
Whether it's a drink.
Whether it's a drug.
Whether it's an act of sex without love.
It's time to recover,
It's time to discover,
You.
It's time to discover,
Who,
You really are.

9
Facing Codependency

THEN, I STOPPED WRITING. I TURNED inward to reflect on the line I had just written: whether it's an act of sex without love. When I wrote that line, it struck an inner cord.

I knew I had spent most of my adult life having sex without love. I started looking more internally at my own shortcomings and not just at Ryan's. I was starting to see my own dysfunctional, codependent behaviors. For so many years, I focused on Ryan's issues and never truly stopped long enough to look at my own. Color me blind. I just didn't see. Better yet, I just could not emotionally allow myself to see the truth, so I remained deep in denial.

Denial is the mind's way of protecting us. It is a self defense mechanism employed by the subconscious mind in an attempt to protect our emotional and psychological wellbeing. Now, through writing, my buried memories and truths that I had denied for so many years, were surfacing little by little. I suppose little by little was the amount I emotionally could handle. I summed up my feelings in this way:

Now, I'm going to tell you our story.
About my son,
My only child,
Who became addicted to drugs and alcohol.
No, it didn't happen over night.
It happened over many years.
I suppose at some level I must have known,
But, denial blinded me.
When he did wrong, I made excuses.
When he was in debt, I bailed him out.

When he needed food, I fed him.
A roof over his head I would always provide.
He'd lie—I'd justify.
He'd steal—I'd make an excuse.
He couldn't hold a job, so I hired him.
I'd pay him wages for doing almost nothing,
For, at least he put in the hours.
I was enabling my son to be dependent.
I was enabling my son never to grow up.
I was allowing my son to live a life of an addict,
Without realizing it—for I was in denial.
Until the hardest day in my life arrived,
When, I did—tough love.

How does a mother turn her back on her son?

That question continued to prey on my mind throughout my journey. And, that is why I continued to write. My writings were my answers to doing tough love. My writings were the *wind beneath my wings.* My writings told me I was on track. I used my writings to confirm in my head that Ryan was okay, or that Ryan needed help, or whatever I needed confirmed at that moment. My writings were my saving grace.

My writings were also my way of not dealing with reality. Through writing I was creating a new reality for both my son and my *Self.* I wrote how I imagined Ryan felt, when I did tough love. I wrote in my imagination. I was able to sense imagined emotions and visualize imagined events, and it was those imaginings and possibilities that gave me *hope.* I needed *hope.* I clung to *hope.* I projected what I needed in order to keep my sanity. Writing my visions was keeping me positive and moving forward in unknown waters. Waters, where my own truths were slowly surfacing. Waters, where I could choose to drown in denial and codependency, or learn to swim as a healthy, fully functioning woman.

10

Everybody Needs a Michelle

I THINK ONE OF THE BIGGEST BLESSINGS both Ryan and I had was Michelle's influence on Ryan's life. I knew Michelle was a gift from God, which led me to write the following projection of Ryan's thoughts:

When my mother did tough love,
I hated her,
She hated me.
When my mother did tough love,
I was truly scared,
I could barely see.
I wanted to drink myself to death,
But, couldn't afford even a beer.
By the grace of God I was rescued,
By an old friend very dear,
Her name was Michelle.

Now, Michelle actually knew me,
From twelve years before.
We had been childhood sweethearts.
She had known me when I was clean and pure.
She had known the innocent child,
Before I closed my emotional door,
Before I tranquilized my pain,
Before I went a bit insane—she had loved me.
Michelle reached out to me when I was drowning in self-pity.
She threw me a life preserver,

But, I had to swim to it.
It was always a few strokes away.
She showed me a light at the end of the tunnel,
But, I had to find my own way.

Yes, Michelle was sent from heaven as an angel in my life.
Yes, Michelle was sent from heaven,
Perhaps, one day she'll be my wife.

There's a Michelle out there for everyone.
Your Michelle will be there too.
Michelle can come in many forms—
A friend, a teacher, a stranger on a bus,
Yet, it's up to each one of us,
To want to change,
To want to rearrange,
Our priorities.

Yes, Michelle was there for my son. Without a doubt, I know her actions were a huge factor in aiding Ryan to save his life. She was the one always throwing the life preserver, but Ryan had to save himself. Michelle could not save him. Ultimately, Ryan had to make the personal choice himself. He had to choose sobriety over drugs and alcohol. Ryan was adamant when he told me, "Michelle did not save my life." He firmly stated, "I saved my own life."

One thing I have had to learn is that *no one can save an addict but the addict.* This is an extremely valuable lesson for anyone, who loves an addict, and that is why I will repeat it throughout this book.

Whenever I stopped to think about how lucky Ryan was to have Michelle in his life, I thought how everyone needs and deserves to have someone who will love them unconditionally, and in spite of one's behavior. I had never witnessed anyone like Michelle who continuously showed love to Ryan with her sweetness, her patience and her compassion, and who just responded to Ryan in soft, loving, and gentle ways. I'm certain there was a halo over her head.

One day, I wrote these simple, yet meaningful lyrics about Michelle:

"Michelle's Song"

Everybody needs a Michelle,
Everybody needs a helping hand.
Everybody needs a Michelle,
Someone, who will understand.
And loves you,
And loves you,
And loves you,
Even when you don't—love you.

Whether it's a smile,
Whether it's a listening ear,
A shoulder to cry on,
A friend to rely on,
Someone, who'll lend you a dime.
Everybody needs a Michelle,
Everybody needs a friend.

Everybody needs a Michelle,
Someone, who will see you through.
Everybody needs a Michelle,
Someone who knows the real you,
And loves you,
And loves you,
And loves you,
Even when you don't—know who you are.

Michelle's maturity was way beyond her years. Yet every once in a while, when she felt she was dealing with something over her head or out of range of her understanding, she'd contact me. Together we'd formulate a game plan, and move forward in our efforts to guide Ryan through his recovery and into a life where he could not only start to dream about a future, but one where he, in fact, could create a future for himself.

When one starts using and abusing drugs and alcohol during their teenage years, one stops growing emotionally at that age. In my opinion, Ryan stopped growing emotionally around age fifteen. Though he was chronologically twenty-six when he first got clean, he had the emotions and maturity of a teenager. Once clean and dealing with life sober, the addict can start to grow and to mature at a pace they can handle, and/or at a pace they choose. It's totally about choices, and the effort one puts into their recovery (assuming there is no permanent brain damage or other issues beyond control).

11

Relapse

IT WAS NOW SUMMER, 2003. RYAN had been sober for eight months and doing quite well. His hepatitis virus had gone. His color returned to normal, and he began acting human again.

Though Ryan had no history of paying his own bills and no sense of the value of money, Michelle decided it was time for him to learn. Upon finding a well paying job, Ryan opened his first checking account in an effort to learn budgeting and how to handle his own finances. His bank had a policy where your account could be overdrawn $300 without penalty. That policy became a double-edged sword for Ryan.

Ryan found a job, as a restaurant manager, which gave a tremendous boost to his ego. However, he claimed he didn't enjoy the job, so he quit after only a few nights. I imagine he didn't feel capable of handling the day-to-day pressures associated with restaurant management at that point in his sobriety. And, that was okay. I'm glad he recognized those feelings and left the job before they had invested more time and money into his training.

After being clean for around eight months and after getting his new job and quitting, Ryan felt extremely good about his *Self* for the first time in a long time, and he was on a bit of an ego trip. I believe he thought he could conquer the world and part of his conquering included being able to handle drinking a beer. At this point, Ryan had never attended any Twelve Step programs. He had just quit drinking and drugging by using his own, sheer willpower.

Sometime in August, Ryan attempted to drink just one beer. Unfortunately, sheer willpower proved insufficient. The intended one beer led to two, then three, and then more. Within a couple of days, Ryan went to the nearest ATM taking $300 out to buy cocaine; his drug of choice. The disease returned full force. I found out a few weeks later that Ryan had come close to dying that night.

Michelle called me a few weeks later out of sheer panic and frustration, telling me of Ryan's nightmare with coke. She tried to handle Ryan herself, but he became too much of a burden to carry alone. She told me his throat swelled up so much he barely was able to breathe. Michelle thought he was going to die. She begged me not tell Ryan she told me as Ryan didn't want me to know. So, to respect Michelle's wishes, I didn't let on to Ryan (for a short time) that I knew.

Needless to say, Michelle took all she could tolerate of Ryan's drugs and lies. She reached the point I reached one year earlier, when I began tough love. She finally told Ryan he needed to go into a rehab facility.

Michelle and I began the search for a facility. Ryan told Michelle he was willing to go, but was only doing so to appease her. Time kept ticking away, and Ryan never entered rehab. Then one night Michelle realized Ryan wasn't being honest with her. In rebellion, inside their home, Ryan started lighting up a cigarette with a screw you attitude towards Michelle's rule of no smoking inside. She freaked out on Ryan. This action, along with her memory of seeing him nearly overdose was the straw that finally broke Michelle's back. Michelle finally gave Ryan an ultimatum.

Michelle told Ryan, in a fit of anger, that he needed to put his butt into rehab or she would kick him out of her home. Period. There wasn't any negotiating. She was done! Michelle finally did her own version of tough love.

Ryan knew he was in big trouble. He begged her not to kick him out. He handed her his car keys and swore he would go into rehab. He finally admitted to being an addict and agreed to seek help.

This time he truly meant it. I believe this time, considering the fact he nearly died, scared Ryan clean again. Michelle and I began searching for an appropriate and affordable facility, and in the meantime, Ryan agreed to go to his first NA (Narcotics Anonymous) Twelve Step meeting. He didn't go immediately, but in time, he did go!

As a parent struggling to understand addiction, I tried to imagine what went on inside of Ryan's head leading him to drink and do drugs again after doing so well with his sobriety. I tried stepping into Ryan's shoes on the night he nearly overdosed and in so doing, created the following conversation:

"Time to Celebrate"

Ryan
No drugs, liquor or beer,

I'm clean for one solid year!
Just got my first high paying job,
I'm not a "loser" anymore.
Kicked my habits, I'm pure.
It's time to celebrate.
Michelle, it's getting late.
Let's go out for a drive,
I'm feeling so alive.

Michelle
Ryan, I'm so proud of you,
When I think of all you've been through.
Yes, let's go for a ride,
I'm so full of pride!

Ryan
So, we went for a ride, and we walked in the night,
And, we spoke about what we'd been through.
When we came home I put Michelle to bed,
That's when the disease re-entered my head.
I looked in the mirror.

Drug Counselor
And, what did you see?

Ryan
A clean and sober me.

Drug Counselor
Then, what did you do?

Ryan
I celebrated.

Drug Counselor
Celebrated?

Ryan
I picked up the phone,
Then, I went for a loan,
From my local ATM.
I drove to a street,
Where we planned to meet,
The dealer and me.
I had the devil on one shoulder,

The angel on the other was gone.
I said, there's no way he has a hold on me.
I said, I've been clean for one year,
There's nothing to fear.
So what if I want to get high—I'll get by,
'Cause I'm not addicted any more,
And, I just want to celebrate.

The next thing I knew I was flat on my back,
I was lying in bed,
I thought I was dead.
I barely could breathe,
I barely could move,
It was all I could do to hold on to my life.
It was all I could do I was slipping away,
Thought I'd seen my last day.
Thought for sure I would die,
As Michelle looked into my eyes, and cried—

Michelle
What did you do?
What have you done?
You're dying my love.
Breathe.
Breathe.
Breathe.

Ryan
One breath at a time is all I could take.
One breath at a time, I thought I would break.
One breath is all I had to give—to live.
I took one breath at a time—until I could take two,
Then I could take three, then four.
I don't know how I lived.
I don't know how I survived.
I should have been dead.
But was alive—alive instead!!

12

Birthday "Presence"

WHEN RYAN'S TWENTY-SEVENTH BIRTHDAY rolled around in September 2003, he still had not entered into any rehab program. I wasn't feeling good about his ability to handle money, yet I knew he always could use money for something. After debating what to do, I sent him the following letter, inside a moneyless birthday card.

Dear Ryan,

I'm not sending you money for your birthday. I will perhaps buy you a gift card at a bookstore. I want to send this card to you in hopes you get it by your birthday, so at least you know I remembered!

I am enclosing a local newspaper story, written by a high school student about the boy she loved—who overdosed on drugs.

I know you did coke again. I know it almost killed you. Don't get mad at Michelle for telling me. You are putting her through hell. As far as I'm concerned, Michelle is now enabling you to do drugs, just like I did. You either get help or I will insist you move out of her life. You are not going to destroy her. She doesn't deserve to be abused by your lack of self-control. What this girl wrote in the article is correct. People, who do drugs, are selfish. They care about nobody—including themselves.

I am not mad at you for using coke again. I understand why you did. You most likely thought after nearly one year you were "okay," but Ryan, you will never be okay when it comes to drugs and alcohol. You just need to admit, first to yourself that you have a problem, and then GET HELP. There are many places where you can go for free help. Drug addiction and alcoholism are rampant in our country.

You are not alone in your battle. Once you seek help, others will be there for you to share your thoughts and feelings. It's okay. Being an abuser of drugs and alcohol doesn't make you a bad person. It makes you do bad things to get money when you are out of control. Do The Twelve-Step program. It works.

You are not out of control right now. You could end up out of control, and you could end up killing yourself if you don't get help. Ryan, you never really know what has been cut with the coke. Who the hell knows, what these clowns put in with the coke! Don't be an idiot. You will end up like Coke Head Bob on the Howard Stern show if you don't stop taking chances with your brain.

Do you understand that your brain is who you are? Without a brain, you might as well be dead. Stop fucking with your brain. Get help! Deal with your issues. Deal with your anger. Deal with your self-esteem issues. Stop denying you have problems and get help. Read my lyrics. You have a copy of them. Maybe they can help you.

I am your mother. I want to see you healthy and prosperous, but you are the only one who can change your life. I am helpless. You resent me when I try to talk with you, just as you probably resent this letter.

I did "tough love" with you in Florida, and I am prepared to do "tough love" again. You need to face your truths, whatever they are. Deal with them and get past your issues. You can do it. If not having me in your life will help you turn around, consider me gone. Whatever it takes—JUST DO IT!

Love, Mom

Here is the newspaper story I sent with his letter:

Drugs Really Do Kill

Every year hundreds of teens die from overdoses. Everyday students hear, "don't do drugs," but they hardly ever listen. My ex-boyfriend, Randy chose to learn his lessons the hard way.

When Randy was very young, his father was arrested for

the possession of 11,000 marijuana plants and for participating in a drug ring. Left fatherless, with a mother who worked day in and day out, Randy was forced to raise his younger sister. Randy told me about his father. He said that he was so much better than him and would never end up in the same position.

We met in eighth grade at Walter C. Young Middle School in Pembroke Pines; Randy was sixteen and failing school. In December 2000, he dropped out, promising everyone that he would get a job and his GED. I was aware of his "minor" drug problem prior to his dropout, but I had no idea how serious it really was.

We spoke every day once I moved to California in May of 2001. Soon, I realized the drug problem was becoming more severe. Randy did not go to school or work, and he soon was kicked out of his home. In July 2001, while living with his grandmother, he was arrested for possession with the intent to deal marijuana.

Each time we spoke, he said that he was trying to quit smoking and that he no longer did drugs. As any young girl "in love" would do, I believed him.

When I moved back to Florida in January 2002, we spoke once, and I was told everything was great. Seeing partially through this, I said I needed time to think, and I would contact him when I sorted things out.

Sticking to my word, we did not speak again until January 15, 2003. This was the last time I ever talked to Randy. On January 28, 2003, he died of a drug overdose. Coworkers of a small appliance delivery business found him dead in his living room.

I did not understand how this could have happened. Just two weeks before, Randy told me he was not doing drugs, had a good job, was working towards his GED, and was happy. I truly did not realize how drugs could take over one's mind until the night my father told me the news of my first love's death. I now know that people who use drugs are selfish; they care about nobody except themselves. When an individual does drugs he gambles with his life and takes the chance of dying each time.

Unfortunately, the night Randy gambled with his life, he did not realize that he would never wake up. He never had the opportunity to say goodbye to loved ones, let alone do all the things he wished to do.

I can only pray Randy went peacefully, yet I hate him for all the pain he caused. I hope others realize that life is worth so much, and life should be lived to the fullest day by day.

Written by: Jessica Adcock

A student at Cypress Bay High School

Needless to say, my heart bled for the young girl, who wrote this story. My heart was still aching for my own son in his battle with drugs and alcohol. I knew all too well that Randy's story tragically could become Ryan's, as long as he continued abusing drugs and alcohol. They are a deadly duo.

(In hindsight: Anne Salter later explained to me that what I didn't recognize then, was that, in my codependency, I was caught up in my own insanity, by even thinking the addict could understand a logical letter. I also did not realize, by lecturing Ryan, I was continuing to nag him, which further enabled Ryan to rebel. When we nag, they go on the defensive and don't hear any of what we are saying.)

13
Ryan's First NA Meeting

ON OCTOBER 28, 2003, RYAN WENT to his first Narcotics Anonymous meeting! He actually stood up and admitted to being an addict. Michelle sent me an email the next day with the following update:

Good Morning!

Last night was Ryan's first NA meeting. I think it went pretty well for him. The second we walked in the door everyone came up to hug him, which I think was a little overwhelming. It was book study night at that particular meeting and every addict, including Ryan, took a turn in reading parts from the Narcotics Anonymous book, "Hi my name is ___, and I am an addict."

Ryan also had to read a page to the group titled, "Why Are We Here?" Everyone was very nice and very welcoming. He said he felt like he didn't have many things in common with these people, but as I see it, their addiction is what they all share.

Tonight we are going to try a different location closer to home and in a different section of town, possibly in a church. He realized after the meeting last night, held in an apartment community's clubhouse that a program located in a church wouldn't be based solely on religion. There was one woman in particular last night that stated she calls the God in the Twelve Step program "HP" standing for Higher Power. She said she's not into the religious thing, and that she won't go around praying all day the way she was brought up by her mother. It's just not her thing, but that she does believe in a Higher Power. This, I do believe, eased Ryan's mind in the aspect of religion and NA.

Last night the group had a series of chips they gave out representing different amounts of time people had spent in NA. The first chip was for someone, who was coming to his or her very first visit, trying to get help. I was so proud of Ryan. He stood up and said, "I'll take it." Everyone clapped and hugged him. I had to try hard not to cry because this was such a hugely significant step for him. I asked him what he would do with his chip. He said he'd carry it with him everywhere.

Honestly, I feel he has as much determination about being sober as he did last November, when he found out he had hepatitis B. He seems so serious about everything. It's amazing. He thanked me over and over again for going with him to the meeting. He said it meant a lot. I told him there wasn't any other place I'd rather be.

I guess, when you first start NA, the goal is to attend ninety meetings in ninety days. Ryan said he was going to try to meet that goal. We might have to try for that goal after his inpatient treatment.

Well, hopefully I will be able to share many more NA meeting stories with you. I think you are definitely getting your son back! I will try to give you a call later today.

All my love, Michelle

After reading Michelle's email, I wept happy tears. I thanked my Higher Power God for the blessings in my son's life and for leading him to his first NA meeting. I knew there was a Higher Power at work in our lives, and I continued to envision only good things for my son's future.

14

Mom's Letter

AFTER ATTENDING A FEW MORE NA meetings, Ryan and Michelle decided if they were going to succeed as a couple, they needed to work their problems out as two adults, and not have "Mommy" to run to every time there was a problem. Ryan called to say he and Michelle would not be calling for a while. They wanted to detach from me while working on their relationship and asked me not to call them.

I imagined Ryan found out I had been Michelle's sounding board whenever she was frustrated with him, and since Ryan still blamed me for his problems, I was the enemy. I understood. I also felt if Ryan chose to do this as part of his recovery, then I needed to respect his choice. At least he was making choices. That was a good thing.

After we had stopped speaking, I decided to send Ryan a letter in early November explaining why I didn't send him the Marlin's hat I promised to send when the Florida Marlins won the World Series. It may seem strange, but I wanted him to feel what disappointment felt like on a small scale. I hoped and prayed he would read my letter and not just toss it into the trash. I gambled on Michelle reading it first, and then making sure (when Ryan was in the right frame of mind) that he also read it. It was written from a total place of love in my heart:

Ryan,

How did you feel when I didn't send the Marlins' hat that I told you I'd send? Were you disappointed? Did you feel let down by me? I hope so. That's how I wanted you to feel. Your response to me was very nice when you said, "Don't worry Mom, it's no big deal. I can get one off the Internet."

I hope you did get one off the Internet. If you did, it shows you can do things for yourself when you want. When you want something enough, you will get it. If you didn't get the hat from the Internet, it's because the hat wasn't significant enough. Don't use the lack of money as the excuse. When you wanted money for coke, you got it. You got it anyway possible because coke was your priority. The money you owe Michelle, you still owe her, because it's not important to you. You choose what's important. As long as drugs are in your life, drugs will always be at the top of your priority list. Drugs control you. You don't control them.

The slight disappointment you felt with respect to the hat is minor compared to the feelings of disappointment you have caused your family and friends over the past ten years or more. I am your mother. You are my flesh and blood. I endured the disappointment for the longest time because I thought if I kept "enabling" that sooner or later you would grow up, stop doing the wrong things and become the person I knew was inside. But, that never happened. What did happen is that I had to turn my back on you last summer and do what is termed, "tough love." That's where the enabler: me, stops enabling.

So then you moved to Virginia with Michelle, and she became your next enabler. Michelle did this because she loves you. She's not your mother, but she loves you as deeply as I do. Why does she? Michelle fell in love with you when she was a kid of fifteen, when you both were young, sweet and (almost) innocent. I believe you were her first love. This is a big thing for most girls, so you remained very special to her. She felt she might be able to save you, and has put way more effort and love into you than any other person on this earth, besides me. Michelle remembers the "other" Ryan. She remembers the "pre-addicted" Ryan, the sweet, fun and unselfish Ryan.

I remember him also. But, as time goes by and single digit years turn to double digit years of drug and alcohol abuse, the "other" Ryan gets further and further out of my memory. Unfortunately, the "other" Ryan has become the drug addicted Ryan for almost half his life. Now, the real Ryan got buried so deep within that it will require hard and emotionally painful work to dig the real Ryan back out. Twelve years of covering up your true *Self* are a long time.

Can you do it? Absolutely! But you and only you must do the work. Michelle can advise you. She can stand by you, but YOU are the only one who must make the commitment to yourself. A commitment to take off the layers of hurt, pain, rejection, shame, and abuse you have put over your true *Self*. You must peel them off layer by layer until you get back in touch with your true *Self*.

You must learn how to deal with life without drugs and alcohol. Ryan, this is why our country has so many drug and rehab facilities. You are not alone! Millions of Americans suffer the same problem. But you have to take steps to help yourself.

The last time we spoke you told me you weren't going to go into an in-house program. I think that's a mistake. In my opinion, this is exactly how you get out of doing the right thing all the time. You manipulate Michelle's feelings of anger and frustration with you.

She wanted to throw you out. So you told her everything she wanted to hear, and you started to do what she wanted you to do, which was to get in-house rehab. You went to a few NA meetings (to further your clean act), and when the heat was off from Michelle, you calmly and coolly decided you didn't need in-house. Well, I think that's bull crap.

You need intense counseling to teach you coping skills in life. You have the emotions of a fifteen year-old boy. When you started taking drugs, that's when you stopped growing emotionally. The skills you would have learned were never developed.

You need to learn those skills now, at the age of twenty-seven, or you will never be able to cope with life. Okay. I will give a bit. You can still accomplish this if you go to an all-day outpatient program. But, you need to commit to a program, go eight hours a day, and then work at night. You need to NOT sleep all day and be bored. Sleeping is escaping. It's nice to sleep instead of snort, but none-the-less, it is escaping. You need a regime in your life. You need to get up at 7:00 a.m., do something, then do something else, then something else and keep doing things. That is what functional people do. They don't sleep all day. They function.

You don't need to escape any more. You need to deal with life. You need to make your emotional growth your top priority. You have lots of catching up to do. You should look at this as your daytime job. It is your job to work on you. My job for years was to sell computers. Your job is to install coping skills into your psyche. You do this by talking with therapists about your life, your hurts, your pains, and your rejections. Dig deep inside to find your truths. With verbal salves, therapists are trained to respond appropriately, and help to heal your psyche. Gradually, over time, you will find your true *Self.* Just like a body with burns. Over time during the process of healing, layers of new skin eventually replace the lost and damaged skin. It's a painful recovery at times, but the result is what you must focus on.

So, Ryan, I know you and Michelle have decided to do whatever you are doing without me in your lives. I accept that, and, I understand it, but I had to write you this letter. I hope you are still reading it and haven't tossed it aside in anger or frustration.

The anger I saw inside you toward me was absolutely raging. I didn't like being on the other side of your anger. I can only imagine the pain you are suffering. It truly hurts me to see you so twisted and knotted inside. Untie those knots and untwist your mind. Once you face your demons, you will find the inner peace we all deserve. You will find the beautiful person you are. You are wonderful. I know that more than anyone in this world. I bore you and enjoyed your sweetness for many years. Life threw me, and then you, many curve balls. I have worked through many of mine, and now you must begin to work through yours. You can do it.

There is a Higher Power. That Higher Power is in you. There is a universal energy force in this world, and you are part of this energy. We are living beings, just like the earth and nature. We all get our energy from the same Source. Try to find the oneness in the Universe. Then become part of that oneness. Become part of the Source.

With love to you and Michelle,
I am your ever-loving mother

(In hindsight: Today, as I finalize my book, it was pointed out to me by Anne Salter that this letter is written from an angry space and is characteristic of a codependent's mental anguish. I violated Ryan's boundaries of detachment and used this letter, as a passive-aggressive way to express my anger and frustration. Regrettably, this is what enablers do because we feel so angry, hurt, and powerless.)

15

Miracles Continue to Happen

BY SPRING 2004, RYAN AND I began speaking again but usually only when he would call me. I really did try to stay out of Michelle and Ryan's business and to allow Ryan to handle his growth and his issues on his own. But I loved Ryan and I missed talking with him. Finally, with Michelle's help, Ryan came around and the two of them planned a trip to visit me for Mother's Day.

What a fantastic Mother's Day it was! I had my son back. We couldn't have been happier. We spent quality time together and I felt a natural high by having a sober, happy, and healthy son again. I was thrilled. My Mother's Day gift was my son! We kept the four-day visit short and sweet. We avoided any heavy conversations. I must admit I walked on eggshells the entire time, so as not to upset the applecart. Just seeing my son sober was such a joy. It felt so good to hug my son again. It felt so good to look into his eyes and to tell him how much I loved him and how proud I was of his sobriety.

My ninety-year old mother, Celeste, was living with Arthur and me at the time, so Ryan also had a chance to spend quality time with his grandmother. Ryan, Michelle, and I drove Grammy to Miami, put her in a wheelchair, and took her to her first Miami Heat basketball game! We had such a wonderful time together. My mother was so proud of her grandson for being sober, but disappointed to see him still smoking cigarettes. She was so disappointed that she made him a financial offer of $1000 to quit smoking.

At the same time Grammy made Ryan her offer, Ryan asked his grandmother if she would lend him $2,000, so he could purchase a hand-made, mountain bike called the Cannondale Prophet. He knew if he biked, it would clear out his lungs and help rid him of his addiction to nicotine. When new, the bike cost $5,000, but Ryan planned to obtain his used, on eBay.

Grammy agreed to lend Ryan the money. She happily wrote a check for $2,000 the day Ryan and Michelle left. When Ryan departed, she gave him one of the longest and most loving hugs of his life, during which, she said, "I love you, Ryan. I remember you as a little boy, and how much determination you had when putting your mind to something." She stopped hugging him to take hold of his hands. Then, while looking him lovingly into his eyes, she continued, "You already quit drinking and using drugs. I know you will stop smoking cigarettes, too."

"Thank you Grammy. Thank you for your love and for your trust in me. I will make you proud," Ryan said, pulling his ninety-one year old grandmother back into his arms for another hug while fighting his tears. Having his grandmother's trust was a very special and pivotal moment in Ryan's life.

When Ryan returned to Virginia, he sent his grandmother twenty, pre-dated checks for one hundred dollars each. Grammy cheerfully deposited one check into her account on the first of every month. I will never forget the satisfaction on her face each month, knowing she had such a positive effect on her grandson's life.

On May 22, 2004 Ryan stopped smoking cigarettes!! Miracles continued to happen! You can only imagine how shocked and pleased I felt. My own mother knew what three things motivated Ryan: love, trust, and money. I guess, after giving it thought, Ryan went for the money and stopped smoking, cold turkey. He already knew his grandmother loved and trusted him, too!

I must admit, I had told Ryan I didn't think he should stop smoking cigarettes. Quite honestly, I thought perhaps he should continue using nicotine, so he wouldn't get frustrated and possibly turn to drugs or alcohol again. I'm embarrassed to admit to that thinking, but it's the truth. Ryan actually got upset with me when I suggested he keep smoking. He told me he was strong-willed enough to quit, and he could remain sober, too. Ryan eventually told me it took more discipline to quit cigarettes than it did to stop using drugs and alcohol!

In July 2004, Ryan had been sober since October 28, 2003. Nine months were a record length of time! So, with pure joy in my heart, I sent him the following letter:

To my Darling Son,

Do you know how hard it was for me to do "tough love" with you two years ago? Do you know the pain and the suffering I had to endure, when I turned my back on my only child, who I absolutely adored? Do you have any idea, how much I love you?

I spend many hours looking at photos of us together when you were young. We had lots of fun together. We were very close. I don't know if you remember all of the good times. Seems you spend most of your time dwelling on the bad.

Well, today and every day should be a celebration for you and your life! It seems to me you have finally let go of the negative, and now you are focusing on the positive things you have in your life. I am very proud of you.

For you to stop doing drugs, drinking and now smoking cigarettes, really shows me you are overcoming the negative garbage from your past. I am truly happy for you and proud of you. I know it has been an uphill struggle. But, you have made it. You have separated yourself from the dregs of society, who are always waiting to pull victims down into their self-pity clubs.

You have taken yourself out of South Beach, which can be an evil pit for people to party and to escape reality, and now you are away from drug users, who like to hang with other drug users. South Beach is a place to visit and to go to dinner and walk around to watch the sites, but it's not a place for someone like you to live. You didn't live in South Beach. You escaped reality in South Beach. South Beach nearly killed you.

You have stopped escaping reality, and now you must learn to create your own reality. Reality or life is what you make it. You determine your own reality. You do that by making decisions about your life, like what you want to do with your life. Now that you are sober, you can think more clearly and make better choices. Take classes at the local college in anything you think you'll enjoy. You don't have to go for college credits. Take classes to expand your mind, and eventually you will expose yourself to something that really turns you on inside.

Finding life's passion isn't simple. It takes time. Not everyone is as lucky as Michelle who loved math and knew what she wanted to do since high school. But, I wasn't lucky either. I created my own luck by working hard and setting goals for myself. Because I wanted to invest in myself, I put myself through four years of college in my twenties.

Figure out what classes you'd like to take and I will help you pay for them. I have always wanted you to be educated. There is no better investment than education. That's why I went back to college in my fifties and finally got my degree. When you feed your brain knowledge, no one can ever take that information away from you. Knowledge equals power—the power to control your destiny.

If you decide to receive counseling, I will gladly pay your fees. I will not buy you another car. I will not just give you money. If I have the financial ability to assist you in getting on with your life as a sober and responsible person, I will help you. I happen to adore you. I also believe in you. Since you now believe in yourself, the sky is the limit.

I don't like the mean and angry Ryan who resided inside of you. I don't like the Ryan who blames the entire world for his problems. I don't like the Ryan who says, "Fuck you" to me, instead of dealing rationally and having a mature conversation. I like the good-hearted and kind Ryan I know is inside. I like the sensitive and funny Ryan. I love the witty, creative, and charming Ryan. I love the artsy Ryan. All of those characteristics are inside you. You just need to choose the Ryan you want to be. It's all your choice.

I am sending you two gifts. One is wrapped in the box. I know you will love it. At least I hope you will. They were supposed to be birthday presents, so consider them still birthday presents, but also, consider them to be congratulation presents for doing so well with your life. The other gift is the book, *Think and Grow Rich*. If you take the time to read and digest it, this book could transform your entire life. Ryan, if you never read another book, you must read this one. Trust me as your mother, the woman who gave you her blood, sweat, and tears.

Read this book!

I LOVE YOU. Enjoy *your* life. Live *your* life. You can be anything and do anything you want—once you believe you can.

Love, Mom

(In hindsight: You can see how deeply I wanted to help Ryan. I have since learned, however, that trying to teach addicts or lecture them about what is good for them—doesn't work.)

16

No Ifs, Ends, or Butts!

IN NOVEMBER 2004, AFTER NOT SMOKING cigarettes for six months and after being sober for over one year, Ryan asked his grandmother if he could have half of the $1000 she had offered him to quit smoking, as a down payment on a car. His grandmother agreed to send him $500 while letting him know how proud she was of his progress. She also acknowledged that she trusted Ryan to continue his smoke-free life! His grandmother felt extreme self-gratification, believing it was because of her offer that her grandson was smoke-free.

Ryan put the money down on a used, 2001 Toyota Camry, in excellent running condition. This would be the first car Ryan had ever purchased with his own money. He was approved for a five-year car loan. Buying his own car and making his own payments were significant parts of the process in establishing independence, self-esteem, and responsibility for Ryan. He also learned to appreciate the value of money, since he was spending his own and not Mom's. This car was probably the first "thing" in Ryan's life he truly valued and appreciated as he was working for it, paying for it, and maintaining its condition.

(As an aside: Ryan still drives this same car in 2014. The exterior body is near perfect, and it still runs well with over 130,000 miles on the original engine.)

17

College — Another Miracle

BY SUMMER 2005, RYAN HAD DECIDED to go to college. Wow! That was spectacular news. Ryan qualified for financial aid, so his education was paid for by the state of Virginia. He was a full time waiter, but we decided while he was in college full time that he should work only part-time, in order to better focus on school. I offered to supplement his income since I didn't have to pay for college. I sent him the following letter on August 24:

Dear Ryan,

I am planning to deposit $500 in your bank account on Thursday, August 25. You can only imagine how happy I am to do so! I am so proud of you for everything you have accomplished in the past three years. You should be very proud of yourself. What you have overcome is not easy. It shows immense strength in character and determination. I truly believe you have come full circle and are now ready to become whatever you want to be in life!

Life isn't about finding one's *Self.* Life is about creating one's *Self.* I had to create myself when I was alone as a single mother, to raise you. I chose to become president of a computer company and with that, created an entire life and business just because I made up my mind to do so. As you study each day and open your mind to the education, ideas, philosophies and thoughts, these will lead you to creating yourself. You, and only you, know, who truly resides inside your being. It is up to you, to discover your true essence and to become the shining star that has always been inside of you. I have no doubt you are on the best path possible. Enjoy every moment, of every day, of your journey. It's very exciting.

I have always looked at my life as a book, and each chapter has been defined by my relationships and what is happening in my life. Many times I allowed others to write my chapters and to determine what happened to me, and at those times my life was out of control. It is only when you control your own life that you can determine your destiny. I feel you are definitely controlling your life now (along with Michelle's loving influence).

Some of my chapters, like yours, were filled with pain, frustration, financial ruin and a broken heart, but each chapter's ending led me to a stronger, better *Self*, and led me onward and into being a better and stronger person. I didn't lose sight of my values in how I treated other people. Always remember to treat others how you would like to be treated. If you do, then only good things will come your way (most of the time). It's necessary that you can look yourself in the mirror and like the person you see.

This is what I get for my $500—the chance to let my son know how special he is! I thank God every day for the love Michelle gave you, and for how she believed in you and knew the true you, buried deep under your pain and hurtful *Self.* Give her my love.

Love always, Mom

After his first few months of college I wasn't making much money at the time, so I had to drop my contribution to $400 per month. Fortunately Ryan was earning enough money to pay his bills, so the $400 was sufficient.

During one of my visits, Ryan took me to his college campus, showed me around, and I sat in on one of his classes. I was so proud of my son. I just glowed. To reflect on everything we'd been through and then to see him attending college was just heart-warming. Again, I thanked my God for all of our blessings. I thought back to what I had originally written the day I did tough love, when my Higher Power God spoke to me and I wrote the following in *Mom's Opera*:

Son

Mom, you really think I can find out who I am?

Mom

Absolutely.

Son

Do you really think one day I'll be able to stay centered?

Go back to school, get a degree, find out who I'm meant to be?

Mom

Absolutely.

Son

But, I'm near twenty-six, and I just know tricks,

Do you really think I can stop the illusions?

Mom

Absolutely…

The powers of prayer, intention, possibility thinking, music in my head, creative visualization, imagination, and universal energy had all provided the paths we needed to follow to get to this day; to the point in my son's life, where he was *Self* actualizing. Thanks be to our Source.

I realized the many lessons I learned while studying Ernest Holmes' *The Science of Mind* while in my thirties, had been my source of strength over the past years while facing a harsh reality. *The Science of Mind* gives us the passion for new possibilities while showing us how to activate the constructive imagination and how to hold in thought and to feel the intention and energy for healing. Spirit works for us by working through us.

18

Just, Hold-On

SOMETIME IN 2005, WHEN I FIRST read James Frey's book, *A Million Little Pieces*, it affected me tremendously as the parent of an addict. This was before finding out it was not based entirely on truth. Meanwhile, I was very impressed by one of the television interviews with James and other recovering addicts. They spoke about how the words, "just, hold-on" from his book, had helped many addicts when they were in recovery and feeling close to relapsing. The interview made me cry, as it made me think of my own son and how I always wanted him to "just, hold-on." I was so moved that I wrote a poem. My intention was to turn this poem into a song for the musical:

"Just, Hold-On"

When things get tough,
And you think—
I don't think I can last another minute,
Hold-on,
Just, hold-on,
Just, hold-on.
Be smart.
Be strong.
Be proud.
Hold-on,
Just, hold-on.

Live honorably,
And, with dignity,
And just, hold-on.

There's no good or bad.
No sinner or saint.
There simply is, what is,   .
So hold-on,
Just, hold-on.

You can use that—to be.
And, that is enough.
Don't talk about it, or question it.
Just let it be.
Just be.
Hold-on.
Just, hold-on.

When you feel so all alone,
When there's no one in this world,
Who understands you,
Hold-on.
Just, hold-on.

When you feel broken,
Into a million little pieces,
Hold-on.
Just, hold-on.
Just, hold-on.

I imagined how many times my son and other recovering addicts have had to "just, hold-on." Or, how many parents (such as myself), feel they too are broken into a *million little pieces* while helplessly watching a beloved son or daughter destroying their lives with drugs and/or alcohol, who must "just, hold-on." Parents must mostly hold on to their sanity and to their *hope* and faith.

Part of my "just, holding-on" included holding on to the belief, that my Higher Power God gave me a mission the day I did tough love, and that there is a reason for everything that happens in our lives. I also believe the Universe puts people into our lives when we become ready. These people are our earth angels.

For an example, a friend of mine knew an elderly gentleman who wrote music and lyrics for many famous entertainers. She offered to introduce us, to see what he thought of my musical concept. He kindly agreed to meet with me in his home.

After listening, this man told me he didn't think the title *Mom's Opera* was a suitable title for my musical. He suggested changing it to *Tough Love – The Musical*. I loved the sound of it and knew it was the right name for my musical. It had been *Mom's Opera* when I was in pain and "just, holding-on," but I was out of pain by 2005 and open to changing the musical's title. For me, this man appeared as an angel in my life. He gave me his time, he validated my writings with his words of wisdom, and I left his home feeling more inspired and with a true sense of purpose.

19

Ryan's Perspective on His Past

DURING RYAN'S COLLEGE DAYS IN 2006, he wrote a paper in English class, about himself and shared it with me. It was quite interesting and thought provoking for me to read his feelings about his life. I am glad to know he took the time to reflect and to write his feelings about the events that shaped his life. This is what he wrote:

When I was a teenager I did a lot of bad things. My mother always told me there were no such things as bad people, just people who do bad things. So, as I grew up and turned into a teenager I still remained a good person, but the number of bad things I did steadily increased and this behavior eventually led my mother to send me to military school.

As a young child, my parents divorced because of their destructive love. Dad remained a hippie while Mom went from hippie to yuppie. In the end, although my parents seemed to have nothing in common, there was one thing they seemed to both share. Both played tug of war with me, using me as their weapon of choice when they played the game of hurt with each other, but in the end nobody ever won and I was the biggest loser.

At first I lived with my mother, and we were very poor, although I didn't realize exactly how poor we were until much later. Eventually, I moved in with my father and stepmother. This was when I started to rebel. I believe I was in the fifth grade. I think my rebellion had a lot to do with how frustrated I was with my home life at the time. I ultimately moved back with my mom, who had opened up her own computer company since I had moved. She became a very successful businesswoman, and although I knew she loved me tremendously, she never had a lot of time for me because she had a business to run. Her way of showing me how much she loved me was by buying me anything and everything, even in times that we had no money I always got things.

I wouldn't say I fell in with the wrong crowd because when anyone hung out with me, they were part of the wrong crowd. When I was fifteen I was lashing out at everyone and everything that had any resemblance of an authority figure. I hated everything. I didn't really have a drug problem. I smoked pot here and there, but hard drugs were not in the picture. I never went to school, and I never listened to what my mom had to say. My mom was fed up with me, and she was at her wits end. She decided there were only two options for me: drug rehab or military school.

So, she had the bright idea to tape my phone calls to give her a little insight into what my social life was like. She thought she might be able to catch me setting up some big drug deal. Boy was she wrong. The first day she taped me happened to be the day I lost my virginity. What she found out was that her little boy was now a man and not as heavily into drugs as she had first suspected. So now that left only one option, military school.

My mom said, "Ryan, I'm going to give you the choice of any military school you want to attend." So we drove from our home in South Florida up to the Florida Air Academy in North Florida. It was an all boys' school, and it did not appeal to me at all. We continued our search and ended up in Virginia. I totally liked the grounds of the campus and the dorms were a lot nicer than the ones that they had at the previous school. There was one huge difference that really made my choice easy—girls. When I found out that I was going to go to a school full of bad girls, I almost fell over from the perverted possibilities that I was seeing in my near future. I also found out I could smoke cigarettes if I went there. I was sold.

I moved up to military school in August of 1991. The first day was a big shock for me. As a new cadet, I had to visit the school barber and get all of my hair shaved off. Then, all of the new cadets were moved into their dorms. There were five different companies in the school, Alpha, Bravo, Charlie, Delta, and Echo. I was put into Charlie Company. It had the youngest of the cadets, ages twelve to fifteen. I moved into my room with my new roommate named Daniel F. I thought he was cool. He was a lot like me. He came from a broken background, and he was also very rebellious.

For the first three weeks, I was in boot camp with the other new cadets. We had to wake up at 4:30 in the morning and shower in less than two minutes. We ate three square meals a day and had to learn all of the cadences. The hardest part for me, personally, was when I was forced to hold my arms out by my side for what seemed like an eternity.

I got in so much trouble while I was there. Every time I would get caught doing something I wasn't supposed to be doing, I would receive demerits and then walk with the D Squad. D Squad was where all of the bad cadets had to go to serve their punishments. Some days it would be cleaning the school grounds and other days it would be cleaning the mess hall, but most of the time they would just make us march, up and down in an outdoor amphitheater. Up and down, hour after hour, was almost enough to make you want to be a good person.

A lot of bad things happened while I went to school there. There were a few kids, who tried to commit suicide. Others tried to run away. A lot of kids got caught drinking or doing drugs just so they could get kicked out, but most of the kids just did their best to lay low. We knew sooner or later the year would be over, and that we wouldn't have to come back until the end of summer. So that's what I did. I just tried to make the best of it. Don't get me wrong, there were also fun experiences for me. I got to go rock climbing and learned how to shoot all sorts of weapons. It was sort of ironic that they were teaching the "bad seeds" how to use weapons.

When the school year was over I was so happy to return home. I swore I would never go back to that place again. Finally, I had convinced my mom that I was a reformed rebel, and she allowed me to return to public school back in Florida. That lasted for about five weeks and then I found myself begging to return to military school. To the dismay of my mother, I had realized my feelings of missing the school outweighed the disgust and hatred I had for it while there.

20

Hindsight is 20/20

TODAY I CAN SEE MORE CLEARLY, from re-reading Ryan's paper, how he internalized negative thoughts of himself and defined himself as a "*bad* seed." Unfortunately, these are the harmful messages children receive because of dysfunctional situations that are beyond their control. Over time, children believe these negative messages about themselves and then their behaviors reinforce them until eventually they act out in different forms of negative behavior and become "bad." Unfortunately, it becomes a self-fulfilling prophecy.

As an example, when an angered parent tells their child, "You are good for nothing," that child believes his parent and becomes "good for nothing" in his mind, and then acts out "good for nothing" behavior.

When my high school sweetheart broke up with me, I was nineteen. At that painful moment, he added insult to injury by telling me that I was stupid. I believed him, so I started doing stupid things. I lost my self-confidence at that point, and it took me years to realize I was not stupid.

If only we could tell ourselves when we are five, ten, fifteen, or twenty that we are perfect, whole and loveable just the way we are, we could resist all the *vices* we use to stop feeling our pain. We could choose to win and not lose ourselves to the words and/or actions of others. These are the *Self* imposed negative thoughts everyone needs to recognize and to let go of, in order to recover.

Being in college added tremendous value to Ryan's self-worth. He was getting terrific grades and gaining self-confidence in the process. He majored in graphic design, which is what he had studied years before in Miami while he partied and snorted himself up with cocaine. Now he was able to focus on his education drug free and complete a two-year program.

When Mother's Day rolled around in May 2006, I again had the pleasant surprise of Ryan and Michelle coming to Florida to visit. Mother's Day couldn't have meant more to me than it did for the past two years. I was always painstakingly aware how very easily I could have lost my only child.

21

Tough Love — The Musical

AS I EDIT THIS BOOK, FOR WHAT SEEMS to feel like the thousandth time, I realize even more so how the entire experience of writing my "musical" and this "book" have been major therapy for me. Writing kept me truly positive while dealing with an extremely negative reality challenging my heart and soul. Writing allowed me to focus my energy on creating a positive reality and a happy ending, by applying the principles of creative visualization, possibility thinking, and manifesting my dreams.

Manifesting is an ability of consciousness, at an inner level, where there exists a world in which everything is possible. Most know this as dreaming. When we dream we can create a world of wonders and miracles. While I was writing, I was manifesting (dreaming) how I wanted the future to be for my son and myself. Though I was dealing with the disease of addiction, I manifested that my son will overcome his addictions and make healthier choices for his life. In order to do that successfully, Ryan will have to see the disease of addiction first and then admit to being an addict. That is the visualization I held onto. That is what I projected into the Universe.

Another visualization I held onto was that one day, when I am ready, and when the time is right, the person(s) meant to write the musical score will manifest into my life. Since the first day I began writing *Mom's Opera*, I always knew a musical is meant to be, and that my Higher Power is behind it. I have never doubted its eventual materialization. Whatever I needed to move the musical forward has always been put into my life, from people to ideas. It is just the way the Universe works.

As an example, back in 2003, I told my husband, Arthur, I would love to have Andrew Lloyd Webber write my musical score. He laughed and told me I was crazy, and that there was no way I would be able to contact him. I told him I wasn't crazy. I knew how powerful manifesting was; after all, I had manifested Arthur into my life back in 1999 (which I will share with you later in the book).

Sometime in 2005, I happened to meet a woman in Weston, who mentioned that since I was writing a musical, I might consider going to New York City and participating in musical theatre workshops offered by The ASCAP Foundation (The American Society of Composers, Authors and Publishers). Serving as artistic director for the workshops was/is Academy Award and Grammy Award-winning composer lyricist Stephen Schwartz, whose credits include the hit Broadway shows *Wicked, Godspell* and *Pippin,* the Walt Disney films *Enchanted, Pocahontas* and the *Hunchback of Notre Dame,* and the DreamWorks film *The Prince of Egypt.*

Fast forward.

In June 2006, I took a bold step. I flew to New York City, by myself, to attend my first ASCAP Workshop, where Stephen Schwartz provided attendees with insight into the writing of a musical. The workshop included prominent guest speakers, such as producers David Stone and Adam Epstein. Storywriter, Joseph Stein, who wrote *Fiddler on the Roof, Rags, Zorba, Raisin,* etc., spoke and shared his writing wisdom. Over three enchanting nights, I was fortunate to be exposed to many, well-known professionals, associated with Broadway musicals.

While attending, I sat next to and became friendly with a woman named Janice. I learned she was a talent agent for children. Months after becoming friends, Janice mentioned she had recently flown one of her young singers out to Los Angeles to meet with (are you ready?) Andrew Lloyd Webber! Janice then told me she most likely could get my script into Mr. Webber's secretary's hands, and possibly into Andrew Lloyd Webber's, if his secretary saw potential.

Though I never sent anything to Mr. Webber, the Universe *did* provide a vehicle through my friend, Janice! That is exactly how the Universe works! And, since I do know how the Universe works, that is how I know when I am ready, the right people will be put into my life and *Tough Love - The Musical* will be actualized.

In late 2006, after attending The ASCAP Workshop, I finally began working with my dear friend Karen, putting music to my writings. (I had been planning to work with Karen since 2003, when I put it on my "to do" list in New York City.) When I told Karen I had met someone, who could connect me with Andrew Lloyd Webber for my musical, Karen got quite concerned. She told me she would make time in her schedule to work on the musical since her first love was composing original music. Though I am an extremely positive thinker, realistically, my chances of working with Andrew Lloyd Webber, at that point, seemed rather slim, so it was thrilling to begin working with Karen!

Karen and I originally met while playing tennis in 1999. Over time, we became very close friends. Karen's passion for writing music and lyrics began at an early age. At nine, she was selected to appear on local, New York television with her original compositions. While attending summer programs during her teenage years, Karen composed the musical scores and lyrics to well received musical productions, garnering awards over seasoned professionals. During her college years, she was part of a rock band, playing current hits, as well as original pieces. After college, Karen opted to employ her gift for words in the legal profession, earning her Juris Doctor in 1978. As a family lawyer, who had too often seen the effects of addiction upon the family, Karen knew this story must be told.

Until working with Karen, I had never picked up one book to read about recovery. My writings and thought processes were entirely from the inside out. I wrote from my gut. Once I heard the songs taking shape with actual music and voices to my words, I realized how important it was for my musical not to offend anyone in recovery.

It was then I started reading books on addiction, recovery, and codependency. I saw glimpses of myself, as a dysfunctional person, but didn't focus on myself (yet). I was focused more on the addict and understanding the addict's recovery. It was at that point; however that I became aware that addiction is a family disease and that I too, had *issues*. At this point though, my issues still remained buried deep in denial, while I primarily focused on Ryan's. Denial had a cunning way of keeping me in denial!

It's one thing to know you're in denial, but it's another to pull your head out of the quick sand. Admitting to oneself that your child is an addict is one huge step and unbearably painful. As Ryan's mother, I was in deep, deep, deep denial as to the part I played in his addiction. Karen and I discussed my denial in depth. Later that night, Karen wrote a lighthearted song based on our talk:

"Denial"

Addicts
I have no addiction,
There's nothing that I lack.
Ignore my dereliction,
Just give me some more smack.

Denial—Denial, just give me one more score.
Denial—Denial, then I will need no more.

I am not addicted,
I could stop at will.
But, gonna steal your wallet,
To buy a few more pills.

Denial—Denial, I just need one more fix.
Denial—Denial, then I can surely quit.

Parents
Though his eyes are glazy,
His words are somewhat slurred,
He's just a little lazy,
Addicted! That's absurd!!
Denial—Denial, it simply cannot be.
Denial—Denial, not in this family.

So his nose is runny,
His conduct too aloof,
Cocaine, don't be funny,
Just needs some chicken soup.

Denial—Denial, he's going through a phase.
Denial—Denial, it's different in our case.
Denial. Denial. Denial. Denial. Denial.

Since I had successfully applied tough love to Ryan, we discussed
the many fears I had to overcome, as a fear-based, codependent mother.
Then, Karen and I turned my experience into an inspirational song, using the voice of an angel, to speak with me:

Angel
Listen to me mama,
'Cause I don't tell fables,
I'll tell you what to do,
If you think you're able.
That boy will never win,
As long as you enable him,
So, let the boy,
Follow his path.
Mom
But, what if he's hungry,
Needs fruit or some bread?
How can I say no,
Turn my back instead?
Angel
He must hit rock bottom,
Don't heed every call.
He will never rise,
If you cushion each fall.
Mom
But, what if he's cold,
Needs a hat for his head?
How can I say no,
Turn my back instead?
Angel
He will never recover,
If he doesn't have need.
The road to recovery,

Is one, he must lead.
Mom
But, what if he's tired,
And needs a clean bed?
How can I say no,
Turn my back instead?
Angel
Let him find his own way,
You've done all you can do.
Sometimes, tough love,
Is the path you must choose!
Mom (almost spoken, pleading, begging)
But, what if he dies?
That's my biggest fear.
I gave him his life,
He's my baby, dear.
Angel
Don't let this fear control,
He's as good as dead right now.
It's time tough love,
Scares him to life, somehow!

I knew when Ryan was older he met up with the wrong people. It's impossible for parents to know whom their children are with and what horrible things are happening to them when out on the streets. That thought, along with the idea of the inner pull of good versus bad, led me to imagine what it must be like when our children are using drugs out on the street. I tried to write from the perspectives of both the demon/disease of addiction, and of angelic goodness. I gave all the goodness of the world, and all the voices from guardian angels the name Celeste (after my mother), to represent all celestial and divine spirits surrounding us:

Ryan and other drug addict
So, here we are,
It's here that we meet.
You and I,

Out on the street.
You're angry,
And, so am I.
Doing drugs to get us by.
Doing drugs to numb the pain.
Doing drugs to keep us high.
Depression is anger turned inside,
Why, oh why, oh why?
We have no answers,
We have no reasons why,   •
Our lives just keep unraveling,
Right before our very eyes!
Demon (disease)
I just love it,
I'm in my glory.
Two more down
My path to hell!!
Angel Celeste
Don't be so quick,
I'm in this story.
I'm still around,
To ring the bell!

Time out boys,
Go to your corners,
Open your hearts,
Let love back in.
You both slipped,
And you both fell,
Pick yourselves up,
Don't go to hell.
Demon (disease)
I just love it,
Alcohol and drugs cover the pain,
While I climb in.
Time out boys,
Here comes the pusher,

Score more drugs,
Keep yourselves high.
You both slipped,
And, you both fell,
Snort, drink and shoot,
Welcome into hell!
Ryan and other drug addict
So, here we are,
It's here that we meet.
You and I,
Out on the street.

Hey man, we're looking to buy.
Hey man, we want to get high.
Doing drugs is better than sex,
Of course, sex could be next.
Perhaps, we'll find a coke whore,
Hey man, we're ready to score.

We have no answers,
We have no reasons why,
Our lives just keep unraveling,
Right before our very eyes!
Angel Celeste
You can hear me—if you try!
Don't buy.
Don't buy.
Don't buy.
Demon (disease)
You can hear me—I'm inside!
Score more.
Score more.
Score more.
Angel Celeste and Demon (disease)
Time out boys,
Make your choices,
You're hearing both of our voices.

Angel Celeste
Will you listen to your disease?
Demon (disease)
Or will you let your angels in?
Angel Celeste
Will you choose my wings of glory?
Demon (disease)
Or will you choose my road to hell?

I continued visualizing the disease of addiction as a *demon* focused on possessing our children. And how, as parents, we think our children are strong enough to resist the many temptations put in front of them. We can't imagine our children consuming so much alcohol and/ or so many drugs that they become addicts. I think, as parents, we just believe our children are too smart to allow themselves to become victimized by drugs and drug pushers. We think our children know better than to put harmful drugs into their young bodies. This led me to continue writing from the demon's voice:

Demon (disease)
Who are you kidding?
Surely you jest.
What makes you think he's not like the rest?
Given the chance,
While out on the street,
As long as kids breathe,
I pull at their feet.
I turn them into liars,
I turn them into thieves,
You never know,
What's up their sleeves!!

They push all your buttons,
They spend all your dough,
With no remorse or shame,
They know—you'll never know.
They party like the Devil,

Raising hell both night and day,
And they know they can do it,
Cause they know—they always get their way.

Look, here comes a poor mother now.
She's been worn down over time, somehow.
She's so fed up with all his lies,
And yet, not to my surprise,
She'll reach into her purse,
To provide him with more cash—
She thinks it's for food, clothing, or rent,
But instead, it's for his stash.
He'll give her a smile, a hug, and a kiss,
And the poor mother feels so loved, by this.
She's there to love and to provide,
That's how and why I continue to thrive!!

Since the first day I started writing, I always believed there was an angel on one of Ryan's shoulders and the devil/disease on his other. Unfortunately, for many years, the devil/disease had won out. It seemed that the only way one can get clean and stay clean is to find a way to get the devil of a disease off one's shoulder by first admitting to the *disease* of addiction, and then by listening *only* to the angels in one's life. Angels or guides have always been there, waiting to be heard. After all, life is about choices. Once we realize we all have the power within to choose right from wrong and we recognize that power, life becomes so much easier.

I understood how Michelle felt when Ryan nearly overdosed. We both loved him. It's disappointing to love someone and believe in them more than they believe in themselves. Michelle kept giving Ryan chances, just as I had for years and years.

Empathizing with Michelle's broken heart and the pain of her extreme disappointment in Ryan's repeated destructive behavior, took me right back emotionally to the day I did tough love with Ryan. All of my feelings of anger and frustration resurfaced. Those feelings led me to write about the fight we had on that day. It was painful for me to write those lyrics and recall my gut-wrenching pain. Just like with Michelle,

Ryan had kept making promises and more promises he never kept. I gave what I wrote to Karen and together we wrote:

"One More Promise"

Mom
Look at your face, eyes read and glazed.
Where did he go, the boy I raised?
Look at this place, squalid and bare.
One more excuse, I will not hear.

He told me I could trust him,
One more promise that was broken,
One more lie.
A simple, honest word, never spoken,
My heart's broken,
Why, oh why?
Ryan
Mom, it's simply a depression,
I cannot cope with rejection,
One more chance, I'll find direction,
Don't expect to find perfection.
Mom
You told me no more drugs and no more stealing,
My appealing to your heart,
Has fallen on deaf ears,
I've no more tears,
And, no more feelings to impart.
Ryan
I am tired of your complaining,
And your love you must be feigning,
If you say you'll leave me stranded,
Once again, I feel abandoned.
Mom
You told me if I bought you one more car,
One more guitar, you'd change your ways.
You told me that these medications,

You were taking, were a phase.
Ryan
I know I have been resistant,
I promise I will get assistance,
I've told you all this before,
Give me some money—I'll do more.
Mom
Look at this place, squalid and bare.
One more excuse, I will not hear.

You told me that you would clean this mess,
You confessed that you were wrong.
The apartment is destroyed and what is worse,
The things I bought you have been pawned.
Ryan
Come on Mom don't get unglued,
Just need some money for some food,
A little more to pay my rent,
I'll pay you back all that I've spent.

Come on Mom don't blow your cool,
You're acting crazy, like a fool,
Remember, I'm your only son,
I'll change—just give me some more money.
Mom
No more. It's over. I want you out!!

He told me I could trust him.
One more broken promise, and one more untruth,
A simple honest word, never spoken,
My heart's broken,
I am through!

Karen and I eventually recorded "One More Promise." When we
played it for a few mothers of addicted children, it brought tears to
their eyes as if the song were about them. I played the song for some
addicts in recovery, and they told me the same thing. The scene is

usually the same between frustrated parents and their addicted children. I'm sure the further you read into this book the more you will realize you are not alone in your feelings of anger, fear, frustration and distrust.

In studying the structure of a musical, I read there is usually one song, known as the "I Can" song. The protagonist (Ryan) gets aroused to assert his conscious will and directs it towards a goal, caused by the inciting action. The audience must understand the goal and the possibility of its fulfillment. The "I Can" song states his goals and expresses those feelings.

In 2002, when I did tough love with Ryan, I knew he hated me that day. I wanted to write a song capturing Ryan's feelings of hate and anger, and one where Ryan expresses his goals while packing his bags to move out. This is how I heard Ryan's, "I can" song:

"I Don't Need You"

I don't need you,
I don't love you anymore.
Can't believe you'd,
Push me out the door.
I can make it on my own,
I can make it through—
Cause, I don't need you.

All my life she's never been there,
That's why this bullshit is unfair.
I don't need this crummy old place,
I can't stand her fucking dumb face.

I don't want you,
I can't want you anymore.
Can't believe you'd,
Throw me to the floor.
I will make it on my own,
I will make it through—
Cause, I don't need you.

the family — transmission of the faith
militate against evil —

2461 Emma Lane
Mansfield
44903

The Skyway East

She'll see I am my own strong man,
I'll prove her wrong the best I can.
I don't need to take her bullshit,
She's so fucked up but can't admit.

I can make it on my own.
I will make it on my own.
I will leave this lousy home.
I will finally be ME.
I will finally be FREE.
Cause, I don't need you!

I started thinking about a poem I had written about myself years before, when I started to question why my life had gone so wrong and so off track. It is too bad I didn't seek professional counseling in my early twenties, when I was writing this poem. I had all the symptoms of depression and fear based behavior, but in the early 1970s going to see a therapist just wasn't something one did. When my life started unraveling, this is what I wrote:

"The Unraveling of a Life"

The unraveling of a life,
How does it happen?
The unraveling of a life,
Where does it go wrong?

Your security blanket's tattered,
Your security blanket's torn,
Your blanket starts to shred,
In the middle of the storm.

Thunder is in your ears,
Turmoil is throughout your home,
Lightning strikes your heart,
As, your family explodes.

Thread by thread it disappears,
Right before your very eyes,
The blanket that held you tight,
Also shielded many lies.

Please don't let me crumble,
Please don't let me fall,
Mother, Father—you're the family I know,
Where, oh where, did you both go?

Your security blanket's tattered,
Your security blanket's torn,
Your blanket starts to shred,
In the middle of the storm.

I'm sure Ryan, along with most troubled children, had similar, confused feelings going on inside as I felt, but couldn't share or verbalize in my teens. My son drank and did drugs to escape his painful feelings. I started writing poetry at nineteen, to vent mine after my broken heart.

I still have my first notebook full of poetry. I participated in loveless relationships, where I had meaningless sex, as temporary fixes for my broken heart. Of course, these relationships added more inspiration for my poetry and more negative feelings of low self-esteem.

Unfortunately, many of us participate in self-defeating behaviors because we haven't been taught or trained in how to express our excruciatingly painful and negative emotions, so we take the easy way out and escape them with a multitude of vices.

22

Sweet Surrender

ON FEBRUARY 10, 2007 WHILE flying in and out of beautiful, white, puffy clouds, surrounded by crystal blue endless sky, inspiration struck! I began projecting and creatively visualizing how I envisioned my son's future. I could imagine hearing my son's stage character singing these words once he admitted to being an addict and when he started working The Twelve Step program. Though my son was sober, had attended a few NA meetings, had gotten his first chip, and had stopped using drugs and alcohol; he hadn't started to work The Twelve Step program.

Because I had started reading books on the subject, I knew that to work The Twelve Step program an addict must admit to being powerless over their addiction and come to believe in a power greater than themselves. I see this as surrendering one's ego. Spiritual surrender is giving up control by your Lower *Self* and inviting your Higher *Self*—your divine *Self*, your Godlike *Self*, to become the ruling factor in your life.

I realized most of us do surrender when we are in pain. We give up. However, at first we don't surrender to a Higher Power; we surrender to drugs, alcohol, nicotine, food, loveless sex, pornography, etc. When we do hit our ultimate rock bottoms, it is then (if we're lucky) we finally surrender to a Higher Power, which may or may not be called, God. In The Twelve Step programs, Step One is, "I am powerless over ——." We just fill in the blank with our vice of choice.

Obviously, Ryan never sang this or any other song in his life. As his mother, who continued to creatively project her visions through prose, poetry and song, when Ryan's character is on stage, I believe my son Ryan will also feel this way in his real life:

"I Surrender My *Self* Today"

I have reached my bottom,
I have reached my pit.
I have caused much sorrow,
And, it's time to quit.

I have hurt my family,
I have lost my friends,
I have begged, stolen, lied,
And, it's time this ends.
I admit I am powerless,
I admit to no control,
There is no more denying,
To the depths of my soul.

God, grant me the serenity to accept the things I cannot change; courage to change the things I can; and wisdom to know the difference.

I will face my demons,
Do battle to win,
Over the disease of addiction,
That holds me prisoner within.
The chains that bind me,
Will be cut away,
For, I surrender my *Self* today.

Hear my words,
See my pain,
I am ready to abstain.
I am ready God.
I am ready to trust my Higher Power.
For, I surrender my *Self* today.

My life is in your hands,
Though, I don't totally understand.
I'm just a child gone amiss,

I never, ever thought my life would come to this.
Smoked some pot, drank booze and beer,
Used more and more drugs each successive year.
But, it's clear where it has lead,
I surrender my *Self* today—
I surrender before I am dead.

I also wrote this next poem during the same flight. I sometimes wonder if my inspiration for these came because I was thousands of miles out in space and closer to heaven:

"Believe"

I believe there's a power greater than me,
I believe this power will restore my sanity.
Belief is an awesome force,
Belief makes you change your course.
Christopher Columbus believed the Earth was not flat.
The Wright Brothers believed they could fly.
Belief, yes belief, got them by.

Believing is a choice.
Believe and hear God's voice.
Believe there is a power greater than you.
Believe, believe, and believe—because it's true.

Whatever you believe you will become; good or bad.
Whatever you believe will become your happy or your sad.
Believing is the starting point,
Know that it's true.
Just dare to believe.
Just dare to conceive.
Just dare to believe in a brand new you!

In thinking about recovery and in both the physical and emotional pain an addict goes through while getting sober, I was inspired to write a love song that either Michelle or I might sing to Ryan as a motivation to search within his heart and soul, and not to be afraid of what he'd find. I think the message is beautiful and very true and that anyone who loves an addict would feel this way:

"Once You Go Within You Will Never Go Without"

Once you go within,
You will never go without.
Let your day begin,
Just let go of every doubt.
When you go within,
You'll let go of all your fears.
Find out who you are,
Shed buried, childhood tears.

You will never go without,
Once you go within.
Your God is there for you,
Just listen as you do...

Once you know your *Self,*
No better friend than you,
Will treat you as you do.
Once you go within,
You will never go without.

I'll be there for you,
Waiting here for you,
When you go within.
Because, I never want to live,
Without,
You.

23

Okay, I'm Sober — Now What?

I REFLECTED UPON A CONVERSATION I had one time with Ryan. He had been clean and sober for over three years, so I asked him, "Ryan, do you ever worry about drinking or using drugs again?"

"Never Mom," he quickly replied.

"Really? How are you that certain?" I continued asking.

"Mom, all I need to do is remember what my life was like when I used drugs and then look at how great my life is now. There is no way I will ever go back to that other life." As a result of our conversation, I put myself in his shoes and wrote:

"Do We Listen or Turn a Deaf Ear?"

Staying sober isn't easy.
Sometimes, I get queasy.
Sometimes, I ache deep inside.
Then, I look to my left,
And I look to my right,
And I think of my life left behind.
I remember the pain,
I remember going insane,
And I remember the hell in which I lived.
Then, being sober gets easy,
I explore the queasy,
Open the threshold to my pain,
I breathe deep and let it drain.
I breathe deep and remain,
Clean and sober,
In a world I choose.
I choose to be a winner and no longer to lose,

At this game called life.
For in this game of life—
It's the choices that we make,
It's the paths we choose to take,
It's the people we choose to forsake.
It's our choices.
It's our voices.
Do we listen or turn a deaf ear?

Another time while listening to the Larry King show, I heard someone talking about being a Michelangelo, and it triggered an idea for me to write about with respect to self-realization and personal growth. Once one surrenders and spiritually understands what it means to become part of the universal power of Spirit, I believe all things are possible:

"Sculpt Your *Self*"

You are the masterpiece of your own life.
You are sculpting you!

Sculpt your *Self,*
Be your Michelangelo.
Sculpt your *Self,*
Re-design from head to toe.

Re-design,
Re-align,
Put your *Self* together.
That's the only way to be,
Who you really are—
Not your mother, father, or family tree.

To create your day, or to find your way,
Sculpt your *Self,*
Knock the chips off your shoulder.
Sculpt your *Self,*

Be true to *Self*, as you grow older.

Re-direct,
Re-respect,
Put your *Self* together,
So you can weather,
Every storm,
Every norm.

Re-new,
Re-do,
Put your best foot forward.
Sand away those rough, hard edges,
Find the David in you.

We're not talking perfection,
Just change your direction,
Chip away—peel back layers,
Uncover—
Discover—
Re-lease the pain,

Sculpt your *Self*,
Chisel your *Self*,
Down to your bare bones.
Put new meat on your feet,
Make your *Self*—prime.

Re-align,
Re-design,
Inject new blood into your veins.
Pump your heart.
It's the start,
Of a brand new you.
Just feel the love in your soul,
Allowing you to feel whole.
Feel the love of being true to you.

Sculpt your *Self,*
Be your Michelangelo!

I hope this poem becomes a song because I absolutely love the message. I do feel my son, along with everyone who struggles with addiction or any emotional challenge, must become one's own Michelangelo. In fact, anyone, who wants to grow and to become a better person, must become one's own Michelangelo. I think we all have the responsibility to sculpt ourselves as often as possible, until the day we die. I have certainly been my own Michelangelo! We all hold our own chisels, not in our hands, but in our minds.

24

Good versus Bad

I WANTED TO WRITE A SONG ABOUT the torturous pull of goodness versus evil that one must feel when attempting to stop using drugs. Honestly, I can not fathom what it must feel like to have one's body crave a drug to the point where one steals, lies, and does whatever it takes to get that drug, and especially knowing, at some level, there is always the possibility of dying.

I envisioned a feeling of having thousands of demonic creatures climbing inside your body, and tempting you into this deep, dark tunnel where there is no light at the end, just for another moment's pleasure. While your true, inner child, angelic *Self*, struggles to resist the demon's pull in an attempt to recover. I wrote it as a conversation going on inside of my son, Ryan.

"Don't Do The Twelve Steps"

Demon/Disease
Don't do the Twelve Steps,
He's all ours.
Inner Child
Strip your *Self* to your soul child,
Strip your *Self* and be whole.
Demon/Disease
Don't do the Twelve Steps,
Just numb your brain.
Inner Child
Deal with your fears,
Stop holding in tears,

Drain your *Self* of your pain.
Demon/Disease
Don't do the Twelve Steps,
Go back to the streets.
Angels
You know where to start child,
Your heart, your heart, your heart.
Demon/Disease
Don't do the Twelve Steps,
Sober is no fun.
Angels
If you stay steady,
If you stay strong,
Your life will be in your grip.
Demon/Disease
Don't do the Twelve Steps,
Get ripped instead.
Angels
Your best friend will be your *Self* to know.
Ryan
Temptation has a hold on me.
Temptation won't let me be free.
Temptation is tearing me apart.
Temptation is beating on my heart.
Temptation is under my skin.
Temptation is trying to win.
Temptation is pulling on my strings.
Angels
Don't give in.
No, don't give in.
Stand strong.
Stand firm.
Don't give in.
No, don't give in.
Be strong.
It's wrong.

Demon/Disease
Want some pot kid?
How about some crack?
Have another shot of whiskey,
With your old friend Jack!
Would some uppers turn you on?
I've got meth, cocaine, and kegs of beer,
Come along kid and share some cheer!
All in Recovery
Temptation once had its hold on me.
You are powerless over your addictions.
Take your first step and set your *Self* free.
Turn your will over to your Higher Power and you'll see.
Don't let your demons keep a hold on you.
Don't allow them to tell you what to do.

When I sang the song for Karen and her husband, Michael, Michael suggested having a tap dancing demon/disease, as a play on the words, Twelve Steps. As a former tap dancer, I thought that was a fabulous idea. I went home, looked up tap dancing terms, and then proceeded to write another version, where the demon/disease tap dances. I didn't want the song to be rude in any way towards NA or AA as I thought it could be misconstrued as being disrespectful to The Twelve Step programs; programs I started reading about and fully respected.

Because I didn't want to insult anyone, I suggested the demon/disease tap dance and sing to create a nightmare effect on Ryan during his sleep, the night before going to his first NA meeting. Karen then took what I had written, added some of the lyrics from my original *Mom's Opera*, and together we recreated the following song, which we ended up, recording:

"Don't Do The Twelve Steps"

Devil
Don't do the Twelve Steps.
Don't do the Twelve Steps.
Scuff to the right,

Keep getting high each night.
Don't do the Twelve Steps.
Don't do the Twelve Steps.
Cramp roll, right now,
Keep smoking dope somehow.

The Musical interlude while Demon/Disease tap dances towards Ryan.

Don't do the Twelve Steps.
Don't do the Twelve Steps.
Stomp the idea,
Or, no more Jack I fear.
Don't do the Twelve Steps.
Don't do the Twelve Steps.
Shuffle, hop, ball-change,
Snort a little more cocaine.
Take it from the devil,
Who used to be an angel 'til I overdosed to hell!

The Musical interlude.

Michelle (*speaking*, *upon hearing Ryan screaming*)
Ryan wake up. You're having a dream.
Ryan (*speaking*)
Michelle, it's not a dream. See the devil.
He's right there. Don't you see him?
Demon/Disease (*singing*)
Only you can see me Ryan—'Cause I'm the devil in you!
Michelle (*speaking*)
 Come on Ryan, go back to sleep. Forget your demons. Remember
the angel in you. You need your sleep. You have your first NA meeting
tomorrow.
 (*Ryan goes back to sleep. Angels enter and surround him.*)
Archangel
Don't give into temptation,
Rehabilitation,
Requires dedication,

Or, your demons will take you in.

Angels

If you stay steady, stay strong child,
And, don't give into your pride.
Over your fears, you will win child,
Or, your demons will take you in.

Archangel	**Angel**
Heed your Higher Powers.	Strip your *Self* to your soul child.
Stop to smell the flowers.	Strip your *Self* and be bold.
To the past—don't cower.	Get life into—your grip child.
Or your demons will take you in.	Or your demons will take you in.

Chorus

Drug's illusion can breed confusion and lead to a deadly conclusion.

Archangel

We all have imperfection,
Vices of election,
Admit your dereliction,
Or, your demons will take you in.

Angels

Deal with your fears,
Reveal those tears,
Drain your *Self* of your pain.
Don't give up or give in child,
Or, your demons will take you in.

Archangel	**Angel**
Hear the angel inside.	You know where to start child.
Face each day with new pride.	Your heart, your heart, your heart.
Make amends—no more child.	Let forgiveness—begin child.
Or your demons will take you in.	Or your demons will take you in.

Chorus

Drug's illusion can breed confusion,
And lead to a deadly conclusion.
Don't give in to temptation,
Rehabilitation,
Requires a dedication—

Demon
Or, the devil will take you in!

I decided to keep both versions of the song in this book because it shows the total progression of my mind, along with how another person with a true sense of musicality can pull the essence out of my work to create meaningful lyrics, rhyme, and rhythm.

25

I Still Love this Boy

ONCE WE ATTEMPTED TO PUT THE MUSICAL'S story in sequence, it became necessary to write new songs whose purposes were to connect a series of events. Once again, I thought back to 2002, when I kicked Ryan out of the townhouse and how he called Michelle. He called her because he knew Michelle had loved him once and hoped she still held a place in her heart for him. It's those beautiful memories that keep us imprisoned as enablers and provide the desire for us to continue helping our addicted loved ones. Michelle was the harbor in Ryan's storm. I heard a duet in my head, so I wrote the following:

"She Had Loved Me"

Ryan
Michelle knew me from twelve years before,
When I was clean and pure.
Before I tranquilized my pain,
Before I went a bit insane,
Before I closed my emotional door,
She had loved me.
Michelle
When Ryan called on the phone,
I knew he was not clean and pure any more.
I knew he tranquilized his pain,
I knew he went a bit insane,
Before he closed his emotional door—I had loved him.

Ryan	**Michelle**
Will she reach out to me?	Should I reach out to him?

Will she still be my friend?   Should I still be his friend?
I have no one,   He has no one,
And nowhere to turn.   And nowhere to turn.

Michelle

How can I turn my back on my friend?
When my friend is lying in the gutter.
How can I turn my back on my friend?
When I know he truly has no one other.

Ryan   **Michelle**
You can't.   I can't.

Michelle

I won't.
I shan't.
I still love him.
I still love this boy.

I remember his silly, comic ways,
I remember our belly laughing days,
I remember his innocent touch,
I remember how he made me blush,
I remember our very first kiss,
I remember, I remember the bliss.

I'll be there for you my friend—I'll be there.
I'll be there to hold you up—I'll be there.
I'll be there to dry your tears,
I'll be there to ease your fears,
I'll be there to lend an ear,
I'll be your forever-burning candle,
I'll be the shoulder you lean on.
I'll be the person, whom you turn to,
When you feel you can't go on.

Can I save him?
I really don't know.
Can I blame him?
When he suffers so.

Can I guide him to a life without woe?
I don't know.
But, I'll try,
For, he's my friend.
Ryan
When I was drowning in self-pity,
She threw a life preserver within my reach.
I had to swim to it—if I wanted to survive.
I had to swim to it—if I wanted to stay alive.
It was always a few strokes from my reach,
But, life's survival lessons, it helped to teach.

I am the first to admit that I clearly am not a songwriter. I believe I was a painter using words to create a picture of an event. Then, once Karen read my written artwork, she'd cut through the fat, to the meat of what I was saying to write an amazing song. This is what Karen pulled out of "She Had Loved Me," to create a sweet love song for Michelle to sing:

"This Boy"

I remember his silly ways—this boy.
Our belly laughing days—this boy.
His tender touch, that made me blush—this boy.

I remember our first kiss—this boy.
I'm remembering the bliss— of this boy.
The playful ways, I passed the days, with—this boy.

I'll be there for you my friend,
I'll be there to dry your tears,
Be your shoulder to lean on, I'll be there.

I remember his sweet smile,
His unassuming style,
Put me at ease, eager to please—this boy.

I'm remembering his face,
Its innocence and grace,
And, how his gaze could make me crave—this boy.

I'll be there for you my friend,
I'll be there to dry your tears,
Be your shoulder to lean on,
I'll be there.

I'll be there for you my friend,
I'll be there to ease your fears,
Be your shoulder to lean on,
I'll be there.

Shortly after Karen started working with me, she asked if we should change Ryan's name, in case he didn't like his real name being used. I told her I would ask. Ryan told me he was very proud to be in the musical and liked his name being used in the story. Still, his feelings have always been, "Mom, this is your story—not mine. If this is what you need to do—just do it."

So I must remind you as you read, this is my story, my journey, my way of turning a negative into a positive and the way I handled and processed the pain I endured. Over time, I changed my son's name to Ryan. Once he actually started working The Twelve Step program in 2010, my son preferred his anonymity be respected.

26

One's Higher Power

SOMETIME IN 2007 I SPOKE TO RYAN about his Higher Power. Ryan had never believed in God and was totally turned off to formal religion, so I wondered how he dealt with finding his Higher Power. Ryan proudly told me his Higher Power was his dog, London. At first, what he told me, bothered me, until I did further reading.

Ryan and Michelle loved animals and both donated time to local animal shelters after adopting London. Since most pets die before their masters, I was a bit concerned about what might happen to Ryan and to his sobriety when little London went to doggie heaven.

Ryan very maturely gave me his answer, saying he and London had a mutually beneficial relationship. London's life was horrible before Ryan adopted him. Ryan was there for London when London needed a home, and London was there for Ryan when emotionally Ryan needed way more than just a home. What London gave to Ryan I tried to sum up in the following poem:

"London the Dog, Not the City"

London the dog, not the city,
Became my son's Higher Power.
London the dog, not the city,
Stayed at his side, by the hour.
London, little London,
Bridged my son's life together.

London wagged his tail between his legs,
Responding happily to Ryan's gaze.

London licked his face every day,
While Ryan questioned his life's way.
It was London's tower over my son at night,
It was London's power as he calmed his fright.
It was London's love, for he was always there,
It was London's gaze that took away despair.
With a bark,
With a spark,
To ignite Ryan's fire.
With a lick,
With a stick,
Ryan kept his desire.
It was London the dog, not the city,
Who became Ryan's Higher Power.

•

My prayer: May London's bridge never fall down!

During my quest to further my knowledge of one's Higher Power and especially within recovery, I needed to recognize and to accept that one's Higher Power can be whatever works; be it a dog, a tree, or an invisible entity who has many names, such as, God, Jehovah, Mohammad, Shiva, etc. I received the following email (author unknown) that provided the reassurance I needed. Again, nothing is by accident.

Why Humans Live Longer Than Dogs

Being a veterinarian, I had been called to examine a ten-year-old Irish wolfhound named, Belker. The dog's owners, Ron, his wife Lisa and their little boy, Shane, were all very attached to Belker, and they were hoping for a miracle.

I examined Belker and found he was dying of cancer. I told the family there were no miracles left for Belker, and offered to perform the euthanasia procedure for the old dog in their home. As we made arrangements, Ron and Lisa told me they thought it would be good for their four-year-old Shane to observe the procedure. They felt as though Shane might learn something from the experience.

The next day, I felt the familiar catch in my throat as Belker's family surrounded him. Shane seemed so calm, petting the old dog for the last time that I wondered if he understood what was going on. Within a few minutes, Belker slipped peacefully away. The little boy seemed to accept Belker's transition without any difficulty or confusion.

We sat together for a while after Belker's death, wondering aloud about the sad fact that animal lives are shorter than human lives. Shane, who had been listening quietly, piped up, "I know why." Startled, we all turned to him. What came out of his mouth next stunned me. I'd never heard a more comforting explanation than his.

He said, "People are born so that they can learn how to live a good life—like loving everybody all the time and being nice, right?" The four-year-old continued, "Well, dogs already know how to do that, so they don't have to stay as long."

*   *   *

Then shortly after that, as if my Higher Power led me, I read the following statement about a family's relationship with their dog. "He taught us the art of unqualified love; how to give it, how to accept it. Where there is that, most of the other pieces fall into place. Mostly he taught me about friendship and selflessness and, above all else, unwavering loyalty."

After doing research, I learned this was one of John Grogan's quotes from his book, *Marley and Me; Life and Love with the World's Worst Dog*. I think those qualities are what my son needed to learn. If London is his teacher, then may God bless London and all dogs. There are many more wonderful quotes written by John Grogan, about dogs that I would love to have included in this book. Unfortunately, I was not successful at getting through to Mr. Grogan's publisher for permission.

I wrote the following in an effort to write a cute, whimsical song that London could sing, about one's Higher Power:

"In Case You Hadn't Noticed"

London
Since this is a story of truth,

I won't tell you a tale.
My name is London.
I'm a dog,
In case you hadn't noticed.

I won't take the stage for long,
But, I want to bark a song!
The truth is…
I said, the truth is,
I became Ryan's Higher Power.
No, I'm not a G-O-D.
I'm a D-O-G.
I'm a dog,
In case you hadn't noticed.

It's funny how three letters rearranged,
Make one mighty or on four legs.
What's important here?
I beg your ear.
I'm good at begging.
I'm a dog,
In case you hadn't noticed.

When looking for something greater than *Self,*
Something or someone to believe in,
It doesn't have to be G-O-D.
A, D-O-G can set you free!
Just look at me!
I'm a dog,
In case you hadn't noticed.

Ryan
London—the dog, not the city,
Became my Higher Power.
She was there for me,
Unconditionally.

London
When I needed to be fed,

Ryan jumped out of bed.
'Cause I'm a dog,
In case you hadn't noticed.
Ryan
London—the dog, not the city,
Licked my face without pity.
Licked my face with laps of joy.
London
When I couldn't hold it any longer,
In came my boy to let me out.
'Cause, I'm a dog,
In case you hadn't noticed.
Ryan and London
I needed him/her,
He/she needed me.
I could provide,
What others did not see.
London
I gave a wag.
Ryan
There went my sad.
London
I gave a bark.
Ryan
There came my spark.
London
I needed to chew.
Ryan
Gave her my shoe.
London
I needed to run.
Ryan
Took her out in the sun,
Took her out to the doggie park.
London
'Cause I'm a dog.

Ryan
No, you're my G-O-D.
London
No, I'm your D-O-G.
Ryan
That's what I said,
They're both the same to me.
I'm in recovery,
In case you hadn't noticed!
(London whispers in Ryan's ear, while crossing her legs.)
Ryan (*to audience*)
Excuse us. London needs to go out for a walk.
London (*with more exaggerated crossed legs*)
In case you hadn't noticed!

2 7

The Secret

I AM COMPELLED TO MENTION AGAIN that the entire process of writing *Mom's Opera* and then *Tough Love - The Musical* and putting them together in this book of *hope* has been a tremendous spiritual journey for me. It's a journey I attracted into my life back in 2002 when I asked my Higher Power God and the Universe, *"How?"*

When the book, *The Secret* came out in 2006, written by Rhonda Byrne and based on the earlier film of the same name, it just reinforced every principle I had been practicing since I was around thirty-six years old, when I first applied the power of my thoughts to my professional life; then when I was forty-nine when I applied them to my personal/romantic life, and again at fifty-two when I began doing tough love with Ryan.

The belief of the film and the book are that the Universe is governed by a natural law called, The Law of Attraction, which works by attracting into a person's life the experiences, situations, events and people which "match the frequency" of the person's thoughts and feelings. Therefore, positive thinking and feeling positive are claimed to create life-changing results, such as increased wealth, health, and happiness.

Rhonda defines *The Secret* as the law of attraction, which is the principle that "like attracts like." Rhonda calls it "the most powerful law in the Universe," and says it is working all the time. "What we do is we attract into our lives the things we want, and that is based on what we're thinking and feeling." The principle explains that we create our own circumstances by the choices we make in life. And the choices we make are fueled by our thoughts—which means our thoughts are one of our most powerful possessions.

Although I will eventually decide to publish this book before completing the musical, I continue attracting people into my life who will help to move the musical forward, when I am ready. My vision is being realized right before my eyes, every day. I recognize this in my life. And throughout this journey and process, both my son and I are recovering; which is the ultimate goal of my thinking and writing. We are where we are meant to be, now. Truth is we will be recovering for the rest of our lives while being our own, Michelangelo's.

When one attempts to create something as immense as a musical and expects to put the musical on stage, it is an accomplishment one cannot do alone. It takes love, energy, commitment and a vision from many dedicated and talented people. It also takes lots of money. I know when I am ready everything I need will materialize. The manifestation process and the ability to create whatever reality one desires are powerful tools we all possess and can be applied to any part of one's life.

Until each of us "is ready" and creates the frequency to transform our behaviors with respect to addiction, sobriety, codependency, or familial dysfunction, we will not attract what we need into our lives. (These beliefs will make more sense to you by the end of my book than they might now.) The power of one's intention works hand in hand with the manifestation process.

As an example, before Karen worked on the musical with me, I had located a very talented, young man, named Caesar who had recently graduated from college as a Music Major. He jumped at the opportunity to compose. However, his wife was due to have twins within a few months so Caesar could not make the required commitment. What Caesar did do was contribute his unused piano, stored in his mother's house. She was extremely happy to unload it! With that, I have had Caesar's piano in my living room from the first time I began working on music! I never focused on having a piano. The piano manifested once I focused on creating music. That's how the Universe works!

*   *   *

After Karen and I worked for over a year on writing our musical we had a handful of songs we thought were ready to be recorded. We just needed to find some talented singers. The Universe again provided. Just by making a few phone calls and with singers knowing other singers, we magically had my living room full of very talented vocalists, passionately wanting to move the musical forward. It was amazing to hear the songs take shape. The songs brought tears to my eyes.

In March 2007, Karen and I went into a recording studio and recorded our four favorite songs. With our hearts filled with hope, we submitted our musical concept to ASCAP as part of their 2007 Workshop for Musical Theatre. Each year ASCAP chooses four original musicals to be professionally developed in a workshop environment by Stephen Schwartz and other professionals. We hoped ours would be one of their four choices for the summer workshop. We would know within six weeks. Hopefully the Universe's Law of Attraction would work in our favor!

2 8

Hope to Reunite Father and Son

WHILE WAITING TO HEAR ABOUT THE musical, I flew up to Virginia to visit Ryan and Michelle in April. As I was flying, I again projected into the future to creatively visualize what I imagined could be the ending song for the musical. I heard it sung as a beautiful duet between mother and son:

"Miracles Happen"

Ryan
You were right, Mom,
It's all about choices.
You were right, Mom,
It's all about the voices— in my head.
If I had not heard the angels, I'd be dead.

You were right, Mom,
It was all about me.
You were right, Mom,
I was too selfish to see.
Mom
I was right son, in my heart son,
But, being right could have ended wrong.
God put angels in your life,
And, thank God, your Demons moved along.
Ryan and Mom
But, now we're both past the pain,
And, now our lives are whole again,
And, now together our lives are joined,

In love, forgiveness, and understanding.
We will both grow strong.

You/I dug deep into my heart and soul,
You/I faced the demons keeping me/you from being whole,
You/I started giving and not taking,
You/I started feeling and not faking,
You/I created a future for yourself/myself,
You've/I've been blessed by angels,
The demons in you/me are gone,
For, you/I chose life instead.

Like a baby starting to crawl,
Like a new born crying,
You/I started trying.
Today—Today you're/I'm clean.
Today—Today you're/I'm on your/my way.
Today—One-step at a time is your/my motto.
You're/I'm on your/my way.
You're/I'm taking your/my family with me.

Miracles can happen,
Just believe in Love.
Miracles can happen,
Just believe in a Higher Power up above.
Miracles can happen,
When you release your pain.
Miracles can happen,
Miracles do happen,
Just look at my son/mom and me.
Miracles can happen,
Went from words of hate to love-r-lee.
Miracles can happen,
When love is sent from above.
Miracles can happen,
Especially when there is love, in *tough love*.

I realized I was able to write upbeat lyrics like this because my son had been clean almost four years. It would be four years on October 28, 2007. So the pressure was off. I didn't even think about Ryan relapsing. He appeared so level headed. He seemed to have finally acquired self-esteem and an understanding of his innate talents and strengths.

When I returned home from seeing how wonderful Ryan was doing, I decided to send his father, Johnny and his wife, Beth, a letter, hoping to rekindle their relationship with Ryan. I knew Ryan was still deeply hurt by not having his father in his life. This is what I wrote in May and sent:

Dear Johnny and Beth,

A short note to you, in hopes of rekindling your relationship with your son, Ryan:

On October 28, 2007 Ryan will be four years clean of drugs and alcohol. You would be very proud of him. He's in his second year of college and only has a few more courses before he graduates in graphic design. He's turned out to be quite an artist—like his dad! He even quit smoking cigarettes nearly three years ago. He is engaged to a wonderful girl named Michelle who was instrumental in his recovery. They knew one another when they were fifteen, before Ryan's addictions possessed him. They were childhood sweethearts. They live in Woodstock, Virginia, where she was raised. Ryan has even taken up mountain biking to stay in shape.

Johnny, you and I gave birth to a wonderful little boy who has finally gotten through his pains of being from an anger filled, split home. I am sorry for my part in our troubled relationship. I have learned so much since I was in my twenties. You and I both came from dysfunctional childhoods, and we both had much pain of our own to recover from before we could be open to a healthy and nurturing relationship with another person. You were very fortunate to meet Beth, who came from a loving and functional family. I was forty-nine when I finally felt whole and met a healthy man to whom I am happily married and who gives me wings to fly.

Meanwhile, I said this would be a short note. I want you to know when I did tough love on Ryan, when he was twenty-five, it was the hardest day of my life. I had been a total enabler. I started writing to keep my sanity, fearing our son could die without my financial assistance. My writing led to a musical that will hopefully be produced called *Tough Love – The Musical* based on writings I originally wrote called, *Mom's Opera*, where I wrote poetry and lyrics to deal with my pain. Then, eventually I wrote a story to tie everything together.

Ryan didn't die. He made the choice instead to become a unique, young man. A son you would be very proud of. A son whose only missing piece of his puzzle is that he misses having a relationship with you—his father. He has such fond memories of you from when he was young. Michelle tells me how much he misses having you in his life. I know you don't owe me anything. But, if I may, I would like to ask you to please contact your son. I think you both would find fulfillment. I remember how much it meant to you when you reconnected with your own father after so many lost years.

I have learned through this entire process that life is about choices. I have chosen to forgive you, Ryan, and myself. We are all human. We were all just little, innocent and perfect babies once, and life threw us all a lot of curve balls. I hope you will choose to throw your son a ball straight from your heart. Call him. Let him know how much you did and still do love him. Let him know the man you have become. I know he's already proud of you. He reads about you on the Internet, and he loves you so much. He wants to know you so badly. Your son is a man now. He's not a lost boy any longer, and he has so many of your good qualities. He's a gift to behold.

The only reason he doesn't contact you himself is that he's afraid of being rejected by you. He's afraid of the pain he would feel. He doesn't know I am sending you this letter.

With love, Deni

I provided Johnny with Ryan's contact information and prayed for him to open his heart to his son. Five years ago I didn't know if we would even have a son when I did tough love. Ryan deserved to know his dad. All I could do was put my prayer into the Universe and wait for the Universe to provide.

(In hindsight: I have since learned from Anne Salter, that writing this letter is another example of the codependent's need to fix everything, and that I had totally unrealistic expectations; which is a large part of codependency. BUT, in my defense, I believe the writing of the letter was also part of my creative visualization and power of intention.)

After mailing the letter I thought about the "Fessin' Up" song I had written back in 2003, and was inspired to add the following verse for Ryan's father to sing:

"Fessin' Up"

Father
I should 'fess up too,
I'm fessin' fessin' fessin' up to the truth.

I'm your daddy—I fathered you,
I loved you too,
But your momma and me,
Just didn't agree,
I pushed and pulled you,
Bestowed upon you, so many lies.

Out of anger, desperation and frustration,
Stopped fulfilling my obligation,
To you my son.
Deserted you and your momma too,
And now I'm fessin' fesssin' fessin' up to my crimes.

I just didn't see,
I just couldn't see,
Your life was my responsibility.
I let you down,
Was not around,
I was not a father.

Son
You're still my father.
Father
It's not too late?
Son
It's never too late to tell your son that you're human.
It's never too late to tell your son he is loved.
Father
I am human,
But was not humane.
Had my own pain,
It made me blind,
Just couldn't see,
Your life was also left to me.
And, I loved you so,
Now I'm fessin' fessin' fessin' up to my crimes.
Parents
We just couldn't see.
We just didn't see..
Blinded by our hostility.
I'll keep fessin' up.
I'll keep fessin' up.
Ryan
I'll start fessin' up too.
All
If we all 'fess up,
And, we all give up,
We will all begin to grow.
We can all begin
To forgive within
And, love we will know.

I felt it appropriate that Ryan's father should own his part in our dysfunctional past. It all has to do with forgiveness; the forgiveness of *Self* and others. Once we remove the ego, forgiveness is possible.

29

Recovery: The Never Ending Story

AS YOU ALREADY KNOW OR AT LEAST figured out by now, *Tough Love – The Musical* wasn't chosen for the 2007 workshop. (If it had been, I'm certain this book wouldn't have been written and my journey would have gone down an entirely different path.) But, that's okay. It wasn't meant to be—then. No biggie. Nothing ventured, nothing gained. At least Karen and I tried. There is a reason for everything!

Today as I continue writing in May 2007, the recovery process feels somewhat like the never-ending story. My son will be in recovery for the rest of his life, and at some point, our story will become a musical on stage based on our lives. These writings represent one woman's journey from hell and back. I am that woman, so I know it is possible.

Ryan will be turning thirty-one in September. He is sober nearly four years. He is prospering. He has completed all but three credits in college, has turned in his final portfolio, and is working full-time as a graphic designer. He plans to take one remaining class next year at night in order to receive his Associates Degree. Ryan is making $30,000 per year as a graphic artist. He uses his creativity every day. He gets up seven days a week feeling good about himself and his accomplishments.

Ryan has always been an artist. Unfortunately, his God-given gifts had not been nurtured. All of us receive gifts at birth. Gifs require nurturing. Some of us, who are fortunate, receive nurturing, while others do not. Ryan's angels made sure his innate truths, gifts, and talents were revealed.

Most every day Ryan calls me on his way home from work to share his enthusiasm about his life. He is making new friends at work and building a network of positive relationships. His company gives employees golf memberships, so on Wednesdays Ryan plays golf after work. Then, on most weekends, he plays golf. He also continues to mountain bike. He can't believe how good his life is today. He doesn't focus on his past. He looks to the future but lives in the now.

He always tells me, "Mom it's all good. You need to stop beating yourself up about your past. You were an awesome Mom. I did stupid things. It wasn't you. It was me."

The fact Ryan could own his poor choices made it possible for him to move on in his life. He paid the price and has forgiven himself. He has forgiven me. I had to own my poor choices too. It's not easy to look back and admit to all of one's poor choices. But, I can guarantee that once you take an honest inventory of yourself and own your shortcomings and your dysfunctions, it truly is a freeing experience. You own it, deal with it, and let it go. Feelings of shame, blame, and guilt need to be replaced with pride, compassion, and forgiveness.

Recovery is an ongoing process of healing and growth. It doesn't happen over night. We have to be patient with ourselves and with one another.

*   *   *

Karen and I are off on an adventure in the Big Apple! It will be interesting and fun to see which musicals were accepted. This will be Karen's first ASCAP experience, so we are both excited to keep growing. We have a lot to learn!

PART II
2007 - 2010

There Are No Accidents

30

Divine Intervention at its Best

STRANGE IS OUR SITUATION HERE UPON EARTH. EACH OF US COMES FOR A SHORT VISIT, NOT KNOWING WHY, YET SOMETIMES SEEMING TO A DIVINE PURPOSE. FROM THE STANDPOINT OF DAILY LIFE, HOW-EVER, THERE IS ONE THING WE DO KNOW: THAT WE ARE HERE FOR THE SAKE OF OTHERS—FOR THE COUNTLESS UNKNOWN SOULS WITH WHOSE FATE WE ARE CONNECTED BY A BOND OF SYMPATHY. MANY TIMES A DAY, I REALIZE HOW MUCH MY OUTER AND INNER LIFE IS BUILT UPON THE LABORS OF PEOPLE, BOTH LIVING AND DEAD, AND HOW EARNESTLY I MUST EXERT MYSELF IN ORDER TO GIVE IN RETURN AS MUCH AS I HAVE RECEIVED.

—Albert Einstein

ONE OF THE BIGGEST LESSONS THROUGHOUT my journey has been that Spirit truly works in mysterious and miraculous ways. We need only be open to God's goodness and to recognize those moments when divine intervention is opening doors. We have to listen always to that still, small voice we all have inside. That voice will guide and lead us in the right direction, and I truly believe nothing is by accident.

Karen, Janice, and I attended the ASCAP workshop over three nights. Karen stayed with her husband and family while in the city, and I stayed with Janice. Janice and I went to see a Broadway show on my last night there. Divine intervention was about to take place in a grand and magnificent way.

After the show, we went to the Stardust Diner, where all the waiters and waitresses sing Broadway tunes. Two, well-dressed women entered and sat next to our table. The four of us literally sat shoulder to shoul-der. Being an open, friendly person, I naturally said, "Hello." With that, the four of us started chatting, only to discover they lived just forty minutes away from me in Florida, and that the three of us were in New York City because we all loved Broadway musicals. When I shared I was writing a musical about addiction and recovery, they shared they were Addiction Specialists and Marriage and Family Therapists.

Meeting Anne Salter and Carey Matthews would appear to be the result of divine intervention, universal energy, and The Secret all coming together in my life at their crowning points—their zeniths! I would never be the same again. My life was destined to change forever.

During the conversation, I asked if either Anne or Carey would be interested in consulting with me on my musical as I didn't want my lyrics to insult anyone in recovery. It turned out that Anne had always wanted to write a musical, so she said she would be thrilled to participate.

Our first meeting would not be until October 26. We met for lunch and mostly chatted about our personal lives so we could casually get to know one another and feel comfortable. I filled Anne in on my background and what led me to writing my musical. I showed Anne a few pages of songs and she was captivated by the lyrics and by my overall mission. When Anne left, I gave her a copy of what had been written thus far, so she could read at her leisure and make notes.

During our second meeting on November 13, Anne went over some of the lyrics where I called addiction the devil, and she explained to me how addiction is a disease and that those in recovery don't like it referred to as the devil. I had a hard time understanding because, as a writer I was only drawing an analogy of the disease as if it were a demon. As an addict's mother, it had certainly appeared as a demon in my son's life! To compromise, I would eventually call addiction a devil of a disease!!

I learned that Anne works with families, adult individuals, couples, groups, and even conducts group retreats. Her focus is always on emotional healing of the *Self*. She specializes in relationship work using family of origin therapy and experiential techniques such as psychodrama, Gestalt, and family of origin sculpting. She studied family and group work from many masters, including Virginia Satir, Sharon Wegscheider Cruse, and John Heider. Anne is an addiction specialist, certified by John Hopkins University in 1978 and previously taught addiction courses at Barry University.

A recovering alcoholic for over forty years, Anne also has personal experience dealing with her own addicted children. She now presents addiction seminars around the United States, while working as a consultant to treatment centers training other therapists. She is also a family of origin relationship specialist, who conducts interventions.

And now, there I was meeting to discuss my musical with this brilliant and experienced addiction therapist! If that isn't divine intervention at its best, then I can't imagine what else you'd call it!

By our third meeting on November 26, I finally convinced Karen to attend. Karen and I had hit a writing wall after New York City. Our relationship was a bit strained, so our collaborating began deteriorating. I had a hard time trying to figure out the story line, and Karen didn't want to continue writing songs without a developed story, and especially without an ending. I was hoping we could find some encouragement and inspiration by meeting together with Anne.

Meeting together didn't help our writing relationship as I had hoped it might. If anything it seemed to go further downhill. By late December, when I met with Anne again I knew my writing relationship with Karen was over. We had both given it our best efforts. It was time to let go.

31

My Parting Message

DURING THE SAME TIME I HAD BEEN meeting with Anne, I also was working as a realtor. In September 2007, I had closed on a large real estate transaction and made a nice commission.

Ryan had a serious passion for watches and lusted for a Rolex. I too had a serious passion. Mine was for the collection of the paintings he created in 2003 while coming off drugs and alcohol. I envisioned projecting his artwork onto the stage during a scene in the musical. I also anticipated hanging his original paintings in the lobby of the theatre, but in the meantime, hanging them in my home-office. Ryan's artwork was a true expression of his soul during his recovery, and I wanted to preserve and make them part of the musical experience.

Like Pablo Picasso's "Blue Period," between 1900 and 1904, when he painted monochromatic paintings in shades of blue and blue-green, which seemed to reflect his experience of relative poverty and instability, I felt Ryan's paintings represented his "Blue Period" as well. I could not imagine Ryan ever painting that way again. I had an idea. I offered to give Ryan a Rolex in exchange for all of his artwork.

In November, Ryan agreed to sell me his paintings for a Rolex. I then knew his artwork would be protected, preserved, and available to share with others. We both got what we wanted, and we were both happy. Ryan wished me much success with my musical and was full of pride putting a Rolex on his arm.

Sometime in December, an inspiration came to me to write an opening song for the musical. From my background in children's theatre, I understood a child singing on stage creates tremendous impact. I also knew Johnny, and I broke Ryan's heart when he was a little boy, so I wrote the following:

"Mom's Opera"

Mom
This is Mom's Opera,
This is my story.
This is a mother's tale,
Heart felt and teary.
I gave birth,
As mothers do.
All my dreams,
Wrapped up in you.
I breastfed my son,
Did all that I could,
To give him good health,
Like a good mother should.
But,
I was dysfunctional,
And his father, too,
We were at each other's throats,
The marriage was all but through.

During all of our strife,
We fought, screamed, and yelled,
Upon his young ears the violence fell.
And then one day on our battlefield,
Our darling young son held his hands to his ears.
Little Ryan
Stop your fights you're hurting my ears!
Stop your fights you're creating my fears!
Stop fighting,
Stop yelling,
Stop pulling me apart.
It's hurting me—Mom.
It's hurting me—Pop.
It's hurting my heart.
Stop.
Please stop!

My little insides just crumble,
My little insides just ache,
I don't have words to say how I feel,
But my pain, my pain is very real.
Stop your fights you're hurting my ears!
Stop your fights you're creating my fears!
Stop.
Please stop!!

Karen did not like what I wrote at all and refused to work on turning it into an opening number or on writing any songs at all until I completed writing the "book" for the musical. I realized I just needed to relax, knowing the Universe would lead me to where I needed to be.

Then, mostly for myself to have an "ending" to my writings thus far on these "chapters" of my life, I wrote the following:

A Parting Message From Deni

My wish to anyone who is an addict, or to anyone who has lost their inner child and/or *Self*, is that you find your Spirit given, divine talents and put them to use in a positive way. Strip your *Self* to your soul. Dig deep and get in touch with your inner child. Peel off those layers of pain until you uncover your heart, your soul, and your essence. Don't cover up the pain any longer. It's okay to experience pain. Paint. Write. Dance. Sing. Sculpt. Find something artistic that allows you to express your Spirit *Self*. Work through your feelings. Cry. Share. I promise you ecstasy does wait on the other side of suffering.

Only you can stop using and abusing yourself. Essentially, it's all about choices, and the voices you choose to follow. Once you are sober, trust me—your family and friends will be there again for you with open arms to welcome you back home.

Home is a place inside of yourself, where you find the real you, that original child of God's who got hurt and lost.

Strip your *Self* to your soul child,
Strip your *Self* and be bold.

Deal with your fears,
Stop holding in tears,
Drain your *Self* of your pain.

*   *   *

When I wrote the above "parting" message, I believed my son was in a good place with his recovery and I even thought I was recovered too, as his codependent mother. I couldn't have been further from the truth concerning either one of us.

The bottoms both Ryan and I hit before turning our lives around were still over two years away. And it seems what I wrote as my parting message to others, was in actuality subliminal messaging to my own, wounded child *Self*. I still needed to strip my *Self* to my soul. I still needed to deal with my fears. I still needed to drain my *Self* of my pain.

Denial is blinding. Denial is cunning. Denial must be denied!

3 2

To Everything There is a Season

AS DISSAPPOINTED AS I WAS, THAT Karen and I had a falling out over the musical, I also knew I was not ready or capable of writing an ending. I was still evolving and felt my personal journey was still unfolding. I knew not what the future held, but I did know that I had not reached the end of *Mom's Opera*. I had not yet found all of my answers because I had not yet recovered my *Self.* How could I explain that to Karen when I didn't even understand what I was going through?

I met with Anne on January 16, 2008 to continue our discussions on addiction and recovery. By this point, it was obvious to me that I had major issues as a codependent enabler. Anne didn't try to be my therapist, but she gently let me know I had underlying issues that needed resolving.

Anne and I spoke about a book she had started writing back in 2004, called *Family Stew: Our Relationship Legacy*. She told me my writing had inspired her to begin working again on her book. Ann realized if she didn't put the seat of her pants to the seat of a chair to write at age seventy, she might never fulfill her dream of publishing a book. Anne's New Year's resolution was to finish writing her book!

My resolution for the New Year was to spend time organizing the many poems and songs into their proper sequence, based on when they were written. In this way it would eventually be easier to create and plot out the story line for *Tough Love – The Musical*.

When we left our meeting that day we both vowed to achieve our goals. Throughout the rest of the year, Anne diligently worked on her book and I diligently worked on organizing my writings. As I put my writings in order, I felt it necessary to explain what had inspired me to write. Over the course of the year before I knew it, I had laid the groundwork for this book.

Anne and I stayed in touch over the phone throughout the year as we cheered each other on and I think we may have met for a social lunch once or twice, but basically it was noses to the grindstone for us both. We stayed focused.

*   *   *

Time passed. It was now 2009. I didn't even consider publishing a book after I thought it was finished in 2008. I still intended to produce a musical, not publish a book.

Anne called in early January to tell me she had finished writing her book. We met on January 7, 2009 to celebrate her accomplishment! Since I had a bachelor's degree in English, I decided to put my musical aside to focus on organizing and executing Anne's book editing. *Family Stew* represented the past thirty years of Anne's professional work in the field of addiction and recovery. I offered to do this as a gift to her, and as a way to gain real life editing experience. Little did I know it would end up being a tremendous gift to me!

It wasn't until I started meeting with Anne and discussing addiction with a professional for the first time that I started to get that I was in major denial as to how my family-of-origin had been dysfunctional. I realized that until I begin to examine and deal with my own pain filled past, I'd always remain ill, as a codependent. This newfound awareness all started surfacing while working on Anne's book.

Because of our schedules, it would take over one year to read through *Family Stew* with Anne, make changes, and get her book finished and ready to be professionally edited. I must say *Family Stew* shed more light on familial dysfunction than anything I had ever read. It is because of what I learned from Anne's book, and by speaking with Anne that I was able to honestly examine my life and share my dysfunctional past with you in part 3 of this book.

I found forgiveness of *Self* and of others, and learned how to reconnect with my authentic *Self*, so I could begin to build healthy relationships with my son and other loved ones. *Family Stew* is a must read for anyone wanting to heal a wounded past. Anne's book provided the keys for me to eventually unlock doors that had been sealed closed for over forty years on my emotional truths.

As an example, Anne writes in chapter two: Relationship With Our Family-Of-Origin and Adaptive Roles, "The Adaptive *Self* is something we form somewhere in our childhood, when we are traumatized or just don't feel safe. We form adaptive parts of *Self* when we become fear and/or shame based. One of the saddest things about our adaptation is that we continue to go through life as an actor. We are, in fact, like a spider caught in the web of our parents, our ancestors, and all their stuff, and our wounds and defenses have been formed from all of this. We feel strangely unfulfilled and try to fill the void with all sorts of external people, places, substances, and things. We try drugs, fancy cars and houses, power careers, food, shopping, sex, gambling, money and more. Yet, because it is the true *Self* and the love of it that we are missing, none of this works. Saddest of all, these efforts to fill this void, aid the abusive and negative behaviors toward the true *Self*. Real value of *Self* and *Self*-care is not something we are even aware of as adult children, and we, therefore, tend not to nurture and do healthy things for ourselves. The adaptive child's job is to protect the inner child's pain, and the adaptive child will be the part that becomes the addict."

How could I read something like that and not see the light? As Anne writes in her introduction; "*Family Stew* will clarify how we are trapped somewhere in the core of our relationship with our *Self*, protected by layers of wounds and defenses, and especially by lack of trust. Thus, we only know what we are aware of knowing. By beginning to realize, learn, and understand one's dysfunctional, personal, behavioral themes, and roadblocks (defenses), one can then discover what is required to change in all areas of relationship, to have a more fulfilling life."

Divine intervention did take place back in New York City the night I met Anne Salter. It's as if all of the universal powers I had attracted into my life joined forces and spoke to me saying, "Deni enough already! We hear you! And, since you want to write a musical on addiction and recovery, we're putting Anne in your life in order to help you with your own recovery!"

33

The Universe Keeps Providing

IT WAS WHILE WORKING WITH ANNE on her book that the Universe put Mitch, my second composer lyricist into my life. It's quite funny how we met.

As a realtor, I paid twenty-five dollars to promote myself at a local, business-networking, breakfast meeting. What this means is I paid to make a business presentation, in front of the group, for ten minutes. I spent one minute promoting real estate and the next nine speaking about addiction, recovery, tough love, and my musical. I was trying to raise the consciousness of others to addiction and to ignite conversations about a family disease that most people don't openly discuss. I tried taking the shame out of something almost *common* in today's world. Two other people shared they had addiction and/or alcoholism in their family, and one person asked me to become their Realtor!

After the meeting, a man close to my age approached me and introduced himself. Moved by my story, Mitch said that he had been a former rock and roll keyboard musician who also had a background in song composition and that he would love to work with me on my musical. I shared with him about my relationship with Karen and how we had hit a dead end because I didn't have my story completed. Mitch said he'd love to help me with both my story and my music. He shared that his family had dealt with addiction years before, and in the 1980s his own mother had been heavily involved in the "Just Say No" anti-drug movement. Mitch had the passion and the background I was looking for in a musician.

Shortly thereafter, Mitch came to my home. When he sat at the piano, he overwhelmed me with his talent. I was excited to see what we could create together. Mitch took my pain filled story, added his creative ideas and together we wrote some highly spirited, yet solid lyrics and rock and roll music. We took the musical from being serious but light, to almost a comedy, where it pointed out much of my dysfunction as an enabling mother.

I wasn't comfortable having the musical being so funny and wanted to add some spiritual songs into the show. Mitch just wouldn't go there, at all. He flat out refused to write anything spiritual. Mitch even told me he didn't think my son was an addict, but that he only liked to party. (That was only a few months before Ryan went into rehab in 2010 after relapsing on amphetamines.) I realized Mitch, and I had two totally different visions for the musical, and we were worlds apart.

In early December 2009, we ended our collaboration. During our time together, we did write and record three impressive songs. And, we actually came up with some very humorous yet poignant scenes. For the most part, I honestly loved working with Mitch. We just differed in the overall message of the musical.

Truthfully, I was not emotionally ready to write a humorous, non-spiritual musical in 2009. Yes, I could laugh at many of my dysfunctional behaviors and see the humor in some of my enabling ways, but the story I wanted to tell centered on the seriously dangerous disease, of addiction, that destroys families and ruins lives. In 2009, it was hard for me to find anything humorous about addiction, or to find any humor in my life's story.

Today, as I work towards finishing this book, ideally, I would like to see both Karen's and Mitch's songs in the musical. I think it would make for an interesting balance. Though I am open to whatever story works (as long as it provides *hope* and encouragement to parents and motivation for youths to stay clean and sober), I am still insistent on including some spiritually based songs! Without my Higher Powers guiding me through the battles I had faced, and still had to face, I'm most certain I would not have been the victor.

Mitch and I recorded a song for our story, where Ryan was sitting in his apartment with his dealer friend, Keith, getting high together and commiserating over why they were so screwed up. This is just before *enabling* Mom pays a surprise visit to her *sober* son who swore to her he was clean. This song was definitely based on our lives:

"Getting High"

Ryan
My parents were always fighting ever since I was three.
I cried for them to stop, but they were way to angry to hear me,
To hear me, to hear me—

I would hide in my room and blame myself for not being good.
Deep down inside me, I felt like no one understood.
The pain, I felt betrayed and angry.
I hated my life more and more each day.
To escape, I smoked—I drank—and snorted.
To deal with my life,
I was always getting high.
Keith (*spoken*)
At least your parents cared enough to fight over you. My parents
were always too busy socializing, rubbing elbows with the rich and
famous. Nannies took care of me.

Keith (*singing*)
Well, I was just a little rich kid.
Let me tell you—was a bitch kid.
Mom and Dad always gave me lots of money.
It was easier than loving me.
They didn't care that I was acting so cool.
They didn't even notice I was always skipping school.
They never hassled me for staying out late.
They never punished me for getting bad grades.
Ryan
What? You had tons of friends and all the hottest chicks.
Keith
When you've got cash, you have all the friends you need.
My friends all loved me, as long as I had the killer weed.
Both
The pain—I felt unloved and angry.
I hated my life more and more, more and more each day.
To escape—I smoked—I drank—and snorted.

To deal with my pain I was always—I was always—
I was always—
Getting high.

Mitch and I also wrote and recorded a title song called, "Tough Love." This song was positioned to take place after the fight song, "One More Promise," that Karen and I wrote and recorded, where Mom finally has had enough of Ryan's lies and self-destructive behavior and begins her tough love by evicting Ryan from the apartment and out of her life. While Ryan is off stage packing his bag, Mom sings:

"Tough Love"

Seems like the more I give in to you,
There's just more that you take from me.
There's never an end, to all that I spend,
I try to help you break free.

Whatever you want from me, I give it to you.
But, I've had enough,
It's time to get tough, with you,
Tough love, tough love,
I'm giving you, tough love.

There's always a problem, it's part of your plan.
You know I'll be there with a helping hand.
Whatever you want from me, I give it to you.
But I've had enough,
It's time to get tough, with you,
Tough love.
Tough love.
Tough love.
Whatever you want from me, I give it to you.
But, I've had enough,
It's time to get tough, with you,
Tough love.
Tough love.

All that I do,
I do it for you.

The third song Mitch wrote, and then recorded on his own, was an extremely heartfelt song, where Ryan storms out of the apartment after fighting with his mom, is alone, and walking by other lost souls while pulling his suitcase through the streets of the city. I love this song. I have played this song for many people in recovery, and everyone said they'd download this song right now if it were available. I think it captures many of the feelings inside our suffering children:

"Shadows of the City"

The streets are busy—people pass me by.
Out here all alone—the city feels so cold at night,
And, I am looking for somewhere that I can hide.
And, I am looking for a brand new life,
In the shadows of the city,
No one knows me,
They won't care.

Mom will be sorry, when she realizes I'm really gone.
I won't be looking back, so I just keep moving on.
And, I don't really care which direction I go.
And, I won't think about my home anymore,
In the shadows of the city,
Is where I'm meant to be—
I can be free once more—I will be free.

No, I won't be turning back,
No one will ever find me,
I'll just fade away—
Into the shadows,
Into the shadows—
Of the city.

I continued moving forward in my life's healing journey. Karen and Mitch were a huge part of the healing process that was going on in my life. In fact, they were both crucial in aiding me to keep my sanity while supporting me in my vision. I tried not to focus on negatives. I focused on only the positives that could come out of Ryan's and my experiences with addiction and familial dysfunction. Working on the musical was my mental therapy.

At this point, I now began visualizing my journey leading to publishing a book. I put the musical on the back burner again. My new vision was to publish the book first and then work towards a heart-felt musical. I continued to apply the principles of successful manifestation. Possibility thinking had gotten me this far, and the benefit of possibility thinking is that anything truly is possible!

Things remained quiet in my life for a few months while the true miracle of recovery was preparing itself to take place for both my son and me.

34

Expressing Motherhood

IN AN EFFORT TO RAISE AWARENESS of addiction, codependency, enabling, familial dysfunction, tough love, and recovery, I was part of a stage production in September 2009 in New York City called, *Expressing Motherhood*. It was a very off Broadway show comprised of fourteen mothers writing their own unique monologue about motherhood. We performed three consecutive nights.

At the time of publishing this book, *Expressing Motherhood* was still being performed in major cities throughout the country. The show's producers continually invite mothers to submit their personal monologues onto their website: www.expressingmotherhood.com.

Most of what was in my monologue you have previously read in various parts of this book. However, I felt it was important to include my monologue in its entirety since this was the first significant step I made in getting my message out to the world. It was a ten-minute verbal snapshot of our lives. And I will tell you, at fifty-nine this was a significant challenge to memorize, but I did it and was very proud of myself for accomplishing the task. This is what I wrote and performed:

Expressing Motherhood: Tough Love

On September 10, 1976, I gave birth to my first and only child. We named him Ryan Michael. And I never imagined, while gazing into the eyes of my angelic infant son, during the wonderful year I breastfed, that one day, those same two eyes—my son's eyes—would become the bloodshot, glazed over eyes of a depressed, drug addicted, alcoholic.

How could this happen? How did this happen?

I'll never forget the time he stood in our living room, just three years old. Placed his tiny hands over his little ears, looked up at me crying, "Mommy stop fighting—you're hurting my ears." That was before his father, and I had divorced before Ryan turned four.

But, it wasn't only his ears that would suffer. Ryan would witness major chaos in his home while his immature, dysfunctional parents battled over custody, allowing their problems to filter into their innocent son's psyche. Where once our little boy felt secure— loved by both parents—he was now being pulled in two directions. His heart torn—he bled internally—for he truly loved us both. He understood nothing of our differences. All he wanted was to play, to be a little boy, and to be loved.

What do children do when their hearts break? Where does that pain go? When a bone breaks, it's put into a cast to heal—but not so with one's heart.

Children swallow their pain. In between their tears and fears, they gasp for air, crying as they push their pain deep within. That pain, that buried pain, festers over time, fostering low self-esteem, anxiety, despair, depression—all of which manifests into all types of dysfunctional behaviors, such as tantrums, overeating, not eating, underperformance in school, fighting, lying, stealing, rage, rebellion—and eventually—to escape—our children anesthetize.

At first, it was experimenting with pot and explaining it away by saying, "Mom, don't worry, I'll never do anything but pot." At some level, I think we both believed that at the time. I didn't live under a rock. I knew teenagers tried pot. But, really—I should have said, *"No, you will not smoke pot."* But, I didn't. By not saying, *"No!"* I gave him permission. Was this the beginning of my denial—of burying my head in the sand?

Motherhood, as a single mother, trying to be a father, a mother, a friend, a confidant, a financial provider becomes so overwhelming that one forgets what a child needs most.

Unfortunately, by the time Ryan reached twenty-five—I had no son. He was no more than a shell of a person, but he was such a skillful liar and thief.

By this time, I had spent fortunes putting him in schools, apartments, cars, clothing; you name it—I provided. But, it wasn't these *material* things Ryan needed. The things he needed most—I never gave—

boundaries, consistency, and discipline. I never knew how or when to say: no. "No, I will not give you $200 for designer jeans; No, you are not staying out all night with your friends; No, I am not buying you another car." I never knew how—until I discovered tough love.

Tough love felt as if I had turned my back on my son. It nearly killed me. But worse—I feared it might kill him. Eventually, I learned tough love is not turning one's back. Tough love is staring your adversary right in the face—facing your demons—looking at them square in the eyes and saying, "No, I will not continue to enable."

My back was turned as a codependent mother who enabled her son by financing his decadent lifestyle. My back was turned when I was in denial.

When I started my recovery, it was the first time I faced both my codependent behavior and my son's addictive behavior, AND that was when my healing started! I've learned that being a non-toxic mother is a non-ending process.

We had a horrible fight that day. Ryan's parting words: "I hate you Mom. I'll never speak to you again. You'll be sorry," devastated me. I cried for hours. To vent my pain, I wrote. We didn't speak for over six months. I didn't know if Ryan would live or die. When the phone rang late at night, my heart would skip a beat, for I feared the worst. The worst never happened. Only the best did!

Without *Mommy* to lean on, Ryan was forced to lean on himself. He had the disease of addiction on one shoulder— acting like the devil. On his other shoulder were angels. Over time and to my eternal gratitude the angels triumphed and the devil moved on. We had been blessed!

I am also well aware that hundreds of thousands of families around the world still suffer with addiction and that is why I choose to share our story. To give *hope* and encouragement that recovery is a possibility.

I told Ryan if he stayed clean two years, I'd help financially again towards college. Today, Ryan is clean over six years. He quit smoking cigarettes one year after he quit drinking and using drugs. He graduated as a graphic designer and is gainfully employed. He does mountain biking for his health. He appreciates life. He's engaged to marry his earth angel and his best friend, Michelle, who stood by him in his darkest times. I have a son again! Michelle has a good man with a heart that is healing. It takes time. Recovery is a process—a journey.

I am so proud of my son. Of the courage, strength and willpower, Ryan showed in staring his demons in the face and in conquering them one by one in order to save his life. Ryan saved his own life! No one can save an addict, but the addict.

My son Ryan will always be in recovery. I will always be in recovery. A part of recovery may include relapse. We are both very aware of this. Every day I fight being an enabler. Every day Ryan fights the disease of addiction. Today, most importantly, we both know we have a choice!

And after all, aren't we all recovering from something?

*   *   *

Ryan and Michelle attended the last night of the show. Ryan previously had read most of my monologue and said he was "cool" with it. However, saying he was cool and being cool while sitting in the audience listening, were two different things. My monologue struck a nerve with Ryan, and that is precisely what I hoped would happen.

Only days before the show I learned from Michelle that Ryan had started to drink again over the previous few months. She said he got wasted once per month drinking beer. Then Michelle would pick him up and drive him home, so he did not drink and drive. With the occurrence of these drinking binges, Ryan had unknowingly started down his path toward relapse, so I "cheated" a bit and customized the ending specifically for my son.

Ryan worked with a group of graphic designers, who went to happy hour on Fridays. For the longest time, Ryan refused offers to join, but eventually accepted. He wanted to be part of the office camaraderie. He had never told any of his peers that he was a recovering alcoholic or addict. I don't think he had yet defined himself as one either. Jokingly, Ryan told me he wasn't an alcoholic because alcoholics went to meetings and that he was just a drunk because he didn't attend meetings. This was his way of emotionally avoiding the truth and staying in denial.

During one of my many conversations with Anne Salter, I learned Ryan is considered a *"dry drunk,"* meaning someone who has quit drinking and using drugs, but who has not dealt with any of their underlying problems, their adaptive selves, or their wounded child issues.

Because Ryan wasn't working any program like AA or NA, Anne said he would relapse one day; that it was just a matter of time.

I wanted Ryan to hear that message in my monologue, so that's why it was put there. I wanted him to understand relapse can be part of the recovery process. Not every addict needs to relapse before they hit their actual rock bottoms, but many do. I wanted Ryan to know it's okay. I wanted him to know that he would be okay.

35

Attention Deficit Disorder or Addiction?

RYAN AND I STOPPED SPEAKING after the *Expressing Motherhood* show. Michelle told me it had been hard for Ryan to hear the truth about himself and that he felt hurt and angry. Then shortly after Christmas, my phone rang on December 29, 2009 with Ryan on the other end. His voice was very positive and energy filled.

"Hi Mom. I've got excellent news!" Ryan beamed.

"Tell me," I replied. "I can't wait to hear. You sound so excited!" The happiness in his voice was music to my ears. I hadn't heard him this happy in years.

"I was not focusing at work and made costly errors for my company, so I went to a therapist to see if I had ADD (Attention Deficit Disorder). He said I did. Then he asked a medical doctor to prescribe Vyvanse, as a treatment. Now, I'm doing incredible work, Mom. I'm so happy!"

"That's wonderful, Ryan. I'm happy to hear you're getting help." My immediate response was pure joy as it thrilled me to hear he was seeing a therapist. I even welled up inside with happy tears. All I focused on hearing was that Ryan was receiving therapy. Therapy, that I assumed would help him deal with his anger and other wounded child issues. I thought counseling might prevent him from relapsing.

"Thanks, Mom, I feel so secure now. This medication saved my job. It's amazing. I'm now totally focused at work!"

Ryan sounded so thrilled with his life. We chatted for a few more minutes as if no time had lapsed since we had last spoken, and then said our goodbyes. As soon as we hung up, I went online to read everything available about Vyvanse.

Shock and anxiety overcame me. Vyvanse is an amphetamine. Amphetamines are synthetic stimulants that are similar to adrenaline, the hormone that the body produces when it's either excited or scared. Because amphetamines are creations of the chemistry lab, and not of Nature, they're dangerous. On the street, amphetamines carry the nickname of Speed, and people can go to jail for selling them. People can also go to their graves for using them, and amphetamines can cause addiction and psychotic symptoms.

My son already was an addict and an alcoholic. He should not be taking amphetamines after being clean and sober for so many years. As a concerned parent (and *yes,* still a codependent mother), I immediately phoned Ryan back, in hysterics.

"Ryan, you cannot take Vyvanse. Vyvanse is an amphetamine. I went online and read about it. You are an alcoholic and addicted to drugs! You should not be taking amphetamines," I cried out in panic. There was an extended moment of dead silence. "Did you tell your therapist you were an addict or alcoholic?" I asked.

"Yes, I did!" Ryan snapped back defensively.

"Well, if you did, then your therapist is a quack because he clearly should not have prescribed an amphetamine for you," I rapid fired back at him.

Ryan became very angered and aggressive, "Mom, you don't know anything and don't call my doctor a quack. You're the quack! I am totally focused, and I'm doing the best I've done at work because of this drug. I'll be on these meds the rest of my life." Then, I heard the dial tone.

The next day I sent Michelle the following email on December 30, 2009:

Michelle,

As hard as I'm trying not to get upset about Ryan's ADD meds, I need to at least send you an email to share my feelings. I realize Ryan is doing exceptional taking this medicine, but I read the contraindications where it's clear that anyone with a past drug or alcohol problem should not take it. The reason is that it is an amphetamine. Taking Vyvanse would feel like using cocaine, so of course Ryan is going to like the result. It's addictive. Ryan already said he plans to be on this medication for the rest of his life. He said he told his therapist that he was an alcoholic and coke addict. I'm not sure I believe Ryan told his therapist. I don't think an ethical therapist, who specializes in addiction, would prescribe an amphetamine for Ryan once he knew his history.

After all his hard work for seven years, it just seems a total waste for him to give in to amphetamines. I realize he's being more productive, and he is happy and seems well adjusted, so perhaps I'm wrong. I'm willing to admit that, but I'd like to know if he did tell his therapist the truth. I don't want to rock the boat, but as his mother I can't help but to worry. Maybe I'm over fearful. It would be nice if he took something without amphetamines for his ADD.

Is he treating you better? Is he respecting you more? Is he dealing with his anger issues? If he's doing great in all areas, then maybe I need to relax and not worry about his 50mg increasing to 70, then 90, then who knows what? I just fear the worst.

We both love Ryan, and I know you want the best for him, so please give me your honest feedback. And, as not to upset Ryan, let's keep our emails confidential for now. Thank you.

Love, Deni

12/30/2009 Michelle immediately responded to my email:

I only have a minute (I am at work) so I will keep it brief. I understand your concerns about the ADD drug. I too have been doing my own reading. I think the key here is for Ryan not to abuse the drug.

Being responsible with it is important and I feel it is helping tremendously. He thinks before he speaks, is more focused, organized, keeps lists of what he has to do, is less agitated, etc. I don't' think he could do this on his own without some medication. He told me he was upfront with the doctor about his past, and I believe him. I have been reading blogs and other Internet articles, where addicts and recovering addicts with

ADD have been prescribed the drug, as well. The thing that is reinforced and repeated is the importance of correctly using the drug. Ryan was only given a prescription of 30, and he cannot automatically refill the prescription. Ryan has to get a new prescription each time and can only do that every 30 days. He really wants to do well, and, in fact, he is doing well. I must go.

Will write again later today. I love you Deni

30 Dec 2009 I immediately responded:

Michelle,

Thank you, but one more thing. He started with 30mg, and he is now at 50mg. He told me with 30mg he ran out of steam at 2 p.m. Ask him about that. These emails are between us. Ask in such a way so he doesn't know we are communicating.

Love you Deni

30 Dec 2009 Michelle replied:

Ryan and I had discussed the increase of the Vyvanse before he did it. He also spoke to the pharmacist who told him the initial 30mg prescription was a very small dosage, so small that this is a dosage prescribed to young children. It is a starter dosage, and from there you adjust. He has also told the doctor and therapist about the increase. I am not worried at this point. He is consistently reading up on this medication. At the slightest inkling of something going on in his body; for example, he had a nerve twinge for a brief moment the other day, he does research to see if it is drug related. I do think he is being very careful.

Love you Deni

By the way, I should tell you, I spoke with Ryan after your first email to let him know you emailed me and that you asked about him and his increased intake of Vyvanse. I told him you were just being a concerned mother and wanted to get my opinion on things. I also told him I tried to put your mind at ease.

I just want you to know, I am aware of everything going on with Ryan, and if I see the slightest change in anything I will let you know. Your concerns are mine as well, but I think seeing everything in person is reassuring for me.

Love you some more! Michelle

(In hindsight: It is so obvious today, in 2013 while editing, how deep in denial Michelle actually was by this point. Codependents become totally blinded by denial. Surprisingly enough, I will even turn a blind eye to Ryan's use of amphetamines, too.)

*   *   *

Time passed. Since Michelle was keeping an eye on Ryan's usage of Vyvanse, and since they did seem to be helping him, I wanted to support Ryan in his decision. I knew counseling was costing him out of pocket money, so, I called to offer my assistance.

"Ryan, I don't necessarily agree with your taking amphetamines, but since they appear to be helping you, I want you to know that I am supporting your decision." I kindly told him.

"Thanks Mom. It saved my job. They really are helping me, so I'm glad you called. And, my design work is so much better than before."

"Since you are getting counseling I'll contribute to their cost to help you. I've always wanted you to get professional help, so I'm happy you're doing so."

"I'm glad you called Mom, and I'm glad you understand. I really am doing fine now. I love you."

"I love you too Ryan, and I'm very proud of you," I said as I hung up the phone. Inside I wasn't totally sure about Ryan's path, but I needed to trust him on his journey of recovery.

Then, at some point, what evidently happened is that Ryan stopped taking his first ADD medication and was prescribed Adderall. Adderall is a combination of amphetamine and dextro-amphetamine, which is used to treat the symptoms of attention-deficit hyperactivity disorder, also known as ADHD. This drug is classified as a central nervous system stimulant. As far as Michelle was concerned things seemed to be continuously improving for Ryan both at home and at work, and as far as I was concerned, my relationship with Ryan was also going quite well. To all appearances it seemed the Adderall was working.

Sometime in February 2010, Ryan asked if my husband and I would consider lending him money to purchase new computer equipment in order to create his own graphic design business. He was working full time, but hoping to one day leave the company and work for himself. I believed in being entrepreneurial, so I suggested he write a formal proposal with a well-thought-out business plan and send it to us for consideration.

Ryan did as suggested. We agreed to lend him $6,000 as long as he would agree to sign a notarized promissory note, requiring him to give us his $7,000 Rolex as collateral until paying off his debt. Knowing Ryan's passion for watches and especially his Rolex, we felt sure we'd get the money back. We charged no interest and gave him two years to repay the loan before we would sell the watch. He only needed $4,000 for computer equipment, but since he had accumulated $2,000 in credit card debt, I suggested he borrow more, pay off his credit cards, and stop paying high interest.

Life seemed to be going quite well for Ryan. I truly thought he had turned a corner, and the medication was serving its purpose. One of my previous marketing clients, Jerri, wanted me to create and design a postcard for an ad campaign. I asked Ryan to do the graphics while I wrote the message. The card design came out extremely well, and it seemed Ryan, and I might be able to work together as a marketing/graphic design team. I let him keep most of the joint income, hoping to receive the first payment towards his loan from that money. He sent nothing.

We finished the project just before I was to leave for an extensive vacation in China and Japan in late March. Ryan and I stayed in touch over the Internet and had some meaningful conversations while I traveled. In fact, we were getting along beautifully via the Internet.

*   *   *

On April 4, 2010, I received an email from Michelle written at 4:30 a.m. She was concerned after hearing news about an earthquake near Tibet. She wanted to be sure we were safe. She was off to her spin class at 5 a.m., but asked me to let her know we were okay.

I replied:

Yes, we are safe and sound in Japan!! About five minutes ago I learned of the earthquake. Thank you for your concern. I didn't go online here in Tokyo until just now as we landed and hit the ground running. Tokyo is amazing!!! Its way better than NYC in many ways—just can't speak Japanese!!! This has been a great trip, and it has been wonderful to communicate online with Ryan. He seems to be happy and busy. Sounds like things are improving for you both. Again, thanks for your email.

Love, Deni

Then, my world turned upside down, when I received a catastrophic email from Michelle only two days later! Her email started out with a typically pleasant greeting but quickly went downhill.

36

The Relapse

ON APRIL 6, 2010, I RECEIVED the following email from Michelle. I read Michelle's email only thirty minutes before we were leaving our hotel in Japan to fly home:

> Deni,
>
> Glad to hear you're having such a great trip. I think you need to make another trip very soon—here to Woodstock.
>
> I've debated for the past few weeks whether I should even bring up the situation here or not, having written and rewritten this email at least ten times, wondering when and if I should hit the send button. I've tried to handle everything like an adult and not run to you, his mother, every time he took a drink or did a line of coke, but this time is different. Ryan is on a path of destruction worse than I have ever seen.
>
> His time in South Beach and his early years in Woodstock pale in comparison to what he is doing to his mind and body around the clock 24/7. For a couple of weeks, I honestly thought and actually halfway believed he was so close to a turning point; however, I now see no turning point in the future at all. His business is going good, great actually, but everything else is turning to shit.
>
> Currently, I am the only one who knows what is really going on. I've had open conversations with his pharmacist about everything and left messages for his therapist, which might actually have saved his life this week. It's too tough to tell my mom, knowing she will spend countless hours worrying about everything, plus the added strain it will cause her.
>
> In so many ways, you are my mother too, and I really need

your help in assessing this. I know it's short notice, but if there were any way for you to make it here over the next few weeks, I would urge you to do so. Starting May 13, our weekends will be tied up with my sister's graduation, helping my sister move, and possibly a family beach trip over Memorial Day. Although at this point, I don't know if I even want Ryan around my family.

I do not want to fill this email with all the details—there are too many, but things are bad. I have attended Al-Anon and Nar-Anon meetings recently, and I am focusing on not being a codependent person in this relationship due to Ryan's addictions, but the situation is dire. I don't want to scare you, but I am scared.

I do realize at some point I am going to have to walk away, but this is so serious Deni. There are probably only two people in Woodstock, other than my family who would care enough to acknowledge what's going on and try to help him, but these two people work with Ryan and it could damage any career future he potentially has.

How quickly life has changed.

I love you Deni and need your help. I know neither you nor I can save him. He has to want to save himself. So, I'm not asking you to help me save him, just to help figure things out if that's at all possible. He has no idea I am contacting you about this, and I really would like to keep it that way. I hate going behind his back. I know what his reaction would be, but I need insight from someone who loves him as much as I do.

He found out I talked to his therapist and that was no fun to deal with. Maybe I shouldn't even be writing this long-winded email, but I am at a loss. I need your help. Please do not judge him harshly. He is not a bad person, just chemically becoming a monster with a death wish.

Love from a concerned Michelle

(In hindsight: Again, while editing, I would have to say that this is where Michelle finally hit her rock bottom. She was no longer in denial. She was facing the ugly reality and seeing the same monster I saw eight years prior, when I ultimately hit my rock bottom.)

Needless to say, this email came out of nowhere for me!! It hit me between the ears like a ton of bricks. I had been communicating with Ryan from abroad, and he seemed awesome. Little did I realize how close he was to knocking on death's door. I freaked out. I decided not to respond to her email until I got to the airport and had time to think. Then, I sent the following:

> Michelle,
>
> I am at the airport and just read your email. Ryan needs to go into a rehab facility where he can get professional help. Can you start looking for something in the area or nearby? The addict in him is winning over his rational being. If he has to lose his job to save his life then so be it, Michelle. He can always find another job, but he can't come back to life once he overdoses.
>
> Michelle, I need to speak with his therapist. Have you ever asked him if Ryan told him about being an addict and alcoholic? Ryan told me he did. I don't know that I believe Ryan. If Ryan did tell him, then I don't believe he would have prescribed amphetamines.
>
> Arthur is online looking at airfares for me. I think I will fly back to Florida, unpack, gather up all his goodies I bought, fly up with all the stuff and make my visit a real surprise. I will say that I just wanted to surprise him!!! I'm not sure when I will be there. If this Sunday works, then maybe I'll be there Sunday. I just fear waiting too long if he is this screwed up.
>
> Can you start researching rehabs??
>
> I do think you should tell your parents. Perhaps your dad or mom could speak with him. Ryan loves and respects them both, and he knows they love him. If they suggested going to rehab, then he may be more apt to listen.
>
> This is not the time to hide anything from parents. When you read about people who have overdosed, you always hear the same things said by their family and friends, "If we had known we would have done something to help." People need to know! Ryan needs immediate help. He'll be creative straight, and if he's not this creative—who gives a fuck!!!

He can't continue believing he'll lose his creativity if he stops the drugs. Success can't come at the price of death.

Write back to me as soon as you can. I am online for a while.

Love, Mom

(In hindsight: Today, as I look back over these events while editing my book, I wish I had realized before this time that a family intervention was so desperately needed once Ryan started his monthly drinking binges in 2009. This is where hindsight is 20:20. I had another chance for an intervention when he started taking the Vyvanse. I didn't listen to what Anne had been telling me, or to my gut instincts. Codependency kicked in, instead, and I even sent him money.)

17 Apr 2010 Michelle sent me the following email:

I know you are now worried sick while sitting on a plane. I'm sorry.

A surprise would be a good thing. Catch him off guard and with no time to prepare, to try to fake it, or to look healthier. Unfortunately, he can function on the medication, however, he really starts to look like shit and a meth addict when he hasn't slept for days at a time.

Once you get here, maybe you could ask him why he looks like shit, and then in front of him ask me, "What the hell is going on?" Then, of course, I would break down, and things would go from there. He thinks he is superman now. He doesn't need anyone. Only being successful matters to him. I told him I hated him and to get out or get help. He told me to give him money and then he would leave. (Money from the sale of the house.)

He is not the same person at all. No emotions, no feelings, only anger with me. When he was angry, he said, he didn't love me anymore. That hurt, but his life means more to me than him loving me or being in a relationship with him. He wants positive things in his life. I try to stay positive, but it's hard to do when standing by and watching this go on. I am the enemy.

He knows he has a problem and says he will never be able to take just two pills a day. When he first started taking the pills he talked to the pharmacist—was very open with him and did not have a hidden agenda at the time. Ryan told the pharmacist it felt like two pills just weren't quite enough. So, he asked if he might have a tolerance somehow. Pharmacist said, yes, depending on various levels of caffeine use that the body is used to and that maybe two pills a day would not necessarily be a high enough dose. I think Ryan took this tidbit of information to justify taking another one, then two, then three, then four additional pills a day. Ryan drank way too much caffeine before taking the pills, so this was a no-brainer for him.

Also, he did speak in general terms with the pharmacist a couple of times about viable, non-speed like drugs that would help him, but the pharmacist said the alternative would take 4-6 weeks to kick in and was not very promising. Again, this was very early on in medication, so it just seemed as though he was being responsible by exploring these options. He was being responsible actually at the time, but he did not like the answer he got, as 4-6 weeks were too long to wait and try to keep his job.

Ryan also knows if he stops taking these pills he will probably never be as creative again as he is now—pharmacist told me this also. When Ryan didn't have the pills for four days he felt very sick and brain dead, which was even worse because he now believes he'll always be this brain dead when not taking the pills. The problem is really that he was functioning way too high on the drugs for way too long, so when he stops taking them cold turkey his brain turns to mush, and he can't focus.

This is way too much info to put in an email, so I will wait until we can talk via phone. I do feel like somehow there has got to be a plan of action first because he will run, and we will lose the chance to help him at all.

Love, Michelle

As soon as I landed and read Michelle's email I immediately responded:

Michelle,

I want to thank you for hanging in there with Ryan again. I know this is extremely hard for you, and you have been through so much already. Then, to hear him say he doesn't love you, I know it hurts. You are the "mom" right now—not me. Soon I will be the one he hates, but I don't really care if I can help to save his life.

Please let his therapist know what is going on. Have him to the house to help Ryan. Ryan cannot stop using drugs this time on his own. He needs professional help. This is bigger than both of us my dear. We need to do an intervention, and hopefully Ryan will agree to get help.

If people from work will agree to keep his job open and they could be at the intervention, then we could pull this off. We need to gather all the people together that he respects and who love him, to meet at one time for an intervention, where we ask Ryan to please get help. I believe if we all do that, then he will see we all love and care about him and that he needs help. When I get there, I intend to put an intervention to-gether. Maybe I can arrive midweek without Ryan knowing I'm there, and then do all the arranging for the intervention with the therapist, people from work, your parents, and his best friends. If I have to fly up his best friend, Keith, I will. Michelle we need to help to save him.

Love, Deni

I must admit my mind was racing at this point. Though I under-stood why relapse was going to be part of Ryan's recovery process, I so desperately feared if we didn't help him quick enough that he might die—based on Michelle's assessment of the situation and her desperate pleas for help. Only one-month prior, when I thought Ryan was doing so well, I had written yet another, possible introduction to my book. I decided to send it to Michelle on April 18:

Michelle,

I am sending you something I wrote only one month ago on March 14, 2010. I was trying to write another introduction to my book. I found this information on the Internet. Like you said, "How quickly life has changed."

Actor, Corey Haim dies at 38, Canadian "Lost Boys" star dies of reported accidental overdose. A housekeeper found the Oscar-nominated "Brokeback Mountain's" star, Heath Ledger dead in a New York apartment, the apparent victim of an accidental sleeping pill overdose at age 28. Just a week before Ledger's passing, the troubled star of 'The Client" and "Apt Pupil" Brad Renfro was found dead in his home at 25, thought to be the victim of mixing alcohol and Xanax. The onetime Oscar nominee for "Running on Empty" and older brother of Joaquin, River Phoenix was considered one of Hollywood's top young talents in the 80's and 90's. He died of heart failure at age 23, brought on by drug use, after fainting outside of LA hotspot the Viper room. Chris Farley, the breakout "Saturday Night Live" comic and star of the hit films "Tommy Boy" and "Black Sheep" died of an accidental heroin and cocaine overdose at 33. John Belushi, the manic "Animal House" star and "Saturday Night Live" died of heroin and cocaine overdose when he was 33. Robert Pastorelli, television and movie actor who played the portly painter in "Murphy Brown," died of a heroin overdose at 50. Eric Douglas, son of actor Kirk Douglas died at age 46 of a drug overdose. Bridgette Anderson, best known for her role on 1982 comedy "Savannah Smiles" dies of a heroin overdose at age 21. Ashleigh Aston Moore, Canadian child actress who played Chrissy in the 1995 film "Now and Then," dies of a drug overdose at age 26. Christopher Lee Pettiet, an American television and film actor best known for his role as Jesse James in "The Young Riders," dies of a drug overdose at age 24. Anna Nicole Smith, drug overdose at age 30. And, there are many, many more…

My son is not an actor. My son is not a movie star. My son, like most of our children, did not end up famous. But he did end up addicted. He is unknown, but famous to me, his mother. And thank God, he did not ever overdose. This is our story. I pray it helps you along your journey towards recovery. I hope our story gives you *hope*. Recovery is possible.

I thank God I pulled my head out of denial before he became another statistic, another hurt child, who overdosed because he didn't want to feel. He didn't make it easy on me to do tough love. I believed his lies. I wanted to believe his lies. I felt safe living in denial. I wanted to think he was okay. When I did tough love, I thought, I was turning my back on my son. But tough love is facing the truth. The truth is ugly. But it's the ugly truth that saved my son. It's the ugly truth that saved me from having to attend his funeral.

Michelle, now as I read what I wrote, it really tears my heart apart because I had no idea Ryan was abusing drugs again until you sent me the email. Ryan easily could become another statistic. We must do all we can in order to prevent that from happening. I spoke with my therapist friend, Anne Salter who specializes in addiction and recovery. She recommends we have an intervention as otherwise, she says, we'll lose him.

Anne said Ryan couldn't have any idea we are going to do one. It must be a surprise. You need to tell him if he doesn't go to rehab he must leave and move out immediately, and that you will not live with him another day until he is sober. I need to tell him if he doesn't go to rehab I will not support him at all in any way, as long as he is using drugs again.

We need his employer to tell him they will support him all the way, as long as he gets treatment, and that his job is secure. Anne said legally they couldn't let him go over this, so we need to see about his insurance. I also think I would ask his childhood friend's parents, or at least his mom, to be at the intervention and possibly even Marc. I need to know the name of treatment center and contact information so I can speak with them. Anne also wants to know. She said there are lots of treatment centers, but they are not all reputable.

Anne recommended several where she had spent time as a visiting therapist in order to observe their operation. One I particularly like is in West Palm Beach, called Hanley. It cost around $30,000 and takes insurance. If he goes there, then his childhood friends and I can stay involved with him. In Virginia, how much money did rehab cost? I certainly don't have $30,000, so we need to find somewhere affordable. I have some money in my personal checking account, plus I have his Rolex that could bring in maybe $6,000, but I hope insurance will cover most.

Also, do you know if his friends Chuck and/or Danielle are in recovery? If one of them is an alcoholic in recovery, then Anne said that would be great if they were at the intervention, but if not, then they would be detrimental because their business thrives on alcohol and people getting drunk. Anne said Ryan is doing cocaine for sure because as soon as an addict starts using any drugs or drinking they always go back to their drug of choice.

So Michelle, we need to work together to help save Ryan!!!

Love, Deni

Michelle responded the same day:

Okay, treatment facility is close. As for Marc, I think he has his own issues. We can talk about him later. We could figure out if facility takes Ryan's insurance and go from there. I will call you later today. If you have specific questions text me on my cell, and I will respond. I do not have email capabilities on my phone, and I will not be around my computer most of the day.

Love you Deni

19 April 2010 received another email from Michelle:

Deni, I have a few more thoughts. He did not go to sleep last night. It's now 5:40 a.m. and he was been working on his website all night long. When I got up at 5:00 he was so excited to show me his website. This is where this drug starts to piss me off so much. He wasn't drinking, and he wasn't doing coke last night. He was simply working on his business.

Unfortunately, he used his medication to keep him awake last night and will abuse it today to stay awake at work. The cycle is vicious and will probably repeat itself again tonight and tomorrow. Even if he isn't drinking or doing coke, the way he is abusing the drug is horrible and justifies an intervention. On the outside, he seems so normal, but then, once you start to see the cycle after a few days, you realize how bad it is. Talk to you later. I love you.

I responded immediately:

Michelle, I don't want to put an intervention together until I get there and assess the situation. I want to speak with the rehab center first, and then perhaps the intervention will be during the week after I'm there, on the weekend. I will let Ryan think I'm leaving Sunday night, but I will stay at a hotel and work on the intervention.

Love you, Deni

Two hours later Michelle sent the following email:

Just had a good talk with Ryan. He talked about needing help, but said how it was so much bigger than just that. He looked me in the eyes and said, "I don't want to lose you." He also said what a different person he is now, both good and bad. Must go. Have to be at work early this morning. Call you later.

I made plans on April 19 to visit Ryan and Michelle the following Friday. I told Ryan I had paid for a ticket last year that I hadn't used and that it expired at month end, so I wanted to visit. He told me he'd have to check with Michelle as they were attending a wedding that weekend. I knew Michelle wouldn't have a problem since we were plotting this together.

He called back actually excited about my visit. He was relieved that I had gotten him out of going to a wedding. I told him I was proud of his accomplishments, and couldn't wait to see the new computer equipment and home/office environment he had created.

The next day, Tuesday, Ryan called to tell me he was fired from his job. I turned the negative into a positive by telling him being fired was a blessing in disguise, because now he could focus all his attention on his own company. He agreed and stayed with a positive attitude on the phone.

20 Apr 2010 received an email from Michelle written at 6:42 a.m.:

I was still awake when Ryan came home last night about 1:30. It seemed like the old Ryan. He talked about wanting to bike again, trying to quit smoking and about having a sense of relief about not working in the chaos of his old company. We also talked about his night, how he went to his friend's restaurant where he had a free meal, and then went downtown to one of his friend's bar. He said when he walked in he told them he wasn't drinking, but they gave him a free beer, so he drank half of it. I told him my biggest fear was not, not making money right now, but of his continuous downward spiral with drugs and alcohol. I also said I thought he would make a super, sober businessman. He agreed. That was it for our deep conversation. I didn't try to push anything else. By that time, it was 2:30, and he was falling to sleep. I just hope his positive attitude remains. Then maybe, eventually, there will be no alcohol.

Oh, I forgot. I did ask him if he thought he would be going through "detox" when you were here. He said he didn't know. I think tonight I will ask him about the pills. How many he has left? When does he plan to stop taking them? What will he do about the nasty effects of the withdrawal?

Love you Deni

21 Apr 2010 I sent Michelle the following email at 8:40 a.m.:

Michelle,
I sent Ryan the following email last night:

Ryan,
Just finally got to see your design work. Very nice! Love the reflections and the whole concept!! Also, I assume the other graphics are the look of your website. I'm not sure.

Arthur and I both agree that losing your job is theeeee best thing for you! It's hard to work for a big company. I was never able to myself—I'm too creative and so are you. This is your moment Ryan. This is the opportunity for you to take control of your own destiny. Be your own man. Run your own company. Work on jobs you want to work on, and use all your creative energy to do what you create in your mind. You are so talented and creative (like your mom). My client Jerri loved your lemon idea for her marketing. I wouldn't have thought of it.

So, now you need to learn to discipline yourself to stay focused on each opportunity you are given and to do great work and build your reputation. You're a man now. You have experience and knowledge. There's a saying that success happens when preparation meets opportunity. I think you are destined for success now. You are prepared, and opportunity awaits you!

Okay, so bye for now.

Love you, Mom

Michelle, I am trying to be a subliminal, support system for him right now. Since he has no idea I know anything, he can just think I'm saying those things just to say them, but what I'm trying to do is reinforce him as a person who doesn't need drugs. I hope my little emails provide him with insight into himself, and he realizes he doesn't need drugs. Between the two of us—hopefully he'll see the light.

Love to you, Deni

*   *   *

(As an aside: While putting this book together and putting all the correspondence in order, I can't help but to wonder, if when we aided Ryan financially to start his business, how much of the money went to drugs? I had actually never, ever until today (March 21, 2011), put two and two together. I saw the equipment he bought and assumed he had paid off his credit cards with the remaining money. I never checked his credit card statements. I trusted Ryan at that point. I had no idea what a full-blown addict he had become again on ADD medication. I didn't realize how horribly the madness of addiction returned.

In again re-reading all the correspondence from Michelle, I clearly see today (June 2013) the deep denial Michelle was in thinking an addict, using amphetamines, could be responsible. Also while rereading my own words of desperation, thinking I could save Ryan further exemplifies my sickness and how much addiction is truly a family disease. Especially, when rereading, *I believed his lies. I wanted to believe his lies. I felt safe living in denial. I wanted to think he was okay.* It amazes me today how blind we become in denial and how fearful we are of our own truths.

I feel it's important to point out this "crazy-making" behavior to you, at this point in my memoir, though I didn't realize any of this while it was happening.

I also learned from Anne Salter, that writing letters to the addict actually puts an overload of pressure on them, which leads to feelings of shame when they cannot do what is being asked of them.)

37
Seeing is Believing

I QUICKLY FOUND OUT HOW HORRIBLE the disease of addiction was when I first laid eyes on Ryan. It was Friday, April 23, 2010. My son lost between thirty and forty pounds since fall. He didn't even try hiding the fact that he was smoking cigarettes again. He was not real friendly towards me, told me he had lots of issues, and that I shouldn't be there. Because I understood what was happening in his life, I kept my responses appropriate, as I didn't want the situation to turn ugly. He didn't know I knew anything, and I wanted it kept that way.

The first night, he grabbed a beer and started drinking outside while walking London. Michelle thought I should go out and catch him drinking, and in doing so, she thought he might share more of what was going on inside of him. So, I did. He opened up a little but told me not to get involved, and that he'd get through all of his issues. I said little. I didn't want to rock the boat. Later, I took Michelle and Ryan to dinner and kept the conversation light. Once we got home, and I went into my room, Ryan proceeded to go out all night, to score drugs.

I asked one of his high school buddies, Steve, to call him on the phone that first night just to "catch up." Ryan did share with him what was going on in his life, as I had hoped he would. Steve, who already knew the situation, told Ryan he loved him, that he was a very talented artist without drugs, and told him drugs are not the answer. Steve has a younger brother who is in recovery, so he has been down this path. He knew how to support Ryan with kindness and love, and also suggested that Ryan should check himself into a rehab.

As soon as Ryan hung up the phone, he asked if I had anything to do with his call. I acted shocked he would even think so, crossed my fingers behind my back, and told him I hadn't spoken with his friend for at least two years.

(Another aside: In the insanity of my own illness, I started lying to Ryan, and even manipulated others to get involved in trying to *save* Ryan.)

I spent most of Saturday speaking with the rehab center and making plans for Ryan to be admitted. They did have a bed available for Ryan on Monday. Michelle and I worked on the issue of insurance. The good news was his insurance would cover it in full, but I would need to prepay half with my credit card at the time of admittance. Fortunately, I would be able to do so.

After another uncomfortable night at dinner with Michelle and Ryan, Ryan once again went out all night to score more drugs. I knew better than to get involved in his drama until the time was right. I spent Saturday night online reading everything I could find about his medication and its side effects.

I found a blog where people wrote about their addiction to Adderall and how they hated it. One young woman wrote that she started taking Adderall in college just to stay awake and had never before taken drugs. Now she was totally addicted, afraid to tell her parents, and had no idea how to quit. She was scared and said she hated the drug. From everything I read, once addicted, it was not easy to quit.

When Sunday morning arrived, Michelle went off to the wedding, leaving Ryan and me to spend time together. We decided to have breakfast at a local diner. While driving there, I was very quiet. In fact, I was totally subdued and waited for Ryan to respond to my quietness, which he did over breakfast. The conversation went like this:

"Mom, what's wrong? Ryan asked. "You're very quiet."

"I am because I don't know what to say," I said, calmly.

"Say about what? Ryan asked.

"I know you are hooked on Adderall, and I am very scared for your life. I did a lot of research on the drug, and it's not easy to kick," I calmly stated—while ready to puke.

"Mom, I'm scared, too," Ryan honestly admitted.

"You are?" I was shocked Ryan so quickly admitted to his addiction and to his fears. "I don't think you can kick this by yourself this time," I immediately added since he was indirectly admitting to his addiction.

"I know. I don't know what to do Mom," Ryan concurred.

"Well, I've located a rehab, and they have a bed available for you tomorrow if you're willing to go." I took a deep breath and prayed while my heart skipped a beat.

"I will go Mom. I'm ready. I'd go today if they'd take me," Ryan immediately responded.

"They don't admit on Sundays, but we can go and have a tour of the facility if you'd like," I replied while silently freaking out inside with pure joy and relief that my son had so willingly agreed to go to rehab. It was almost too easy. *Thank you God.*

"I don't need a tour. I just need to be admitted," Ryan said as he breathed such a sigh of relief. He didn't have to say another word. His position was crystal clear. He wanted to save his life.

When I told him the name of the rehab, it turned out one of his close childhood friends, Marc, had gone there for addiction. So, when we finished eating, Ryan called Marc and got all the *dirt* on the rehab. Only two things were important to Ryan: the food must be decent, and the staff could not be full of degenerates, worse off than the addicts in recovery. Marc told Ryan that he had a positive experience, the staff was very professional, and the food was surprisingly good. Ryan was pleased with the rehab I had chosen.

We spent the rest of Sunday preparing for Monday. Ryan had his haircut, did his laundry and packed his bag for the next twenty-eight days. It couldn't have gone any better. He even went online to tell his Facebook friends where he was going. For the first time in Ryan's life, he had no problem admitting to his friends, that he was addicted. He did go out Sunday night for more drugs, but explained to me that he didn't have a choice; that he had to get high. I understood. I cried inside, but I understood.

38
The Reality of Rehab

WHEN WE ARRIVED ON MONDAY, RYAN'S admittance went smoothly. We had a tearful, yet happy farewell. I wouldn't hear from him for at least one week. He was out of touch with everyone for one week. Michelle agreed to keep him supplied with snacks and cigarettes. Eventually, he and I had very short phone conversations, just to let me know he was okay. Although we didn't say much during those calls, it was nice to hear his voice and to know he was doing okay.

After admittance, as part of his physical, Ryan was given an electrocardiogram (EKG) to check the electric activity of his heart. The test was given to him on April 28, 2010. Mother's Day occurred while Ryan was in rehab. I didn't expect to see a card from Ryan, so I was quite surprised when I saw a white, letter sized envelope in the mailbox addressed to: MOM, Deni B. Sher. It was from: Ryan/SON, followed by the address of the rehab facility.

Inside was a letter size sheet of white paper folded into thirds, and on the outside was written:

How do you show your mom that you love her on Mother's Day, when you're in rehab?

I unfolded it and found a copy of Ryan's EKG report showing a healthy result. Handwritten and highlighted in orange were Ryan's sentiments:

As long as my heart has a beat it will always have love for you, Happy Mother's Day—Son.

Tears. You have no idea! It remains thee best Mother's Day card I have ever received. I keep it framed on my writing desk.

During week three, family members can attend a four-day counseling session to interact with their recovering addict. We learn how to live with someone just new to recovery, and about the importance of changing our enabling, codependent behaviors.

Ryan and I had joint sessions, which were extremely stressful for me. Ryan vented his anger and openly shared how specific experiences from our past messed up his head, and also why he felt these caused much of his teenage problems. One of the sessions went something like this:

"Mom you have no idea how much you fucked my head up when you lived with Albert. He was married, and you sent me to the same Christian School as his kids. You told me to keep it a secret that their dad lived with us. You invited his son to my birthday party. I knew my mom was living with his dad, and I felt like a big liar. It was fucked up. You were fucked up."

I only could sit there and listen. He was correct. I did do that.

"And when I was younger, you left me with a babysitter, who smoked pot all day. She had all these creepy motorcycle guys in and out doing drugs."

"I never knew she was smoking pot while she was watching you," I responded.

"How could you not know?" Ryan yelled back at me as if I were an idiot.

"I don't know. I thought she was very kind and loving to you," I said in my defense.

"She was, but she was smoking pot all the time. I didn't realize it was pot because I was too young. You should have known!" Ryan argued.

"I'm so sorry Ryan. I really didn't know. I hope you can forgive me."

"I don't know if I will ever be able to forgive you, Mom. I have so much rage and anger associated with my childhood that I just don't know if I will ever get past it," Ryan responded. His eyes were full of hatred and disgust, and focused intently on me.

At this point, I did not think Twenty-eight days in rehab would be enough time for Ryan to work through his anger issues. It seemed crucial that he continued with therapeutic counseling. Ryan must feel his anger and process it in a professional environment. He needs to do that to get past it. It might take years of work for Ryan to work through his anger issues. I only could pray and be hopeful that he will do so.

One thing Ryan told me was that if he were to be honest and to work The Twelve Step program, he must end his relationship with Michelle. He told me he was not in love with her the way a man should love a woman. He loved Michelle as a sister and friend, but not as a girlfriend or fiancé. Ryan acknowledged Michelle's efforts to love and to rescue him over the past years, but he adamantly felt he saved his own life.

Though I knew it initially would break Michelle's heart, I also knew it would be the best thing for her in the long run. No woman wants to be with a man because he feels obligated to her, and I get that. Michelle took my place in Ryan's life, as the codependent, thinking she could love him clean and sober. The harsh reality is: Ryan used Michelle in his disease. Addicts have one or more enablers, always people, who care about them.

I said this before, and I cannot stress it enough: no one can save an addict, but the addict. If the addict wants to use drugs, he will. If the addict doesn't want to use drugs, he won't. It's their choice entirely and not anyone else's.

Upon leaving rehab, Ryan was honest with Michelle in explaining how he felt and why he needed to end their relationship. Thank God, by that point, the feeling was mutual. They continued living together as friends, for nearly four months. They first needed to sell the condo they shared, so each could have enough money to move out and to start over. I was actually quite impressed by how maturely they handled breaking up. I'm sure it was a huge relief for both since their relationship had become extremely dysfunctional over the past seven years.

Each needed to sort out their individual lives and emotions. Michelle acknowledged to me, that she recognized her codependency and that she intended to continue going to support group meetings. Both Ryan and Michelle told me they wanted to disconnect from me totally while processing their lives and while breaking up. I understood.

After selling the condo and moving on they continued to remain friends and to share the responsibility for their pets. Eventually, it made sense for them to disconnect, and for each to build a new life; separate from one another. Michelle certainly deserved to be adored and in a healthy, loving, non-dysfunctional relationship. And Ryan needed time and space to become comfortable with himself, in his own body, without drugs or alcohol, and to work through his anger issues.

It was during this same time period that I started facing my codependency issues head on and began peeling off layers of denial, so I could process my past. In essence, Ryan, Michelle, and I each spent the next several months in our own personal recoveries. Our eyes were now wide open. Our hearts needed to heal. Our paths reached a fork in the road: a place where each of us knew we needed space and time for healing to take place. Respectfully, we gave that space to each other.

I sent Michelle a birthday card in June 2010 with a small check enclosed. I did not get her usual reply of thanks, so I knew she wasn't ready to communicate with me. I didn't attempt to reach out to Michelle again until October 2012, to let her know I was getting close to publishing my book, and to ask if she would consider giving me permission to quote her emails. Without Michelle's permission, I would not have been able to use them verbatim.

Ryan and I would not communicate again until late November. During which time, I continued the healing process started while working with Anne. Surprisingly, it seemed everything I had written, thought and said, over the past eight years, with respect to being a recovered codependent, had been just surface talk. Though I admitted to having problems, I had never addressed any of them internally. I had just talked the talk. Now, it was time for me to walk the walk.

How could I expect Ryan to face his disease and demons, and to become whole and fully functioning, if I weren't willing to face my own? How many times would I need to hear Ryan defend himself by saying, "What about you, Mom? I'm not the only one who's fucked up!"

Like Alice, in Lewis Carroll's book, *Alice's Adventures in Wonderland*, once I entered the rabbit hole eight years ago, there was no turning back. And, to quote Alice, "I can't go back to yesterday because I was a different person then."

PART III
2010 – 2012

The Miracles of
Deni & Ryan

39

Fessin' Up — It Sure Ain't Easy

MANY OF US SPEND OUR WHOLE LIVES RUNNING FROM
FEELING WITH THE MISTAKEN BELIEF THAT YOU CANNOT BEAR THE
PAIN. BUT YOU HAVE ALREADY BORNE THE PAIN. WHAT YOU
HAVE NOT DONE IS FEEL ALL YOU ARE BEYOND THAT PAIN.
—*Kahlil Gibran*

AS MEDLODY BEATTIE WRITES IN HER unique, daily meditation book, *The Language of Letting Go*, "Real power comes when we stop holding others responsible for our pain, and we take responsibility for all our feelings. Things change, not because we're controlling others, but because we've changed."

Honestly examining my past and then writing the following, freed me to change. I must admit I struggled with including part 3 in this book. My fear was that you might think to yourself, *no wonder her son did drugs, look how screwed up she was.* I hope you don't think that way. I hope you use my courage, as a possible springboard, to uncover and to discover your own, divine, authentic *Self* as I have during the course of this entire process. It's never too late to become whole.

I keep a paperweight on my desk with a quote by Ernest Hemingway written inside. It says, *"True writing is honest writing."* Believe me, my writing can't get any more honest than what I am going to share with you now.

If you recall, in 2003, during my first visit with Ryan after doing tough love, I wrote a song called "Fessin' Up." Seven years ago when those feelings first emerged I wasn't ready to face my truth. I wasn't ready to 'fess up when I started writing:

"Fessin' Up"

Mom

I'm fessin' up,
Fessin' up to my crimes,
I want to make—make my life rhyme,
I want to put—put my steps in line.

I'm fessin' up,
Fessin' up to the truth,
Lookin' my *Self* in the eyes,
Dealin'— yes, dealin'—with problems, of my own youth.

Today, I am. I am ready to deal with problems of my own youth. The writing of "Fessin' Up" created the possibility for this to happen once I put those thoughts into the Universe. I allowed my ego *Self* to get in touch with my spirit *Self,* when I tapped into some of my buried feelings of failure as Ryan's mother seven years ago.

I was actually continuing in the process of my own surrender that had begun the day I did tough love, but I had no idea the process that was taking place was termed *surrender.* It is just mind boggling that I could start out writing about my son needing to *'fess up* and come to the realization that *I was the one needing to 'fess up.* This is why writing is very healing.

So here I go, in celebration of my sixtieth birthday, on July 2, 2010, I begin seeking and writing my truth:

While I was growing up and spending part of my teenage years in front of the television, *The Adventures of Ozzie and Harriet* sitcom (1952 – 1966) portrayed the stereotypical, ideal, all-American family as two happily married, loving and communicative parents, living in a home behind a white picket-fence, with two near-perfect children. Deep down, I wished my parents were like Ozzie and Harriet.

As a teenager, I dreamed of one day having my own, "perfect" family, like the Nelsons. Unfortunately, that dream ended abruptly in 1969. I was nineteen, when my high school sweetheart, Ricky, broke up with me and broke my heart. Ricky was my first "true love." I was devastated.

I was actually more than devastated. I fell into a deep, dark depression where I totally lost my self-esteem, self-respect, self-image, self-worth, and my over-all identity and morals. I was literally, a lost soul.

Now, forty years later, my only child is a recovering alcoholic/addict. I am a recovering co-dependent/adult child of an alcoholic father. So, what happened? How did I get here? Why me?

As I reflected on the dysfunctional aspects of my life exhibited over the past forty years, I scratched my head and asked myself how I went so off course at nineteen? How could a broken heart, over a nineteen-year old boy, leave me so devastated, when all he was, was an immature and confused teenage kid? What did I lack? What was I thinking? *Was* I thinking? While growing up, I appeared quite healthy, happy, and successful. On the surface, my grades were above average, and I appeared to have had a busy, fun-filled and well-rounded social life. So, what short-circuited my psyche?

Born in 1950, I was the fourth child and the only daughter of Henry and Celeste. I had three older brothers. Donald was three years older, Arnold was thirteen years older, and my oldest brother, Harry, was fifteen years older. We were never a close-knit family of children. All of us carried our own set of painful childhood issues into our adult lives. Although our parents stayed legally married for over forty years, their relationship was totally dysfunctional, and far from the healthy relationship I had witnessed while watching *The Adventures of Ozzie and Harriet*. Eventually, I would acknowledge, accept, and grow to understand that painful reality.

While growing up in the small, South Jersey town of Linwood, in the fifties and sixties, "dysfunctional" wasn't commonly used to describe families. I don't remember much before the age of ten other than what I see in photos. I remember nothing before kindergarten. I only vaguely remember the feeling of being in my elementary school classrooms, the musty odor of the cloakrooms, and the sounds of the huge, echoing hallways and bathrooms. Mostly, I remember the kindness of my elementary teachers, but I don't remember very many specifics. I do know going to school was always something I anticipated with pleasurable excitement. I was happy at school. As a little girl with three older brothers, I was definitely "Daddy's little girl," and the "apple of his eye." He spoiled me.

As I sit writing the words, *he spoiled me*; I am emotionally struck because I want to add the word *rotten* to the sentence. If someone spoils you rotten, does that mean he has done you a disservice? Today I would have to say: yes. Children don't really want to be spoiled rotten. Children want to be loved in a healthy way. I was spoiled rotten. Being spoiled means there is a lack of boundaries and an attempt to give love through things. In hindsight, I realize I had my dad "wrapped around my little finger," just like Ryan had me "wrapped" around his. Unknowingly, I had repeated my father's behavior with my own son.

I remember really loving my dad when I was a little girl. I remember standing barefoot on his shoes while we danced in the living room. I knew my father adored me. I was expert at making him laugh. I had a responsible, hard-working father, who financially supported his family in a middle-class lifestyle. A happily married father I didn't get. A sober father I didn't get. An emotionally available father I didn't get. A father I could discuss my feelings with—I didn't get either.

While trying to examine and to write honestly about my youth, I realize how self-consumed we are as children. As a child, we live in our own worlds, and we have absolutely no idea what our parents endure to support us financially and emotionally. I had no idea what my father did outside our home when he wasn't working. I had no idea my father was a womanizer. I had no idea he started cheating on my mother shortly after they married. I had no idea what my mother had to tolerate as his wife. I had no idea she knew about the other women, yet stayed married, feeling she had no other options.

Divorce wasn't a choice for my mother. Her own mother had divorced, leaving horrible scars in my mother's memory. In my mother's mind, a divorced woman became an outcast in society, and she did not want to be an outcast. I had no idea how much verbal and physical abuse my mother tolerated. I had no idea what it meant that my father drank a huge pitcher of Manhattans every night and then crashed in his recliner. I had no knowledge of a disease called alcoholism. I lived in my own world. And today I realize more so than ever, why I created my own world. I was escaping.

Fortunately, I didn't drink or smoke. I went another route. I became a tremendous athlete and a dedicated student, who loved going to church and to youth group. I loved school. I loved sports. I loved God.

I loved my teachers. I loved boys. I was out of the house from sunup to sundown. Once I reached seventh or eighth grade I either lived on the phone, in front of the television, listening to the radio, or spending time with friends. I can't remember ever having a meaningful conversation with either of my parents. I argued with my mother, and I totally disrespected her. If she told me I couldn't do something, I would pick up the phone, call my father at work, and he would give me permission. My mother had little control over me. My father's need for total control left her powerless.

I was a very cute teenager and started dating when I was a freshman. Boys were my obsession. I always had a boyfriend, but I would kiss only—going no further. I would have one boyfriend at a time. One or two of these relationships even lasted close to a year. Then I'd immediately have another, another, and another. Still, I would go only so far as kissing—until I met Ricky. I fell in love with Ricky. I gave him my virginity when I was seventeen. Back in 1967 my virginity actually meant a lot to me. I grew up respecting my body as the Lord's temple. After I had sex with Ricky, I stopped going to church because I felt I was no longer pure. *I felt shame.* My temple belonged to Ricky at that point—and no longer to my God, or even to me.

I clearly remember the exact moment my mother asked if I had sex with Ricky. She told me she saw stains in my underwear, and that was why she was asking. I had never lied to my mother until that exact moment. I told her, "Absolutely not!" I acted insulted that she would even think that of me. I told her I loved him, but we were absolutely not having sex. She believed me.

How I wish I had not started lying to my mother, on that day! I wish I had told her the truth. Who knows, just maybe, my mother might have opened up to me and shared how she had accidentally gotten pregnant by my father. Maybe, we would have talked about the importance of not giving our innocent and undeveloped "selves" away to young boys who don't have the maturity to comprehend the value of our actions. But I didn't. I lied. I deprived my mother of her chance to be my confidant. And most importantly, I deprived myself of the parental guidance I so desperately needed at that time in my life. I chose to lie over being honest. How sad.

Today, on my journey toward truth and wholeness, as I peel off and uncover more and more layers of childhood, buried wounds, I can understand how Ricky was providing me with the love, stability, and recognition I was lacking at home, from my father. I understand now that Ricky became my father figure. He would even discipline me in loving and kind ways. I would ask Ricky permission to do something while I almost never asked my parents. I turned him into my world. I turned Ricky into a god. The sun rose and set on him. It was as if I was no longer whole without Ricky in my life.

I will never forget one of the weirdest conversations I had with Ricky, when we were both seventeen. To the best of my memory, it went like this:

"Ricky, I would like to use the 'F' word," I proclaimed. "I have never said it out loud."

Ricky responded by saying, "Okay, I will let you say it now, but after you do, I never want to hear you use that word again."

So, with his permission I said, "Fuck. Fuck. Fuck." Just saying the word felt so weird to me. You have to understand, I had never cursed, as a child.

After the third time, Ricky chirped in, "Okay, that's enough. Now you've said it, and don't ever say it again."

"Okay, I won't," I responded. And, that was the end of that. Of course, I said it again—but never with Ricky!

I look back at that conversation, where I actually asked Ricky permission to say a word, and I can't help but to question, why and how I gave him so much power in my life. I gave him parental authority over me. He became my father. Our relationship was unhealthy and totally dysfunctional.

As far back as I can remember I had always wanted to be a gym teacher when I grew up. I went from being a tomboy to a star athlete. I had been accepted to a few colleges and planned to attend Trenton State, as a physical education major. Then, at the last minute, I canceled my enrollment, so I could marry Ricky. In my mind, I couldn't live without him. As soon as I graduated high school, I couldn't wait to move out of the house. I was tired of hearing my grumpy and usually inebriated father, telling me, I dressed like a whore. In 1968, mini-skirts were the rage. I was fashionable—not a whore! At eighteen, I was hired to be an assistant manager for Elaine Powers Figure Salon. I was engaged to marry Ricky and moved into a trailer with him. I then proceeded to throw away my life. Correction: I continued to throw away my life!

What hurts me most, when I think back to those years, is that my parents allowed me to give up college. They allowed me to move in with Ricky. Why didn't they protect me from myself? I didn't know anything about the realities of life. Why didn't my father take a stand and insist I attend college? I realize now—he couldn't.

He was so buried in his own dysfunction, and so deep in his own denial as an alcoholic and as an unhappily married man, that he wasn't capable of protecting his own daughter. He wasn't capable of parenting me. And today, while working on understanding my own dysfunctional past and how familial dysfunction operates, I totally forgive my father. He too was a victim of inherited familial dysfunction that perpetuated from generation to generation.

The year after I moved out, my parents sold their home of nineteen years and moved to Florida. It was 1969. Drugs were at a peak and along with smoking pot; Ricky started taking LSD everyday and tripping. Once, he persuaded me to take half a tab of LSD, but I really didn't like it, so I never did it again. How could I marry him? I told him I couldn't marry someone who took acid and was high every day. So, we broke up. My "white picket-fence" dreams were all destroyed.

When we broke up, the sun was taken out of my life. That, coupled with my parents' move to Florida, left me with all my "roots" torn out from underneath me. This led me into a deep depression. I had sex with six random guys the first week after we broke up. I became the whore my father said I was. I went from one hundred and twenty-five pounds, to one hundred and seventy pounds in only three months. I ate to fill a void in my heart and soul.

I just didn't care. Dysfunctional! I was in such pain. I just wanted to feel good. I couldn't handle Ricky's rejection. Even though I broke up with him, my "wounded child" *Self* (the codependent teen-age girl), still told herself she loved Ricky and wanted him back again, even as a drug user because she was afraid to be alone. But Ricky wouldn't even give me the time of day. He totally rejected me. I did not have the skills to know how to handle his rejection. I had never been rejected. I became emotionally ill. All of my childhood friends were scattered around the country attending college. All of them—but me!

When we broke up, Ricky told me I was stupid. I believed him. One year later I enrolled in junior college. In my first semester, I made Dean's List. At twenty-two, I graduated junior college with an Associate's Degree, a grade point average of 3.6, and I was on the Dean's List. Realizing I wasn't "stupid" helped me start to get my life back on track. I didn't know where the tracks would lead, but I was down to one hundred and fifty pounds and had an Associate's Degree. They were both significant accomplishments. Unfortunately, however, I was still emotionally dysfunctional.

I could have used drugs. They were there and available, but thank God, I didn't. I tried smoking pot but got paranoid. I felt guilty because I was breaking the law. I grew up respecting the law. Police were our friends when I grew up. I guess in my teenage, hormonal years I could justify sex, but I couldn't justify drugs. I didn't even drink alcohol until I was twenty-one and then hardly drank at all. I still count my blessings I didn't turn to drugs to anoint my pain like so many in my generation. I turned to other salves.

The Vietnam War was raging. It was the early seventies and "Free Love" was the slogan of the times. All my sexual boundaries and religious indoctrination went out the window. I would meet someone, get his name (sometimes), and five minutes later we were in bed. Ricky had my heart and everyone else had the rest of my body. I tried escaping my painful feelings with sex—just like an addict does with alcohol and/or drugs. It was only a sexual fix and had zero to do with my heart or with making love.

I wasn't in love with anyone, but Ricky—and certainly, not with myself. I had lost myself. I had lost my self-esteem. I had lost my identity. I was a lost soul. I still have a notebook full of my writings, mostly from when I was twenty. I wrote the following on June 15, 1970:

Help me. Help me. I'm a lost child, a lonely person, unable to survive alone any longer. I need security. My hope of becoming close to my parents is gone. I have no family to turn to. I want to be loved again by people who will take the time to know and understand me. I want a home life. I want parents. Mother. Father. Where did you go? Why? Why can't they see how badly I need parents, and guidance? There is absolutely no love or understanding between my parents and me. I hate

them. I actually hate them! They are making me hate them. They don't respond
to any of my signs of love towards them. They are very distant, very cold, and very
ignorant. No one else will ever understand because they will never be the daughters,
of these two people. I am the daughter. My eyes are the only ones that can see what
I see. Why am I a victim of this coldness? All I wanted was my parent's love. I need
financial aid for college and I know my father doesn't want to part from his money.
His money is his life. His children aren't a part of his life.

Reading that today, as I process my history, I had forgotten those
feelings I had forty-years ago. I had forgotten how lost I felt at twenty.
I learned to bury that pain and then to cover it over with an amazing
sense of humor and outgoing personality. I learned to cover it up in the
arms and beds of strangers. I didn't know my dad was an alcoholic. I
just knew he drank. I didn't know anything about anything when I was
twenty. I just did whatever needed to be done to keep from hurting.

I turned twenty-one only a few weeks after writing that and shortly
thereafter my mother phoned me. At that time, I was living in Walla
Walla, Washington for the summer. She called to inform me my father
was involved with a girl my age. She was only six weeks older than I
was. My mother had a very difficult time dealing with their relationship. Though she thought it was just another stage my father was going
through, it seemed my dad was being very cruel and wasn't trying to
hide his affair. My mother vented her pain to me, her twenty-one year
old daughter.

He would leave my mother at night while he and his girlfriend
went out on dates. He would spend the weekends in hotels with his
girlfriend. One time a local policeman caught them having sex in my
father's car. My father had the nerve to share that embarrassment with
my mother. And, as if that weren't painful enough, they even had sex on
my parent's patio, where my mother could see them. This relationship
was devastating to my mother and to me. I was the daughter she cried
out to for help. Neither one of us knew what to do or how to handle
my father's disgusting behavior.

At age fifty-seven, my mother, who never drank or smoked a day in
her life, started to take Valium to calm her nerves. She was in such pain. She
continued living with my father for at least another five years before finally
asking him to move out. Though I wasn't living at home then, I know my

father's affair and his lack of respect for my mother's feelings, coupled with my emotional trauma and ensuing shattered morals had a huge, negative effect on my attitude towards men, marriage, sex and adultery. All of these experiences helped to create a very dysfunctional me.

(I have since learned from Anne Salter that my father's sex addiction, throughout my entire life, means I was emotionally abused, in such a way that it helped to create my own sexual dysfunction.)

During the summer of 1971, while visiting South Jersey where I grew up, I met a guy from Pittsburgh named, Frank. Frank physically looked like Ricky. Yep, I found a Ricky look-a-like! Dysfunctional! If I couldn't have the real thing, at least I could have a replica. I scoped him out in a disco, followed him to the bathroom and waited outside. When he came out, I swooped down on him like a hawk on prey.

Frank quickly fell in love with me. He relocated from New Jersey to Florida, and we lived together for the last six months of my junior college. He was a very talented artist who had graduated from Columbus College of Art & Design, and we got along beautifully. He made a wonderful Ricky substitute.

Frank found a carpenter's job in Florida, working for a wealthy family I knew, who also owned a summer home in North Haven Island, Maine. They invited us up for the summer with the intention to continue employing Frank. They were building a custom home on the island using weathered wood from an old barn and planned to use Frank's woodworking skills.

There was only one catch. Frank's employer's, eighty-year old parents, who were the owners of the Maine property, were very *proper* Bostonians. They would not allow anyone living together and unmarried to reside on their property. Enter, husband number one.

When my father walked me down the aisle, he said, "I thought you weren't ever going to get married and that you didn't believe in marriage." I sarcastically replied, "I don't believe in marriage. We can always get a divorce." Now, isn't that exactly what a bride should be saying to her father while approaching the altar for her first marriage? I'd say that's quite dysfunctional.

I would discover talents I never knew I possessed while on North Haven Island. I wrote, cast, directed and produced a variety show for the islanders. Frank designed and built all the props. It was quite a hit. When asked where I taught the dramatic arts, I told everyone I had never done this before. That's when people said I was a "natural," and many New Englanders suggested I attend Emerson College in Boston.

Frank and I had no plans beyond the summer, so we moved to Boston.

I was extremely fortunate. I worked at Emerson College for one year as the secretary to the Athletic Director. During that year, I took one free course per semester. At the end of the year, I applied to Emerson in their Children's Theatre Department and was accepted as a full-time student. I was on an exciting and creative path in my education, but in my personal life I was still not doing so well. I wrote the following poem one day while at work:

"Longing Liaison"

Lady Love
Lies listless
Lonely
Longing Liaison
Loathing logic
Listening for liberty
Yet, liable to laws

Her lifeline lifeless
Limbs in limbo
With limited lips
Lingering
Languid

While
Man makes money
Machinery
Methods
Mad with motion
And, maneuvering manners
Masked meanings
Marked by marquees
Merchants and misers
Merging in markets
Master, have mercy on man
Forgetting his lady

Lying listless
Lonely
Lustful
Longing
Liaison

The first time I cheated on Frank was with my high school sweet-heart, Ricky. I discovered he lived on Cape Cod. He came to Boston to see me, and we had sex. After cheating once, I knew I shouldn't be married. I was twenty-three, back to being thin, attractive and a college student. I wasn't a good liar, so I told Frank I cheated and suggested we part ways. He agreed. We parted friends. He moved back to New Jersey where we had met, and I stayed in Boston. We had no money, so we never filed for divorce. We just separated. It didn't matter because neither one of us was planning to remarry any time soon.

There was a musical at the time in New York City called, *Let My People Come*. The producers were planning to open the show in Boston. The entire student body of actors from Emerson College auditioned for the show. I was the only student from Emerson who was cast. This was actually quite surprising since I hadn't even had an acting class, and quite honestly my singing wasn't incredible (though I could sell a song). But, one thing I did have was tremendous stage presence. Evidently, I truly was a natural. I was actually making money as an actor! But after the first two weeks of rehears-als, the show was banned in "moralistic" Boston because of nudity in the show. It was advertised as a sexual, musical revue. The producer told the cast the ban was temporary, not to worry, and in a short time we would be back rehearsing and earning money. In the meantime, I needed another source of income. The producer suggested I become a "Go-Go-Girl" at clubs around Boston, and in that way, I would get used to being semi-nude on stage. That made sense to me. So, one of my college classmates and I auditioned as danc-ers and were hired. Thus, began my short-lived career as a "stripper."

I was a stripper majoring in Children's Theatre! You can only imagine how silly I was. (Anne Salter has explained how being able to dance near naked was another way that reflected my loss of self-esteem and loss of sexual boundaries.) Personally, I feel being near nude on stage enhanced my abilities as an actress. Any inhibitions I might have had on stage—were gone!

The funniest thing was, I had no breasts. I was barely an "A" cup.

So, when I would go on stage and take off my top, I would make faces and do comedy. I tap-danced, did ballet and would mostly entertain as a "stripper comedienne." My girlfriend and I had no money to invest in wardrobes like all the other "real" dancers. One time, the two of us wore snorkels and fins onto the stage and pretended we were swimming. As long as we took our tops off, we could do almost anything we wanted. Our bottoms always stayed on in "moralistic" Boston.

The show, *Let My People Come*, never *came* back into rehearsal again. Fortunately, I was making enough money dancing to pay bills and to stay in college. This led me to write my own stand-up comedy routine. When summer came, I took off for Provincetown, where I planned to see Ricky again. I was still in love with him, and hopeful we could get back together.

Unfortunately for me, Ricky was dating another woman at this point, and told me he had no romantic interests in me. And then, to pour salt in my already wounded heart, he told me he thought I was terrible in bed and that I didn't know how to make love. Basically, he rejected me, again! This rejection was emotionally sexually abusive and continued to affect my self-esteem.

The next night I performed stand-up comedy in a local club. I wore a one-piece, black girdle and told jokes. That is the night I met Johnny. He was in the audience and fell madly in love with me.

Johnny was seven years older than I was, which I found appealing. All Johnny did was flatter me and tell me how wonderful I was. Johnny was a talented guitarist with a voice like silk. He serenaded me with music and song, and he even wrote a romantic song about me called "Silver Deni," because all of my jewelry was silver and like the moon above, he felt I shined my love on him. He made me feel so good about myself. Johnny's timing was perfect after Ricky's harsh rejection.

I was still in love with Ricky but tried to move on with my life. Sadly, after Ricky, I would never fully give my heart to, or trust another man until I was forty-nine. I was this very attractive female who obviously had many repressed issues, but who could attract males like flies to honey. I was a lot of fun. I was honest. I was kind. I was witty, funny, animated and talented. Besides, it was still the hippie generation and everything was cool. To all appearances, I was a creative, hippie chic! Remember, we don't know what we don't know.

40

The Perpetuation of Familial Dysfunction

WHEN I RETURNED TO BOSTON IN August, Johnny was riding along in my car. He was a lost puppy (like myself), who found a home. Johnny talked me out of going back to college at Emerson and suggested I attend The National Mime Theatre School instead. The program ran for three months, where I studied jazz, ballet, tap, mime, and theatre. I resumed dancing throughout this period to help pay bills.

One day, Johnny caught me on the phone speaking with my husband, Frank. Fearful that I might return to my husband and jealous of my existing relationship with Frank, Johnny said, "If you loved me you would have my baby."

In order to "prove" I loved Johnny, I stopped using birth control, started taking vitamins to prevent morning sickness, and within a month I was pregnant. I put myself on an organic health diet. I ate no processed food throughout my entire pregnancy and followed Adelle Davis' book, *Let's have Healthy Children*. It was my *Bible*. I was extremely excited.

When I was six months pregnant, Johnny began telling me the facts about his background. I became his therapist while he told me horror stories about his childhood. He said his father put him in an orphanage after his mother left him with five young children. While there he had been sexually abused. Then, at eighteen given two hundred dollars and told he was on his own. Feeling embarrassed about his past and not having positive self-esteem, Johnny started making up stories about his past life and creating a false *Self*.

When Johnny started sharing his past, I listened and wanted to help him. After all, I was pregnant with this man's child. I wanted him to be okay. I wanted to be okay. I wanted us to be a well-adjusted couple. I told Johnny I loved him. I wanted to love him. I wanted to be loved. We both tried to make it work. Isn't being loved what we all want? Unfortunately, two dysfunctional people were about to create the most beautiful and perfect baby one could imagine.

I've left many details out of this introduction to the story of my son's childhood, but I feel I have provided enough insight into my background to show how unprepared I was to be a fully functioning wife and mother. I can't say I ever was in love with Ryan's father. I tried to love him, and I even think I thought I loved him. I felt sorry for him, and I tried to give him the same compassion I so desperately wanted and needed. It was like the "emotionally blind," leading the "emotionally-blind."

Believe it or not, Ryan's first two years of life were near perfect, considering our backgrounds. We had moved north from Boston to Newburyport, Massachusetts when I was five months pregnant. Johnny and I truly made an effort at normalcy. We lived in the country. I baked my own bread for two years. I cooked three meals a day. We sat down at night and had family dinners. We ate organically. I nursed Ryan for thirteen months. We had two dogs and a cat. We made friends with other young parents. On the surface, we were a happy family. We were both totally in love with our son. He was the apple of our eyes. He was the common thread that bound us together.

I still don't think Johnny was an uncaring person inside. I think he was just extremely dysfunctional—like me. He was the product of a horrible childhood and didn't know how to turn his life around. Johnny wrote the most beautiful lyrics and music. He was talented beyond one's imagination. His lyrics were brilliant, gentle, and loving. I think if he could have just told the truth about himself to recording companies that he could have made it as a recording artist. Because of his low self-esteem, I believe he fabricated stories about himself and eventually started believing his own stories. I grew to see him as a pathological liar, and I certainly did not have the skills or qualifications to help him.

Though I truly wasn't in love with Johnny, I decided since he was Ryan's father, that I should marry him. Dysfunctional! I divorced my first husband and married Johnny when Ryan was two. We planned to move to Florida, where my now-separated parents lived, so Ryan could be near his grandparents and have a greater sense of family (dysfunctional as it was).

By the skins of our teeth, we were able to purchase a home. It was in a fantastic location, and it was the first time either one of us owned a home. Back in 1979 our home was only $43,000, and it was one block off the Intracoastal Waterway in Deerfield Beach, Florida. When we closed on our home, we appeared to be a quite well adjusted and happily married couple with one adorable and happy little boy. And, should truth be known, we were, at first. Unfortunately, like an iceberg, the trouble floated just below the surface.

Johnny found employment as an electrician. It was a skill I didn't even know he possessed. Okay, so what else did I not know about this man? Because Johnny was such a skillful liar, one could not tell when he did or didn't lie. It became very difficult to live with him. He made me look normal, and believe me I still had lots of my own issues. I was far from perfect, but I was honest. I only had a traumatized psyche from a broken heart (or so I thought). Johnny seemed broken in a multitude of ways.

Once, because we were in debt, he did something totally unethical and involved me in his scheme. I was so mad, but I couldn't rat him out. He threatened to take Ryan from me if I opened my mouth. He said I'd never see him again. I believed him. I loved and adored my son, so I kept my mouth shut, being as I was not in any position to argue. I wasn't working, and I was dependent on Johnny to support our family. I was able to be a stay-at-home mother. But after that, I totally lost any respect I had for Johnny. I realized I was in a very sick (dysfunctional) marriage, and I was being emotionally abused.

Because I had majored in children's theatre, I still had a love of the theatre. When I was twenty-nine, I auditioned for the role of Peter Pan. I got the part. I took Ryan with me to all the rehearsals and tried to make the best of my life. Rather than dwell on my unhealthy marriage, I focused more on being a mother and on my role as Peter Pan. I escaped reality by focusing on theatre.

Then one day on my way home from the show on a Saturday morning, I saw my husband with another woman and eventually found out he was cheating. That was the beginning of the end. For months,

Johnny had been accusing me of cheating on him, and I spent most of my time defending myself, when in reality, he was the one cheating and projecting this onto me. Gee did I marry my father?

For months to come Ryan would be exposed to horrendous fights. He would hear things no three-year-old should hear. He would see things no three-year-old should see. He saw his father punch his mother in the stomach, then run out of the house yelling, "She hit me, she hit me." Ryan was in my arms and watched this all take place. During one fight, I received a black eye. I was now being both physically and psychologically abused.

Once, when we had a horrible fight, I called my father and asked him to come over to get me. When he arrived I started telling him what was happening and rather than listen and understand my hurt feelings, he started to question me. Another conversation I will never forget because it was so "crazy-making."

"What's wrong with you?" Why can›t you stay married? He asked as if this was all my fault.

"What's wrong with me? How can you ask me that question when you're with a girl six weeks older than I am? You cheated on Mom your entire marriage," I tearfully blurted back at him. I was in such pain and disbelief that my own father could be so heartless when I so desperately needed his protection.

"I never planned to get married. I was a playboy when I met your mother. Girls were all over me. Your mother and my sister were friends. That's how I met your mother. She'd come over to our house, and before I knew it we were in bed, and she got pregnant. I did the honorable thing. I married her. I was never in love with your mother," Dad confessed.

Unbelievable! I was twenty-nine, going through hell with an abusive husband, and all my dad could do was tell me how he had been a playboy and had never loved my mother. Thanks for sharing! I had a father I could never turn to for emotional support. I wasn't expecting to hear all of that out of my father's mouth.

These were the buried, painful experiences from my past that I needed to revisit and to process in order to understand myself better as an adult-child of an alcoholic father and as a codependent mother of a recovering addict. I needed to understand how my poor choices in life were the result of the unhealthy ways I buried my painful repressed feelings, and because I didn't know what I didn't know.

There was a time I remember, when Ryan, at age three, put his hands over his ears and said, "Stop yelling you're hurting my ears." I can only imagine how he must have laid in his bed in fear as we fought in the living room just outside his door. We had a cat named Jawbones, who slept with Ryan and kept him company until Ryan was eight, when Jawbones died. I know Jawbones provided Ryan with comfort as a little boy. We also had two dogs Ryan loved during his first two years of life that we left with friends when we moved to Florida.

Since a dog played such an important role in Ryan's recovery, I have to believe there was a link between his childhood feelings of comfort with animals and his adult feelings toward a dog in his recovery process. Animals provide us with unconditional love, which is comforting at any age. I too remember the comfort I received from a Great Dane we had when I was in the fourth grade. I remember feeling like she was my best friend and then one day, without telling me, my parents gave her away. My heart was broken. I remember crying for days.

*   *   *

The ensuing divorce from Johnny was ugly. The judge told us we both needed to live in the house until it sold and until the divorce was final. I don't remember all the gory details, but I do remember that one time I was jumping out our bedroom window to get away from Johnny, when little Ryan walked into the room. It was a first floor bedroom, so I wasn't being suicidal. I just needed to escape his abuse. Many times, just the threat of physical abuse was horrifying. He would corner me, yelling and threatening to hit me with a raised hand in the air as I cowered in fear. We yelled, fought, and raged, all within Ryan's sight. It was not a pretty picture.

Eventually, we sold the house, got divorced, and went our own ways. Granted full custody of Ryan, I took my half of the proceeds, purchased another home with three partners, got a real estate license, and proceeded to give Ryan a stable home life. His father, on the other hand, took off to travel the world, spent his share of the profit, didn't pay child support, and then returned one year later to play havoc in our lives.

Unfortunately, after one year, I had forgotten what a nasty and manipulative person Johnny was capable of being. I should have known better, but when I saw him penniless and homeless, I felt sorry for him. Because he was Ryan's father, I was a *Sucker* with capital S. When he asked if he could move in with us and pay rent, I agreed to let him. He moved in only as Ryan's father, not as a lover.

I did not realize at the time, but this was the diseased, codependent part of my personality in full-blown operation. I was now mirroring my parent's dysfunctional relationship with Johnny. (It would be another twenty years before I learned what a healthy, functional relationship between a man and a woman was like.)

This extremely poor choice on my part began a nightmare that would go on for years. I hesitate to admit, but I do believe we did more damage to Ryan after our divorce than before. Now that Johnny had absolutely nothing in his life, he wanted to destroy everything I had worked so hard to build.

After Johnny had moved in, I told him I wanted to go away for two weeks. Having not had a break all year, I needed to take some time for myself. This meant Johnny would stay with Ryan for those two weeks. When I returned, he told me he would not pay rent. He told me he did not move in with us to be my babysitter. I remember precisely what I said, "He's your son. The son you didn't see for one year. You are not a babysitter—you're his father!"

His anger was such that he refused to pay rent. I told him if he did not pay then he needed to move out. He told me there was no way he was moving out. I called the police. Because Johnny knew the law, he told them we had a verbal agreement and that this house was his residence. The police could do nothing. He stayed. I then moved out and took Ryan with me.

We moved into a studio apartment while I evicted his father from our home. This dysfunctional man had the audacity to stay in his son's home and put him out on the streets for his own selfish needs. It took nearly two months for the eviction to take place. At that point, I hated Ryan's father.

I do not use the word hate lightly, and I almost never say I hate anyone or anything, so for me to hate Johnny, meant something. This man put his son and me through hell. He told me if he couldn't have me then he was going to make my life miserable. And, believe me, he did what he said. My life was chaotic on and off for years. It wasn't until Johnny met a woman named Beth that things began to settle down a bit.

Of course, that wouldn't last long. They decided I was a horrible mother, and they wanted Ryan to live with them. His father took me to court where he would lie and create false stories to make me look bad. They would keep Ryan from me when their visitation times were over and tell me I couldn't have him back. Ryan became a pawn. Meanwhile, this loving father was thousands of dollars behind in child support payments, but I would still let him see Ryan. I felt it was better for Ryan to see his dad, than not. This situation became a double-edged sword, and there was no easy solution.

Things got real ugly when I had a younger man, whose ancestors were from India and Jamaica move in with us. He was a young, college student, majoring in theatre, who was extremely caring to both Ryan and me. Johnny decided to take me to court because we were living together and not married. I then secretly married Scott. Six months later, when we arrived in court, Johnny had no case. Scott became husband number three.

As far as Scott and I felt, it wasn't a "real" marriage, but only a favor. In fact, one year later, when we divorced, it was simple and friendly. This was obviously another very dysfunctional situation Ryan endured when he was between six and seven-years old.

During those times, I wrote various poems that I have chosen to include in this book. I was thirty-one when I wrote the following poems. This was during one of the times I vented my inner pain associated with my inability to love another man:

"Love Knots"

I was seventeen
In love with him
Fourteen years later
My heart still suffers paralysis.
It pumps my blood
But builds walls around the scars.
Every time it begins to feel vulnerable...

Vulnerability…BAM.
The door at my threshold
Abundant with love
Slams shut.

It's all inside of me
Wanting the freedom
That being in love allows.
Tangled
Twisted in knots
Love knots
Wanting to be untied.

"Liquid Hurt"

I'm crying tears.
Bottled in my eyes since my teens.
Tears—liquid hurt.
Liquid pain.
Held back by pride.
Held back in an image of security.
Contained in a vacuum,
That hasn't felt,
Really felt,
Since it first felt rejection.
Total rejection.
And, I didn't know how to handle defeat.
I had always played on winning teams.
Didn't know what it was like to lose at one-on-one.

"Paradox"

I told myself never again.
He told himself the same.

Then, we met.
Should we let our emotions run?
Have fun,
Laugh,
Smile,
Touch,
Feel,
Be real,
And love?
Or, will we choose,
To continue living for our lovers,
Both of which,
Are gone?

"I Want Out"

I'm tired of hurting other men,
Other people,
For the hurts I suffered years before.
I want out of this prison.
A hell that cuts my tongue,
So I cannot utter the words,
I love you.

One time, I remember calling the police because Johnny called me from a phone booth telling me I'd never see Ryan again. They were gone for three days. It was pure hell and pure torture. I cannot even imagine what went on in little Ryan's mind, but I know I sure suffered.

Ryan started sucking his thumb beyond what was reasonable for his age. I thought it was a problem, so I started to put hot pepper on his thumb and bind his arms in large magazines when I put him to sleep so he couldn't bend his elbow while sleeping. I personally didn't see it as anything weird, but as an adult Ryan told me it was child abuse. I certainly didn't try to abuse him. My intention was only to prevent the need for braces later on as I didn't foresee having money for them.

So today, as I reveal my truths, in an effort to reconnect with my divine *Self* and to seek inner peace and forgiveness of *Self*, I openly admit to my part in the many dysfunctional situations contributing to Ryan's emotional and behavioral problems. Children don't possess the tools to know what to do when they are in an unhealthy living environment. My son ultimately turned angry. My son didn't even know why he was angry.

Ryan, though he tested gifted, did poorly in school and developed frustrations because he couldn't keep up with his peers. He was extremely intelligent and yet failing. He became a rebel, taking his frustrations out on himself. Like millions of emotionally hurting children, Ryan would discover nicotine, pot, and alcohol as a young teen to numb his painful feelings.

I started my enabling when Ryan was young. I used to do his homework for him. It was easier to do it, than to fight with him. I was not good at discipline. It was easier to give in to Ryan than to punish him. I did not set boundaries. I lost control of my son at an early age. There was no consistency whatsoever. One word I never learned to say was, no. And usually, when I did say no, I would eventually give in to Ryan's persistency. Ryan learned at an early age how to push my buttons. Because of my pre-existing yet undiagnosed codependency issues, I allowed my buttons to be pushed.

When his father married Beth, Ryan was ten. I allowed Ryan go and live with them because I felt he needed more stability than I was providing as a single mother. I felt he needed a more structured family environment that I wasn't capable of giving him as a single mother. I believed (or at least told myself) his dad had changed for the better, and that Ryan needed male influence. I also felt my mothering wasn't as important as the stability of having both a father and a mother under one roof.

I was still his mother, but I felt Beth also loved Ryan. I was pretty much an emotional wreck by this point after my years of struggling. Out of pure frustration I even kicked Ryan in his butt once when he was ten. Ryan was out of control, and quite honestly I could not discipline him. I hoped his father could do so.

Please, do not get me wrong. It was excruciatingly difficult for me to send Ryan to live with his dad. I cried my heart out, yet I believed it was the right thing to do for Ryan. I spent every other weekend with him since it was extremely important to maintain our relationship. Shortly after Ryan moved out, I couldn't stand to be in our home. It felt empty and depressing without him, so, I sold the house.

After paying off the balance of my Emerson College loan, I invested the remaining proceeds into opening a computer business. I transferred my motherly love from my son into building a company. I needed something to consume me. I didn't want time to focus on missing my son. It was too painful. At thirty-eight, I made up my mind to become financially independent, and never put myself in another situation where I needed anyone for anything, ever again. I decided to *pull my own strings,* as Dr. Wayne Dyer advised in his book, *Pulling Your Own Strings.* I became a workaholic.

I literally worked from sun-up until the time I went to sleep. I was totally under capitalized when I opened my computer company, and most people thought I would fail. I spent every day on the phone doing telemarketing, then followed with a creatively written letter on gorgeous letterhead, containing an impressive business card and a colorful Rolodex card.

Though I was consistent in my follow-up, I made sure not to pester customers. All I asked of potential customers was for an opportunity to quote the next time they had a computer hardware need. I always treated my customers the way I liked to be treated. The Golden Rule was my rule.

I also spent part of my day building relationships with my vendors. Because I was only as good as my vendors, I depended on them providing their finest refurbished products, at competitive prices, and with on time delivery. Without reliable vendors, I could never have succeeded in business. Fortunately, I was a member of an ethical group of business people in the computer brokerage world (ASCDI), and we treated one another with the highest of business ethics. I was truly blessed.

The accountant from my former employer gave me a one-week course in bookkeeping. I did all my bookkeeping manually (the old fashion way), on large, green sheets of paper, in two huge books: Accounts Payable and Accounts Receivable. At the end of each week, I did all my invoicing. When I opened I didn't even have a fax machine the first year. I had to send every contract by Federal Express. In 1988 fax machines cost around $4500. I only had $8,800 to invest in my company after paying off my debts, and $4,500 the day I opened for business. A fax machine was not in the budget.

My business grew month by month and by the end of the first year I had $30,000 in my corporate checking account. I didn't know most companies don't make a profit their first year! Every day when I got up and looked in the mirror, I thanked God for my success. I was extremely grateful to my Higher Power God at that time in my life. I would also give thanks to living in the USA, where I was able to own my own business, work hard and become a success.

Every other weekend, like clock work, I drove from Hallandale Beach, Florida on Friday, to Stuart, where Ryan lived, picked him up and drove back to Hallandale. It was five hours round trip. Then on Sunday afternoon I made the same trip again. I did that consistently for one year until Johnny and Beth moved to Tallahassee. During that year, I only saw Ryan twice because it meant flying, renting a car and staying in a hotel. It wasn't easy for me to do logistically, and it was certainly a significant expense. It was horrible being that cut off from my son.

After being in Tallahassee for one year, Johnny asked if I would take custody of Ryan back. Though I had been consistently paying child support, Johnny said he no longer could afford raising him as he had fallen on hard times and was moving to Colorado. I had been praying that Ryan would live with me again, and my prayers had now been answered! I immediately paid Ryan's airfare back home, and within days we'd be reunited. Both of us were quite excited, and looked forward to living together again.

While Ryan was in Tallahassee, I had purchased a lovely pooled home in Deerfield Beach, near where Ryan and I had previously lived. I was in the second year of running what would eventually become a company grossing three million dollars a year in sales by its fifth year. I worked from home, so "ideally" I was available for Ryan. Though I was there for him every morning to fix his breakfast and to send him off to school, my company consumed me until around 8 p.m. because we did business in California.

By day's end, I was exhausted. It was easy to hand Ryan money and just say, "I love you, go have fun with your friends." After school, Ryan pretty much ran free with his buddies going to the beach, skateboarding, or just hanging out. There wasn't much time in my schedule for mothering until late evening and weekends. He hadn't started drinking or using drugs yet, and quite honestly, they weren't even an issue. He was still quite innocent to the ways of the world.

Unfortunately, when Ryan returned he was going on thirteen and had many emotional problems, which I didn't know how to deal with at the time. If I am to be totally honest, in processing my past, I didn't make the time to deal with them either. At the same time, I also continued making poor choices in my personal life. I was dating a married man when Ryan moved back home, and enrolled Ryan in the same Christian school his children attended. I asked Ryan to keep our relationship a secret. His son even came to Ryan's birthday party.

I was obviously still extremely dysfunctional with respect to my relationships with men. I certainly didn't think about how my actions would affect my son. And as I process these thoughts further, I can see how my behavior totally replicated my father's. Apples don't fall far from the tree and familial dysfunction perpetuates from generation to generation. I am seeing this more clearly as I write and process my past.

Ryan started causing disruptive problems in school, and he refused to adjust. Eventually, I ended up sending him to a military school in Virginia when he was fifteen. I still felt he needed male influence, and I wasn't able to parent him. I also knew he was starting to smoke pot and to drink. He was getting bigger and stronger than me. I couldn't even make him get in the car if he wouldn't choose to do so. The tail was definitely wagging the dog. Military school lasted only one year. Ryan refused to return. It was during that year Ryan met Michelle. It was also during that year I met Diego.

Diego was an ambitious Brazilian who was a very good person and who needed a break in life. I had been single for twelve years, so we married. Diego became husband number four. I told Diego that I didn't love him, but I agreed to marry him nonetheless. After all, not loving and marrying had pretty much become my style, so it was no big deal. I wanted to help him return to his country and to see his aging mother. He helped me to grow my business internationally. It was a win: win relationship. At forty-two, I still had a pretty dim view of love. Two days after our wedding, I slept with an old lover. (No, not Ricky, another former lover.) Three years later, Diego and I divorced. Need I say more?

During our marriage, I sold my home in Deerfield to move to Miami where I could build my exporting business. It was a strategically sound move for my company, and I totally enjoyed the diversity of such an international city. Within a short time, I doubled my office space from 1000 square feet to 2000 and doubled my employees from three to six. My business life was excellent.

Ryan eventually finished his high school years at a small, private school in Deerfield Beach. The man who owned the school was simply fantastic. He took kids who didn't fit into public schools, and gave them the encouragement and understanding they needed in order to succeed. He was a miracle worker for sure, and we felt blessed to find his school.

When Ryan graduated it was a day neither of us thought we'd ever see. He had no desire to go to college. He had a passion for nothing other than skateboarding. Because Mom was making lots of money, I supported him, and enabled him to do nothing. I was a busy executive building her "empire."

Ryan continued living with me after high school and started hanging out with other kids who were also not parented. Ryan and his friends started breaking into cars. He claimed he wasn't stealing, but that his friends were, and he was just a look out. When a policeman came to our door investigating a car theft, where my son's ID was found, I lied to the policeman about my son's whereabouts and told him my son had recently lost his ID. After this incident, I saw the writing on the wall and knew Ryan needed to get out of Dodge.

(What was wrong with me that I would lie to protect my son? When was I going to let him start suffering consequences for his actions? Today, I wish I had let him be arrested. Perhaps being in jail would have shocked some sense into him. I'll never know. But I certainly was one hell of a codependent mother.)

Out of pure frustration, I sent him to live with his dad again. Ryan was nineteen at the time. They hadn't seen one another for about six years, so both of them were looking forward to being together. Ryan also looked forward to the Colorado terrain where he could hike and snowboard in the mountains. I hoped for the best, but things didn't work out. They had disputes over the lifestyle Ryan was living, so Ryan ended up on the streets and homeless.

After about a year, he came back to Florida. Ryan returned with a pierced tongue. I insisted he remove the stud before moving back into my home. The stud came out. Ryan moved in and worked on and off at my company over the next year, which was the continuation of my enabling. He showed up, did nothing and got paid. At least I knew where he was.

Eventually, I moved to Miami Beach near South Beach with Alex, a man I met while divorcing Diego. Ryan was twenty and twenty-one during this time, and he lived with us. At this point, Ryan had a job selling five-dollar t-shirts on South Beach, where he made one-dollar for each t-shirt sold. He was making so much money that he couldn't spend it fast enough.

Unfortunately, he started hanging out with people who liked to party. He was "turned on" to cocaine by an older woman living in our building. He smoked dope, dropped pills and partied a lot while living in South Beach. (Ryan told me all of this, a couple years into his recovery, when he was around twenty-nine. At the time, I had no idea Ryan was using and abusing so many drugs while living with us.)

I was naive when it came to drugs. I couldn't tell when someone was stoned. Ryan always appeared happy and positive, so I assumed he was doing well. I didn't know he was high. I truly don't think I was in denial, yet. Let's just say I was uninformed and ignorant of the signs. I think my true denial was later, when there were more obvious signs of his addiction, and I ignored them. I would see my son living like a pig with glazed eyes, and I did nothing. There was nothing I could do. I gave him money. I ignored the problem. He wasn't living with me, so on a day-to-day basis I didn't see what he was doing. He told me what I wanted to hear, and I chose to believe him. That's major denial!

As I look back today through my *truth serum* lenses I see that I was a "workaholic" mother and a relationship addict, who buried my head in my successful computer business so I didn't have to deal with my failure as a mother or with my repressed pain from my family-of-origin. I created and lived in my own world: Deni's world.

I was a hands-on president, focused on running this successful computer business. I lived in my own world as a respected businesswoman, in a male dominated industry. I had great friends and acquaintances. I helped my parents financially, and I would give money to others who needed financial assistance. (I vividly remembered what it was like to live hand to mouth, so I never put money before people.) Through my financial success, I had recovered my self-esteem, and yet I still was not able to open my heart enough to love anyone. I said the words, "I love you," but I truly did not feel true love for anyone.

I spent my life becoming an independent woman. Sure, I always had a boyfriend or a husband because I liked companionship and safe sex. I didn't want to sleep around because of sexually transmitted diseases. I liked being in a relationship. It felt safe, but the relationships I chose to be in were dysfunctional (to say the least) because I was dysfunctional. It was my way of protecting my wounded heart. It was my way of perpetuating the story I had been telling myself since I was nineteen.

I absolutely loved my son. I knew I wasn't the best mother, but I would do anything to try to make my son's life better. I was financially always there for him. He wanted to go to an art school in South Beach. I paid for him to go to art school. I put him in an $800 per month condo on the Intracoastal Waterway and paid all his expenses. Meanwhile, he was a cokehead, and I didn't know it. He dropped out of school in his second semester and pawned all the top of the line computer equipment I had bought him.

At that point, I admitted him into an outpatient rehab program. Ryan swore to me he wasn't a drug addict. We went every day to the facility, and the entire time my son kept telling me I was wasting my time and money. Eventually, he wore me down. I agreed to stop taking him though the counselors told me all addicts say they aren't addicts. I chose to believe my son. I was definitely still in denial.

As Ryan's mother, I too, met with a counselor at the rehab facility as part of the program. I was still living with Alex going on four years, in a relationship where we had absolutely nothing in common. I told the drug counselor I felt a large part of Ryan's problems were related to the fact that I was always in and out of loveless relationships. As unfulfilled as I was with Alex, I didn't want to break up with him because he and Ryan had such a bond. The counselor strongly advised me against staying in any unhealthy relationship because of Ryan.

"What do you want in a man, Deni?" The counselor asked.

"I don't know." I replied.

"You are forty-eight years old. How are you ever going to get what you want, if you don't know?" He then gave me an assignment. That assignment would change my life forever!

41
Successful Manifesting

HE TOLD ME TO GO HOME AND TO THINK about what I truly wanted in a man. He told me to write down what was important to me and to bring the paper in the next night. On February 23, 1999 I proceeded to write three pages of what I wanted in a man, and I put those thoughts into the Universe:

First, I want to stress that the physical appearance of my ideal man could come in almost any shape, size and color. I have been with tall, dark men and short blonde men, blue eyes, brown eyes, thin, heavy, bald, lots of hair, etc. The outer shell of my ideal man is only the encasement of the spirit. It is the inner spirit of my ideal man that will attract me and keep me by his side.

My first priority is that he has spirituality; that he is in touch with his inner Spirit *Self,* and he is enlightened and in touch with the "energy of the Universe." That he understands, "what goes around, comes around, we reap what we sow, and to do unto others as you would have others do unto you."

I want a man who is kind. That kindness comes from within and will turn blue, green, amber or brown eyes into warm, glowing and kind eyes.

I want a man who is in touch with his inner *Self.* A man, who has struggled to get to know himself, and one who has made a conscious attempt to become a good human being. With that understanding, I want a man who likes himself as a person, and with that knowledge, turns what could be a physically unattractive man into a confident man, who projects that feeling throughout his being, and the result, is a man of beauty both inside and outside—no matter what exterior he carries.

I have met physically gorgeous men, who are ugly because their thinking is ugly. If we think it, and believe it: we can become it. So, I want a man who believes in himself. He believes there isn't anything he can't do if he truly desires it, and he is willing to do whatever it takes to reach his goals. These are my beliefs, and I would like to be with another positive thinker.

At this stage in my life, almost fifty, I would like someone who is financially secure and successful. Mostly for two reasons; so he is not threatened by my earning power and so I do not end up spending all my money to take care of him. In my past, I have always been the caretaker, and I am tired of that role. I'm ready to play a different role. I'm not quite ready to be "taken care of" at least not 100%, but I sure would appreciate being pampered, taken on trips, taken out to nice romantic dinners, and made to feel like I was really appreciated by my mate. My ideal mate should possess the desire to travel and to appreciate the finer things in life. I am at that stage for myself.

Ideally, I would like someone whose work hours were parallel with mine. This way we could wake up together, enjoy early mornings together, work similar hours Monday through Friday, and then have evenings to do the things we enjoy either together or apart, since we all need alone time. I want to eat dinner together, to unwind together, and most importantly to get into bed together. I didn't know how important that was until now as I am in a relationship where we are on two opposite time clocks, and I am slowly losing my sanity to the situation. This is one of the main areas that will force me into changing my relationship and beginning my search for my "ideal man." This time, however, I am writing what I want, and will not settle for anything less, even if it means being alone.

My ideal man will appreciate good health and nutrition. He will take care of his body, and understand, it is his temple. My ideal man will appreciate humor and laughter and have a lust for life. To understand me, he will need a sense of humor. My ideal man will be nonjudgmental. "Judge not, nor be judged." One should walk in another man's moccasins before judging him. My ideal man will know how to love unconditionally. I am not able to do this yet, but I am trying.

My ideal man will not be a moody person. I would like consistency in his personality. I am so tired of dealing with mood swings. My ideal man will be a people person. He will be someone who likes people and who knows how to carry on intelligent conversations, when meeting new people.

My ideal man is adventurous and likes to try new things, do new things, and go new places. He is someone, who is not afraid of the unknown, but relishes it. He is someone, who will try new foods with an open mind.

For leisure time, my ideal mate would be able to know how to relax and do nothing with me and still be content. My ideal mate would be into health and fitness, and we would spend time working out together in a gym or outdoors. My ideal mate would appreciate going to theatre and to live entertainment. It would be nice to be with someone who likes to read in bed together.

So, that man is out there somewhere. Let's hope I find him!

*　　*　　*

I didn't realize at the time, but that night, I created my future husband. I created Arthur, my "Knight in Shining Armor." It was only February. I wouldn't meet him until August 26, 1999. I still had a lot of work to do on me first, so the timing could not have been better!

Within one week of describing my ideal mate, Alex and I agreed to split up after our four-year relationship, and we agreed that I would buy out his share of the condo. It was absolutely the first time in my life I had broken up with someone without having another man waiting in the wings. I truly, truly, truly broke up with Alex because I was tired of being dysfunctional and in dysfunctional relationships. I was forty-eight and ready to face my demons. I was ready to be my own best friend. The truth is, you cannot fully love someone else until you first love yourself. At least not if you intend to have a healthy and fully functional relationship!

One of my girlfriends told me about an organization called, The Landmark Forum. The Landmark teaches how to let go of whatever is keeping us from growing emotionally. My friend invited me to attend the last night of her session. When I did, I knew I had to enroll in the program. I knew I had to end my own self-defeating behavior. The example used by the speaker on stage was, "If you feel like you have this chair strapped to your leg and you are dragging this chair every-where you go in life—Landmark Forum is for you. The chair represents an emotional hang-up that keeps you from becoming whole and from growing emotionally."

Well, gee, I could relate to that! I knew I had dragged an entire dining room set around for the past thirty years!! The furniture's name is Ricky. I knew I had never let go of Ricky. I knew I had never allowed myself to trust in love again. I knew I needed the Landmark Forum. I was ready, willing, and hopefully able. I had become successful as a businesswoman. I had created a fantastic life for myself externally, but internally, I still had a wall around my heart. I was ending a four-year relationship, and I was ready to do the required work. I also knew I needed to get a handle on my parenting skills. I needed to recover me.

I attended the Landmark Forum over three days in late February while Alex moved out of the condo. Briefly, the Forum offers a safe envi-ronment, where a group of between seventy-five and two hundred-fifty people who have all made a commitment to themselves to grow emo-tionally, gather and openly share their innermost fears and feelings. It is a powerful, accelerated learning experience with guiding dialog between the instructor and participants.

Grounded in a model of transformative learning, Landmark's programs give people an awareness of the basic structures in which they know, think, and act in the world. From that awareness, comes a fundamental shift that leaves people more fully in accord with their own possibilities and those of others. Participants find them-selves able to think and act beyond existing views and limits—in their personal and professional lives, relationships, and wider com-munities of interest.

I can honestly say I don't know if I could have gotten past the bro-ken heart story I had been telling myself, and others, for the previous thirty years if I had not attended the forum. I learned how to create new possibilities for myself. What happened in the past; happened. It is complete and over. The only thing that continues in one's life is the story. I learned to have the courage and integrity to relate to my past as a story and only a story.

Shortly after the course, I located and phoned Ricky, who had been married for over twenty years. I briefly explained my situation to him, and then I asked if I could see him again—for closure. He kindly agreed to see me.

Ricky and I reunited on August 1, 1999. It was the first time I had seen him in over twenty-five years. I changed outfits at least six times before pulling into his driveway! We ended up having the best time together. We went to lunch, sat and talked about our past teenage years together, and even shared some belly laughs. Ricky had absolutely no idea how his rejection, along with his unkind and unloving words, had affected me throughout my entire life.

Now, there we were at lunch, laughing over old times together, and I realized like running into a brick wall, how I truly had done this all to myself. It was the stories in my own head that I told myself as a young girl, then as a young woman; that kept me imprisoned. Our psyches can do horrible things to us when emotionally injured. I had never let anyone else love me again. I had chosen not to at an unconscious level because I wanted to avoid the pain of rejection from ever happening again. Therefore, I never gave my trust or my heart to anyone else—just my body. I never wanted to feel that rejection again, or the pain of loss, so I used my story to protect me.

After thirty-years, I truly had closure. When I drove away from seeing Ricky, I felt wonderfully alive! It was like being weightless. My mind and heart were free. I had allowed my *Self* to be destroyed as a teenage girl, and finally I would be able to reclaim my *Self* again, as a woman. Because of my spirituality, I believed all my struggles collectively made me stronger as a human being and prepared me for a blessed future, and blessed, it would be!

The Universe didn't wait long to put my ideal man in my life. On August 26, 1999 Arthur and I met. Five nights later, on our first date, we sat together over a bottle of champagne, sharing our pasts, our present, and our dreams for the future. Within the first week, we both knew there was something magical about our relationship. This time I was free to love again, and I was not going to settle for anything less than I deserved. My walls were down, and my heart was open. We had a magnificent year of dating. One year later we moved in together, and three years later we married. At fifty-three, I had the love, the man, and the marriage I deserved. I finally had my "white picket-fence" dreams!"

On May 24, 2014 we celebrated eleven years of blissful marriage... and life just keeps getting better. I finally am experiencing what being adored and loved by someone truly means. I found out what making love with someone means too! I think respect remains the essential ingredient in our relationship. We have mutual respect for each other as unique beings. At times, Arthur understands me better than I understand myself. He has been my rock. I allow him to be my rock. I trust him as my best friend. Arthur loves me like I have never been loved. There is little (if any) dysfunction in our relationship. The little girl in me often finds herself wishing her father could have been Arthur. While the woman in me keeps thanking the Universe for putting him in my life as my husband and the love of my life!

42

Full Circle

AS I EXAMINE MY LIFE FROM the time I lost my identity and self-esteem to Ricky, until finding closure at forty-nine, the most challenging and painful truth I have had to accept about *Self* is that I had used loveless sex to relieve my pain for thirty years. I never thought of myself, or even considered myself addicted to sex per say, but today, I can understand where loveless sex became my drug of choice. I got high from sex. It was my temporary fix. I was able to forget Ricky's rejection and all my emotional pain during sex. I felt wanted. I felt needed. I didn't need to engage my heart to have sex. Sex was my cocaine. Where did I go? (Anne has explained that what I developed was an underlying intimacy disorder fueled by anxiety, depression or other deep-seated emotional vulnerabilities-not by reason and rationale.)

The song I had first heard in my head about Ryan years before, received a new verse about his mother—me:

"Where Do Our Children Go?"

Where do our children go?
Where do they run and hide?
Who did they grow up to be?
What's their reality?

At the tender age of seventeen,
With no father figure guiding me,
I found love in the arms of a boy.
I trusted him with my heart,
Never dreaming we would part.

Two years passed,
Then, just like my Daddy,
He deserted me.

No, I did not drink.
No, I did not drug.
I buried my pain in sex,
With Rob, Roy, and Rex,
Todd, Tom, and Tex,
Just to name a few.

I buried my pain with food,
As, I became unglued.
Buried my pain in poetry and plays,
Became an actress upon the stage.
Became an actress within my private life,
Four times I became a wife.
I became a mother once,
A workaholic too,
I became a financial success,
Independence carried me through.

But I failed as a wife.
And I failed as a mother.
And in the end,
I lost my company, too.
All because I was born,
Into a dysfunctional, *family stew*!

Where do our children go?
Where do they run and hide?
Who did they grow up to be?
What's their reality?

When I think of the harmful words and living situations my son, and I both endured over the years, it totally makes me shudder. We both need to recover from the damage of emotional traumas, broken homes, poor choices, and verbal abuses. Today I realize more than ever the power that spoken words have on one's psyche. I also realize that parents perpetuate their pain onto the next generation. I repeat: Parents perpetuate their pain onto their children.

We need to put an end to the perpetuation of pain from generation to generation. As parents, we all need to strip ourselves to our souls, deal with our fears and the truths of our youths, and then drain ourselves of our pain. When we do this, we will stop saying and doing things to our children that wound their angelic inner child spirits received at birth.

As parents of addicts who attend Coda meetings (Codependents Anonymous), we learn about the "Three C's." We are taught, "You didn't *cause* it, you can't *control* it, and you can't *cure* it." Unfortunately, I disagree. I do think his father, and I both contributed to Ryan's drug and alcohol addiction because of our own wounds and dysfunctional histories. I think it is necessary that I own whatever part I played in the development of his disease. Owning that truth is not to put blame or shame on me, but rather to enable me to look honestly at my own dysfunctions. Owning that truth is simply what it is: ownership. Yes, I cannot *control* it. And, yes I cannot *cure* it. But it might have been *prevented* if he had been born into a healthier family environment. Unfortunately, Ryan inherited a long line of dysfunctional, familial behavior. Today, Ryan can choose to put an end to his family legacy.

If I could turn the hands of time back, I would do so many things differently in my life, but, unfortunately, I can't. What I can do is write and publish this book; expose my challenging past; share my healing process; and hope my journey to wholeness and to truth will enlighten and inspire others. Perhaps others will be able to see parts of themselves in my story and be moved to heal. Enlightenment and recovery happen only when we are ready.

You don't need to be addicted to drugs or alcohol to go through recovery. I believe most of us all have areas of dysfunction that need to be worked through. Please understand, being dysfunctional doesn't make us bad people, but we perform self-defeating behaviors. It's like the drug addict, who steals money to buy drugs because their addiction is controlling them. The addict is not a bad person, but their behavior is self-defeating and unacceptable. Or, when I had love-less sex, or dated married men; I was not a bad person, but my behavior was self-defeating and unacceptable.

After helping to organize Anne's book, *Family Stew: Our Relationship Legacy*, and while I was processing my life and writing about my childhood and my familial dysfunction, I wrote the following poem, based on all of the insight gained:

"Family Stew"

When I think of my dysfunctional family,
I came from a pretty twisted family tree.
It's as though I was born into a *family stew*.
My *Self*, the meat, absorbed all the juices,
All the "crazy-making" psychological abuses,
Like meat, my soul was flavored through and through,
Absorbing hurt and pain,
Feelings of disdain,
Lies and guises sprinkled in,
A pinch of anger,
A slice of hate,
A fib from Mom why Dad was late.
For Daddy, Manhattan wasn't a city,
Drowned his pain, such a pity.
A womanizer,
A cheating spouse,
Mom stayed married,
Though Dad a louse.
Seems that's just what that generation did.
Kept the truth hidden under the *family stew* lid.
Simmered over time in my *family stew*,
Dysfunction seeped into my very being,
My prime meat (me) toughened and hardened,
Frightened little girl inside became fearful and guarded.
Covered up with laughter,
And, with always being cute,
While I buried my pain,
I kept from going insane.

Buried my fears,
Hid my tears.
Buried my soul,
Buried my relationship,
With who I was born to be.
Yes, I buried me.

My life has come full circle. It took me forty years to uncover and to understand what happened to me in my youth and be able to see how the dysfunctional life I created was a result of my relationship (or lack of relationship) with my family-of-origin; my *family stew*.

A *family stew* made up of an emotionally void, alcoholic, sex and relationship addicted father, who did not provide me with boundaries, who was verbally abusive to his wife, and who had no respect for her or other women. A *stew* with a mother, who allowed her *Self* to be mistreated emotionally and physically, who was subservient and catered to her husband out of fear, and who enabled her husband's alcoholism by her coexisting disease of codependency; a disease not diagnosed nor defined by professionals until the 1970s.

I never questioned why my mother always drove home from restaurants and parties, or why my father slurred his words, walked so foolishly, or spoke so mean to my mother at night. They were my role modeling experiences. I thought that was a "normal" marital relationship. I never witnessed what a healthy, functional marriage looked like. I replicated only what I knew. Without realizing it, I eventually mirrored my mother's dysfunctional, enabling and codependent behavior. And, unfortunately, I also mirrored my father's sexuality and emotional intimacy issues.

Today, as I look back on my journey that began the day I did tough love, I realize most of what I wrote about in poetry, lyrics and scripted dialog were similar feelings I had when I was in my pain filled years with low self-esteem and loss of self. Ryan's pain was my own pain. I could relate because I, too, had suffered and was still suffering. It is not only the addict who needs to recover. We all do.

Being as I am not a psychologist, but instead, a recovering codependent who suffered for years in denial and years as an enabler, I believe I do not qualify to go into depth as to how these psychological disorders manifest or appear in our behavior. Instead, I am going to suggest that you do further research on your own as there are many books written by experts; such as Anne Salter, Melody Beattie, and Pia Mellody on the subjects of family-of–origin and codependency. Codependency, alcoholism, and addiction are severe, interrelated family diseases that can definitely be arrested over time.

43

Ryan Meets Ashley

WHILE I WAS GETTING MY ACT together, Ryan was working on keeping his together. I'm still not sure how long Ryan stayed sober after getting out of rehab, but I don't think his sobriety lasted very long. His wounds from the past were haunting him and for reasons only Ryan knows—he started drinking again.

Evidently, Ryan was slipping and sliding into a dark space when he met another earth angel named Ashley. They were introduced at a party sometime in August 2010. Ashley would tell me later she was extremely attracted to Ryan's personality from his first hello. He was drinking beer that night and she was drinking wine. She knew he had been to rehab for drugs, but she didn't realize alcohol was also a problem. Ashley, who had recently graduated from college, was still in celebration mode herself, and celebrate they did!

After their first night of partying together, they only saw each another randomly at various clubs around town. Ryan and Michelle, though not still a "couple," shared the same condo until it sold, so dating anyone else would have been awkward. Once Ryan moved into his own apartment, he and Ashley began dating and by fall, they officially decided to be in an exclusive relationship.

Over the next six months, or so, Ashley started to see patterns in Ryan's personality changes while drinking. The adorable and funny sober Ryan became an ugly and rude drunk Ryan, and Ashley didn't like what she was seeing. Though he wasn't doing any drugs, his drinking was progressively getting out of control. Ashley told Ryan he needed to quit drinking. In fact, she refused to be romantically involved with him any further if he didn't stop. She told him flat out that she was not going to be another enabler like Michelle! She didn't like him at all when he drank.

What Ashley did next was quite remarkable. She examined her own life and realized she too had started drinking way too much while she was in college. She had graduated nearly one year before, but hadn't stopped partying like a coed. Although Ashley wasn't an alcoholic, by any means, she acknowledged that she did use alcohol to an extreme. Because she liked Ryan and saw potential in him, Ashley decided to quit drinking. She wanted to show Ryan that she had more willpower than he did! So on May 8, 2011 Ashley stopped drinking and boldly put the ball in Ryan's court. Ryan continued drinking, but, not with Ashley

Two weeks later, on May 22, 2011, Ryan played ball. Ryan attended his first AA meeting since relapsing. He finally admitted to being both an alcoholic and a drug addict. This time, I trust he wholeheartedly admitted he was powerless over drugs and alcohol. I believe he truly surrendered. Ryan began working The Twelve Step program with every ounce of his being. He surrendered and accepted his truth.

The first time Ryan called telling me he was in love with a girl named Ashley, I asked if he could be totally himself with her. He told me he was the man he had always wanted to be, when he was with her. Because Ryan is ten years older than Ashley, I believe he truly feels valued in the relationship for his additional years of experience and knowledge. He clearly didn't want another mom. He needed a partner, who was strong enough not to let him walk all over her, yet vulnerable enough to appreciate his strengths.

Ashley knew Ryan's history with drugs and alcohol, but loved him for the man he had evolved into— a sober, functional, caring, and responsible adult. Ryan continued attending AA meetings and stayed connected with his rehab center. At thirty-four, Ryan was decisively becoming his own man. The power of his mind was at work in his life. My son started to recognize the importance of loving himself and was therefore capable to love another person.

44

Divine Intervention Strikes Again

SEVEN MONTHS HAD PASSED SINCE RYAN was out of rehab. I wrote the first four sections of Part 3 (chapters 37, 38, 39, and 40) during those months. I was working on understanding how my family dynamics had affected me as a young girl and now felt I understood why and how I became so dysfunctional and codependent. I painted a pretty horrific picture of myself, as Ryan's mother, but I needed to be totally honest in order to recover and to be present for Ryan in a healthy, non-toxic relationship.

I no longer just talked the talk. I began to walk the walk. It felt good to think differently. It felt good to feel the change inside. It felt good to be whole. As Mahatma Gandi said, "Be the change you wish to see in the world."

I had promised Ryan I wouldn't call him. He said he would call me when he was ready. I missed my son. I missed having him in my life. Every time I'd see mothers with their sons I'd ache inside. I longed to have Ryan want me back in his life. My feelings led me to write the following poem just before midnight on November 23, 2010:

"Let Me Love You Again, my Son"

The reasons why I lost you,
Are as clear as the day you were born.
Cut from my umbilical cord,
You came in crying.
And, today I am crying too.

Let me love you again, my son.
And, please let yourself love me—again too.

Second chances,
Second chances,
We all deserve second chances,
Not just in romances—but with family.
No one is perfect,
We all make mistakes,
Forgiveness heals one's heart,
Forgiveness lets us start—
Anew.

Second chances,
Second chances,
We all deserve second chances,
I'm sorry for mistakes made while raising you.
We can't change our past,
But we can change our futures—through,
Second chances,
Second chances,
If you let me,
Please, just let me,
Let me love you again, my son.

As my Higher Power God is my witness, at 9:30 a.m. the very next morning my cell phone rang and my son was on the other end. I know it's hard to believe, but it's the truth. In a gesture of kindness Ryan reached out to me that very morning for the first time since getting out of rehab!

Over a year ago I had asked Ryan to design a card for Arthur and me for when we traveled and met others; like a social card. I didn't like handing out my real estate business card. Ryan called that morning to remind me to send him what I wanted written on the card. The fact that we began speaking again *that* very next day was an answer to my *prayer* and to my *intention* to let me love him again.

This is one more affirmation as to how essential it is to write down what you want in your life. When writing, your entire being participates in your thoughts (your energy), which together with your heart (housing your soul) and your hands and fingers (aspects of your physical being) allows you to create something tangible, strong and powerful. That something is the written word. Words are most powerful. Words strung together in sentences have changed the world. Words are written thoughts.

Many people would call this a coincidence, but once I grew to my own understanding of how the Universe works, I knew it was divine intervention. Creative visualization, prayer, intention, positive affirmations, and putting what I wanted in my life into writing worked. I am living proof. Just look at the many miracles that have taken place in Ryan's and my life.

As you could see while reading about my history, I am living proof that negative thinking also works equally well. As I reflect upon my entire life, I clearly see how my thinking created my world—be it positive thinking or negative thinking. Our thoughts create our reality. Thoughts are powerful tools.

*   *   *

When Christmas 2010 arrived, I couldn't have received a more meaningful gift from my son. Ryan knew how much I loved his artwork, so he surprised me with the very first painting he painted after getting out of rehab, and after separating from Michelle and moving into his own apartment. He mailed it to me in a cardboard tube. When I unrolled his canvas and witnessed this peace-filled, spiritually centered painting, you guessed it; I cried. These were tears of joy, gratitude, and internal peace

Painting 16

What an amazing contrast to all his previous paintings. Thank you God. Thank you Universe. And thank you Ryan for loving yourself enough to choose life. Recovery is a rebirth of the *Self*. It is a rebirth of one's heart and soul. It is a time to let go of one's past and to create one's future. Recovery is a time of discovery. Recovery is about the recovering one's *Self* and becoming the person you were born to be!

*   *   *

Sometime in 2011 while Ryan was looking for a full time job and sharing his frustrations with me, I wrote the following:

Why Be Clean—In a Dirty World?

As the mother of a recovering alcoholic/addict, it disgust and angers me when I hear my son tell me he can't share his sobriety with others because he'll be prejudged and it will affect his ability to find work. In 2011, when it seems almost every American family has someone who is either an alcoholic, a drug addict, or taking prescription drugs to cope, I would think those in recovery and who are sober could stand up and be proud of their achievements.

In a world full of hypocrisy, where the "well dressed" on Wall Street can steal from investors, where pornography fills our lives through media, where children murder other children, where parents murder their own children, and where politicians continue to be "caught" with their pants down, I would think our society would welcome with open arms, those, who have found their way back from addiction to sobriety.

Just like we turned our backs on our Viet Nam Veterans in the seventies, we are turning our backs on the war against drugs. Why be "clean" in a "dirty" world? That is what I'd ask myself if I was my son and had to face feelings of shame and rejection when looking for employment. If it pisses me off, try to imagine how Ryan and other recovering addicts must feel.

Human nature is such that no one is perfect, and a biblical saying comes to mind, "Why do you look at the speck of sawdust in your brother's eye and pay no attention to the plank in your own eye?" So, I ask the world to please stop judging those in recovery so harshly and give them a chance to regain their dignity and self-worth.

Not one person who is in recovery chose to be an addict or alcoholic. Yes, they made poor choices in the past. It happened. Now, give them a chance to have a future. They earned that right. Recovery takes lots of hard work, determination, and discipline. Ryan went to college and became a graphic designer after being clean two years. I am extremely proud of his accomplishments. There is no reason for him to feel any shame about his sobriety or his past. The only shame is on you, Mr. Employer. Pull the plank out of your eye!

*   *   *

I empathize with my son and with anyone else who is in recovery or who has survived hellacious, dysfunctional pasts, and who now struggle with shame or blame issues. Society is quick to judge and slow to forgive. I believe the first step is the forgiveness of oneself and then of others. Forgiveness is something you do for yourself.

Being sober is not always easy for Ryan. Ryan would love to have a drink. He knows he can't, so he doesn't, but he did tell me, sometime in 2011 that the desire was still there. All I can do is pray the desire goes away and that he stays in touch with his truth.

The truth is Ryan cannot drink. He cannot have only one drink. One leads to two, two leads to three, three leads to four, and before Ryan knows it, days later; he's snorting coke. Unfortunately, that is his reality, his truth. Ryan has come to the conclusion that his primary disease is alcoholism. If he drinks alcohol, he knows it will lead to cocaine. For that reason, he has chosen AA as his Twelve Step program instead of NA.

I have learned to "let go" and to "let God." It was extremely hard to do in the beginning, but it got easier as time passed. Ryan is on Ryan's path. I am on my path. We all recover when we are ready. Each of us has his own rock bottom to hit. It took me fifty-two years to hit mine. Then it took eight more years before I was emotionally ready and willing to understand how my *family stew* affected me.

Hitting bottom is a good thing. Sometimes we must do it more than once. Up is the only way we can go! And, so it is.

PART IV
2012

More Truth

45
How Spirit Worked for Me

IT IS THE LAW OF SPIRIT, THAT WE MUST BE THAT WHICH WE WOULD
DRAW TO US. IF WE WOULD DRAW TO US LOVE, WE MUST BE LOVE, BE
LOVING AND KIND. IF WE WOULD HAVE PEACE AND HARMONY IN OUR
ENVIRONMENT, WE MUST ESTABLISH IT WITHIN OURSELVES. TO DO
THAT, WE MUST ⁵RST LEARN TO LET GO, TO GIVE UP, TO MAKE ROOM
FOR THE THINGS WE HAVE PRAYED FOR AND DESIRE.
—*Charles Fillmore*

IT IS EARLY 2012, AS I ENDEAVOR to reflect on my journey in order to
share the most valuable parts of my healing process. After doing my
own recovery work, I found a place of peace within *Self*. I was no longer
reacting to the drama of addiction and dysfunction, so I no longer had
the need to document Ryan's life with poetry and prose, or to continue
visualizing his healthy future. One had already materialized. Plus, I was
busy organizing and editing this book. After so many stressful years, I
was taking deep breaths full of meditative air. I focused on healing my
own life.

Since the day I did tough love with my son until today, which to-
tals ten years of processing my journey and ten years of evolving into
wholeness, I have grown <u>only</u> because I chose to grow. I found *hope* because I chose to find *hope*. I found *Self* because I chose to find *Self*. My
journey also included rediscovering my Higher Power. My God had always been with me throughout all of my life, but I forgot to listen. Yes,
it's that simple. I forgot what I already knew. Spirit lives within each
one of us. All we need to do is hear our answers in the silence. In the silence, between our breaths, we find our God—our Higher Power—our
Spiritual *Self*. Like the wind, Spirit can be felt, but not seen.

And when an addict or an alcoholic hits bottom and is on their knees, it is then they must choose to seek their Higher Power in order to find inner strength. They must surrender. Surrendering to one's Higher Power is not so difficult for alcoholics and addicts after years of surrendering to lower powers, such as alcohol and drugs. The addict's thoughts, attitudes, desires, habits, relationships and purpose need transformation. The root of the trouble is in the addict-alcoholic thinking—not in their drugging and or drinking!

I believe the reasons The Twelve Step programs, such as Alcoholics Anonymous, Narcotics Anonymous, Co-Dependents Anonymous, and Nar-Anon are successful for many people is quite simple. They are programs based on universal principles and unity of purpose. Principles, which when applied, can help to eliminate alcoholism, addiction, and codependency. These same principles might also help to eliminate war, hate, poverty, greediness and discrimination, just to name a few. All of us, and especially our politicians, would benefit from a Twelve Step program!

Once one's inner spiritual life develops, then such things as emotional contentment, honesty, concern for others, humility, patience, happiness, and core values all fall into place for the recovering addict/alcoholic and also for the recovering, codependent parent or loved one. Many books are available to learn about The Twelve Step programs, and how they work, so I am not going to expound on them further.

From the beginning of my journey, I wrote. To get the dis-ease out of my body, I processed and recorded my pain. I broke the word disease down into two words because internally I was not at ease. I had anxiety. I was crying. I was scared. I felt sorry for myself. I was depressed. I felt lost. I felt hopeless. I felt frustrated. I felt angry. I felt confused. I felt my son might die. But fortunately for me, once I sensed my Higher Power, I never felt alone!

The Universe truly works in strange, mysterious, and miraculous ways. I believe once one is open to universal energy and to the power of one's God and one's divine *Self*, we understand nothing is by accident and that there is a reason for everything. Based on The Law of Attraction, when we are ready, we attract what we need into our lives. It is quite exciting and powerful.

Strange as it may seem the most important person I attracted into my life was my *Self*. Once my mind came out of denial, and I began facing reality head on, I had to look myself in the mirror and to ask myself—who am I? Who am I beyond this face, this hair, and this body? In truth, who am I? And, why did this happen to me? Yes, my son was/is the addict, but as his mother—this situation also happened to me. I questioned my mothering. I questioned my past. I questioned what I might have done in a different way. I tried not to beat myself up because I knew I had never done anything with the intention to hurt my son. And yet, buried inside of me lived this destructive, underlying feeling of guilt that needed elimination from my soul.

There is no room for guilt in the recovery of *Self*. Forgiveness of *Self* is the key ingredient towards becoming whole. You could say I became pro-active. I did not sit home and wait for the Universe to bring solutions to my doorstep. I bravely stepped out and attracted meaningful answers into my world through my openness and honesty.

Once I walked out the door, one of the most important things I did both for myself and other families facing addiction was to verbalize the truth. Rather than putting my tail between my legs in shame when asked about my son (like I used to do), I began sharing that my son was a recovering addict and alcoholic. I shared my pride in him. I shared how I had been in denial and how I had been his biggest enabler. I interjected this into conversations whenever appropriate or possible. I talked about the diseases of addiction, alcoholism and codependency and how they were affecting what seemed like almost every family. Guess what happened?

Inevitably, others shared that their son, daughter, wife, husband, or friend was an addict or alcoholic. I realized opening the door by expressing my truth allowed others to express theirs. A conversation would take place where strangers were able to verbalize and to share their 'story' and to express their 'truth.' They felt safe. They felt a sense of relief by venting their painful feelings. They felt good about not feeling alone. I believe the time is right for all families to share their truths, so that parents and our recovering children and loved ones can live in a world of acceptance and most importantly without shame, blame or guilt.

In 2005, while cruising on the Queen Elizabeth II, I boldly stood on stage in front of at least one thousand passengers and recited what I had written the day I did tough love. I prefaced my poetry with a powerful speech about how addiction is destroying families and how after doing tough love I went home and was inspired to write. I cannot tell you how many people came up after the show to commend me for my courage and to share their stories of addiction. I did this again on a few more cruises during talent nights and received similar responses. They continued to admire my honesty, courage, and openness. The funny thing is I did not feel courageous at the time. I felt I was honoring all families who struggle with dysfunction, alcoholism, addiction and codependence. These diseases are worldwide, and they do not discriminate.

46
New Thought For a New Millennium

IN LATE 2009, I WAS LED TO Unity Church of Hollywood, Florida. I specifically went to hear a particular singer's voice. Mitch and I planned to record songs for *Tough Love — The Musical* on that particular Sunday afternoon and we needed to find a soprano. After hearing Marie Ballard-Blakemore sing, I explained to her about the musical and asked if she would consider singing for us in a few hours. Marie agreed to sing, while sharing she was seven years sober on that very day, so being asked to sing for a musical about recovery appeared as a blessing for her.

Eventually, perhaps five months later, I returned to Unity in 2010. I believe I was led back for a deeper purpose. My intention in the next few paragraphs is *not* to convert you, the reader, to any religious belief or to think the way I think. Please know I only am telling my story and sharing my journey. Attending Unity became part of my journey. In fact, it became a most integral part of my understanding of the path I had been on for the past eight years. I do not want you to think I am preaching. I personally cannot tolerate anyone who tries to blanket me with his or her religious beliefs. I don't consider myself to be religious. I consider myself to be spiritual. There is a difference.

I believe, when one becomes spiritual, we accept responsibility for our own soul's journey in the pursuit of universal truths versus limiting oneself to only one religion's dogma. Therefore, I was attracted to Unity's metaphysical philosophy. As a first time attendee, I was given the book, *New Thought for a New Millennium*.

New Thought for a New Millennium is a book about the potential for humankind as seen through the lens of twelve powers of awakened humanity. Each of the twelve theologians, philosophers, authors and scholars who contributed to this book share from his or her deepest personal beliefs, his or her most innovative, exciting perceptions and projections, and his or her collective vision of the "possible" human. It invites us to go deeper to uncover the powers within ourselves.

According to this book, "Jesus had twelve disciples, disciples to whom metaphysical scholars attribute a power. These powers are twelve expressions of the one Power, the Christ within each of us.

- Love
- Faith
- Understanding
- Wisdom
- Imagination
- Zeal
- Strength
- Will
- Life
- Power
- Renunciation
- Order

Christ, as a fully awakened human being, is the same as the Buddha-Mind or the Higher *Self*, the indwelling Lord, Shiva, and the Atman, to use words from a number of traditions. It is a state of consciousness within us which is completely one with God." (God, as *you* define God.) Christ's purpose was to teach spirituality and love.

In 2002, I began a journey, where I allowed myself to surrender, to feel *hope*, and to have faith again—faith in a power greater than my *Self*. Without a doubt, my Higher Power and my connection to my divine *Self* carried me through this journey. After reading about the twelve powers, I realized those powers had been awakened within me as I wrote and processed my recovery and revealed my truth.

Rosemary Ellen Guiley, author of over forty-five books and one of the twelve contributing authors in *New Thoughts for a New Millennium*, writes about the power of faith. "When tragedy strikes, when the world turns upside down, it is faith that sees us through. Faith is the engine that drives our existence. The greater our faith, the greater results we obtain, the greater works we do. Faith moves in the realm of the unseen. It cannot be measured, captured, rationed or held. It moves us out of the plane of the material and into the plane of the universal Mind. Through faith, we come to terms with one of the fundamental metaphysical laws of the universe that thought creates reality. What we think becomes manifest. What we believe comes to pass. How well and how quickly these manifestations occur depend upon our faith. With faith, we are empowered to make the invisible visible. We can pull our hopes and dreams from intangible into tangible."

Ryan had entered rehab almost one year before I encountered those words in March 2011. It was as if I had been led to read other supportive words, providing for my deeper understanding of what had transpired in my life over the past nine years. The power of our thinking is beyond words. What I thought became manifest. What I had written on the first day of my tough love journey had manifested. I wrote and continued writing for years while creatively visualizing Ryan's future. Eventually, my visions became reality. My faith held me up.

Rosemary continues, "Without faith, we begin to fall into doubt, and from doubt we sink into fear. Fear leads to a breakdown of order and of spirit. Faith enables us to see beyond the physical world, into the world of potential and possibilities. There, all the good that is ours and ours alone awaits us. Faith helps us to see it, reach it, and create from it. We see the possible, even when tangible evidence in the material world tells us otherwise."

I believe *hope* stems from a place of fear. While our addicted children are using drugs, parents do live in fear. I believe one's first step towards recovery and wholeness, therefore, is first to find a little ray of *hope* within one's heart. With a feeling of *hope*, we then become open to the possibility that trust and faith will evolve as we flex our heart muscles, open our eyes to the truth, and "let go" to our God, as we understand and define God. Without *hope*, I would have been lost and would never have searched within for my Higher Power.

The word HOPE became my mantra. I came up with various titles for this book based on HOPE. *How One Parent Evolved* was going to be the title for the longest time because I had changed so much over the past eleven years. This book, however, is about how I engaged addiction and my metamorphosis was a direct result of my total engagement. Had I not fully engaged myself, in the battle for truth in my own brokenness, I may not have survived and, therefore, this is how I came up with the book's title.

Bernie Siegel, M.D., another of the authors found within, *New Thought for the New Millennium,* titled his chapter, "Finding Strength in Our Brokenness." Dr. Siegel writes, "Ernest Hemingway wrote, 'The world breaks everyone, and afterward many are strong at the broken places.' This truth is difficult for most of us to accept. We focus on the brokenness and never take notice that we have become stronger at the broken places. Yes! When fractures heal, they become stronger than the bone. Nature teaches us a principle in the body that is also true in the soul—that pain is a teacher, protector, and definer of one's self. Pain is a teacher that can focus our attention, push us to move beyond our mental/emotional limitations, and ultimately bring us closer to God. Pain helps us to discover our authentic selves and to define our purpose. When you lose touch with your feelings and emotions, both painful and pleasant, you cannot respond properly to life. Acknowledging and responding to our pain is a path to healing. Reacting to our pain by anesthetizing it robs us of its gift—its capacity to bring us to wholeness. Strength comes from using the pain and learning from it."

I think his thought encapsulates what happened to me, to my son Ryan, and to everyone who has suffered from various degrees of emotional illness. It's so important to understand that it's okay to suffer or to lose one's way along life's journey. In our suffering and pain filled experiences, we receive the opportunity to discover how strong we can become from those negative experiences. Getting back in touch with our true selves, and our true feelings are the ways we become whole, healthy and vibrant. Guilt, shame and blame drain us of our powers and need to be replaced with compassion, understanding, acceptance, and *Self* love.

In Dr. Siegel's words, "…we must move beyond the legacy of lovelessness, to forgive and to be reborn." I believe this is the primary challenge for all who suffer as addicts, alcoholics, or with codependency. The rebirth of *Self* is joyous beyond words! Become your Michelangelo!

To say I couldn't put this book down is an understatement. It seems as if I hi-lighted the entire book. I highly recommend reading *New Thought for a New Millennium,* as a vehicle to rediscover your twelve powers, your inner peace, your wholeness, and your purpose.

47

Stand Like Mountain
Flow Like Water

ONCE I STARTED ATTENDING UNITY, I also started participating in their book study classes. I was amazed at how each book seemed to clarify the emotions I had expressed over the past eight to ten years in my writings. I had frequent 'aha' moments. The more I read, the more I knew my poems and songs were on target. Though I wasn't the perfect poet, or even the perfect writer, I knew my poetry and my story was from the heart and, therefore, would be heartfelt by others.

The next book I read was *Stand Like Mountain, Flow Like Water—Reflections on Stress and Human Spirituality,* written by, Brian Luke Seaward, Ph.D. In the book's foreword, author Michelle Naomi Remenit, M.D. writes, "After twenty years of working with people with cancer, I have come to realize how much stress is caused by the sad fact that many of us believe in one way and live in quite another. Perhaps this explains why many people in the face of what one might imagine is the most overwhelming stress, life-threatening illness, often notice their stress level has actually diminished, and they feel more joy. Such people seem to have found through their suffering a profound sense of what is most important to them, and the courage to bring their lives into alignment with it for the first time."

Dr. Remenit quotes a woman with breast cancer, who said, "For the first time I am sailing my boat by my own star. My God, I have sailed it by everything else, and allowed everyone else to take a turn at the tiller. All of my life I've headed against myself, against my own direction. But now I have a deep sense of my way, and I am loyal to it. This is my boat, and it was made to sail in this direction, by this star. You ask, why I seem so much more peaceful now? Well, I am living all in one piece."

While reading only the foreword to this book, it spoke to me. I had found my star. I had found my soul. I was finally at the tiller. I too had found the courage to bring my life into alignment. I too was living all in one piece. Ecstasy does wait on the other side of suffering!

The saying, "Stand like mountain, move like water," is a principle of the Taoist philosophy. To stand like a mountain suggests a sense of stability, resistant to the winds of change. To move like water implies the ability to go with the flow, rather than trying to change things we have no control over. To move like water is to persevere, to yield essentially to gain strength, and to move on once again. The concept of balance is best summed up in the words of Reinhold Niebuhr, now titled, "The Serenity Prayer," and used by every self-help group grounded in the tradition of Alcoholics Anonymous. "God grant me the serenity to accept the things I cannot change, the courage to change the things I can, and wisdom to know the difference." In other words, "Stand like mountain, move like water!"

Throughout Brian's book, I read more and more writings clarifying the journey I had been on and reinforcing my vision. He quotes Poet Maya Angelou as saying, "I believe that Spirit is one and everywhere present. That it never leaves me. That in my ignorance I may withdraw from it, but I can realize its presence the instant I return to my senses." For certain I had withdrawn from Spirit during most of my dysfunctional past years and Spirit had returned to me—all I had to do was listen. All I had to do was ask, *"How?"* All I had to do was return to my senses!

Brian writes: "On occasion you may ask yourself, 'Is there really meaning and purpose to the less than desirable experiences that make me feel victimized and violated?' Caught in the midst of these encounters, it often seems impossible to make sense out of them. As a result, one often feels like the victim; this is a natural response. But when we choose to first listen then learn from the lessons by emotionally detaching from the experience, we mature spiritually—like the rough rock that becomes a smooth gemstone. This process of soul growth is as inevitable as the phases of the moon and as natural as the dawn of each day. So the seasons of the soul offer us the unique opportunity to examine the landscape of the human journey— the spiritual path. In turn, these seasons offer insight into two of the most important questions: Who am I? Why am I here?

Four aspects of the human condition compose the whole: mind, body, spirit, and emotions. Of these four components, the spiritual dimension—more specifically, the evolution of the soul—is the most difficult to comprehend. Perhaps for this reason, it is the most trying. Nevertheless, it is the soul's growth process, our evolution of higher consciousness—the realization of the divine nature of our inner selves—that is the least understood—the most challenging, yet ultimately the most rewarding."

I learned that on the day I did tough love and asked my Higher Power God, *"How?"* was the day I had surrendered. Surrender does not mean to give in or to give up. "Surrender to the will of God," Brian states, "is an invitation to work with, rather than in opposition to, the divine game plan. Think of surrender as flowing with the current." In the words of Sri Ramakrishna, 'The winds of grace are blowing perpetually. We only need raise our sails.' The word surrender is synonymous with detachment, letting go, moving on. To truly align yourself with your Higher Power, you must truly surrender."

While reading Brian's book, it dawned on me, that the poem I'd written in 2003 called, "Once You Go Within You Will Never Go Without," was about the centering process. In Brian's words, "...the centering process, where rather than doing, we take time to simply be. Through the centering process, the conscious mind is encouraged to pause in silence and then listen to the deep-seated wisdom that guides us. To center ourselves is a way to achieve balance, to bring equity back to the soul; we do this by making a concerted effort to reconnect with that part of our consciousness we know as the Higher *Self*, the divine essence or God."

Brian's book has a section about forgiveness. Because the forgiveness of one's *Self* is so critical to one's recovery, I'd like to share a couple more of Brian's quotes. "Every act of forgiveness is an act of unconditional love. If unresolved anger is a toxin to the spirit, forgiveness is the antidote. Where anger is a roadblock, forgiveness is a way to drive around and transcend the experience. For forgiveness to be unconditional, one must be willing to let go of all feelings of anger, resentment, and animosity. Sweet forgiveness cannot hold any taste of bitterness; the two are mutually exclusive. When feelings of anger are released, the spirit once held captive by anger is free to journey again."

Brian continues, "Forgiveness means more than condoning someone's inappropriate behavior and excusing personal violations. It means letting go of the feelings of denial, anger, and indignation and moving on with your life. Forgiveness is a healing process where the wounds of injustice are allowed to fully mend by going from controlling others to empowering oneself. To paraphrase the words of psychologist Sidney Simon, 'forgiveness is not something you do for someone else; it is something you do for yourself. Forgiveness sets you free again.'"

I cannot say enough about how powerful and insightful *Stand Like Mountain, Flow Like Water* was for me. I highly recommend it for all parents of addicts, and for anyone living with stress or in dysfunctional relationships. Stress will kill you. Anger is stress. Anger is fear. Love is letting go of fear. My journey led me home; home to my spirit *Self* and home to the divine nature of my inner *Self*. Reading Brian's book re-confirmed how all I had gone through led to the understanding of my soul's purpose here on earth and to furthering my true, inner peace.

PART V
2012 – 2014

More Truth

48

How the Universe Worked for Me

CRITICISM IS SOMETHING WE CAN AVOID EASILY BY
SAYING NOTHING, DOING NOTHING, AND BEING NOTHING.
— *Aristotle*

I SPENT MUCH TIME DURING 2012 AND 2013 organizing and editing my manuscript for publishing. Still, there remained this internal fear I needed to overcome with respect to exposing my life to the world in a book. Finding the inner strength to publish was not coming easy. I believe the Universe picked up on my fears and started putting additional books and television shows into my life in order to reinforce and support the publishing of this book.

One such book is *Believable Hope: Five Essential Elements to Beat any Addiction,* written by Michael Cartwright. Michael was instrumental in establishing addiction treatment centers across the United States and has successfully been using his unique five-point approach for seventeen years with recovering addicts. His first ingredient, necessary for lasting change, is to find believable *hope.* That blew my mind! *Hope* was the one thing I always held onto, became my mantra, and even integrated it into my book's title!

Michael's second ingredient shot me to the moon, with a boost of confidence, when I read, "Specifically visualize or imagine the new world you desire to create." Wow. Wow. Wow. I spent over ten years visualizing, imagining, and creating a new world for both my son and myself based on the *hope* and faith I maintained. Now I was reading an entire book, written by an authority, supporting what had worked. He even has a chapter titled, "Thank God for Grandma!"

Since I was only a recovering, codependent parent, having no credentials like Ph.D., M.D., or LCSW after my name, I needed additional confidence to share my story. Sometime in 2012, I started to record shows on Oprah's new station called, OWN, but never seemed to find time to view them. I happened to watch my first Super Soul Sunday show on October 21, 2012, where Oprah interviewed Gary Zukov, author of *The Seat of the Soul*, and his spiritual partner, Linda Francis. After listening to the interview, I purchased *The Seat of the Soul* and two other books Gary co-authored with Linda Francis: *The Heart of the Soul*, and *The Mind of the Soul*.

Page after page of reading continued to explain the journey of my soul. Each book shed more and more light on what I had experienced and provided me with a better understanding of the healing path I had chosen. Their books fueled my fire to publish.

To top it off, the fact Oprah created a show called, Super Soul Sunday, at this point in my life was not only magical, but also uncanny. Oprah states, at the beginning of each show, that her show is, "food for the soul." Oprah wants a place, where people can go every Sunday, to wake up, thought provoking, eye opening, and inspiring. As far as I can see, Oprah is achieving her goal.

Oprah's interviews include such people as authors Eckhart Tolle, Llewellyn Vaughan Lee, Don Miguel Ruiz, Dr. Wayne Dyer, Marianne Williamson, Iyanla Vanzant, Tony Robbins, and Jean Houston. Every one of her shows focuses on some aspect of spirituality, love, forgiveness, one's soul, living in the now, or on what truly matters in life. All of her shows helped in reinforcing that my message was a valuable part of the new age of awakened spirituality and that what I experienced needed sharing.

Then, on May 5, 2013, author Brene' Brown, Ph.D. appeared on Super Soul Sunday. Brene' had written three books: *I Thought it was Just Me, The Gifts of Imperfection,* and *Daring Greatly. Daring Greatly* is about how the courage to be vulnerable transforms the way we live, love, parent and lead. "To 'dare greatly,'" Brene' said, "means having the courage to be vulnerable, to show up, to be seen, to ask for what one needs, and to have hard conversations. You can't get to courage without walking through vulnerability."

While listening to Oprah's interview with Brene' Brown, I realized that my biggest fear was *vulnerability.* It didn't take long for me to understand the real power in being vulnerable. In fact, had I not been vulnerable back in 2002, I would never have surrendered. I would never have taken the first step of my journey from darkness into light. As Brene' stated to Oprah, "Being vulnerable is not weakness. It is the key to having meaningful human experiences. One can be brave and scared. One must have clarity of values and faith."

To borrow from Brene' Brown's title of her book, *Daring Greatly*; it is from Theodore Roosevelt's speech, *Citizenship in a Republic*. Here is the passage that made the speech famous and provided the title for her book:

> *"It is not the critic who counts; not the man who points out how the strong man stumbles, or where the doer of deeds could have done them better. The credit belongs to the man who is actually in the arena, whose face is marred by dust and sweat and blood; who strives valiantly; who errs, who comes short again and again because there is no effort without error and shortcoming; but who does actually strive to do the deeds; who knows great enthusiasms, the great devotions; who spends himself in a worthy cause; who at the best knows in the end the triumph of high achievement, and who at the worst, if he fails, at least fails while daring greatly. . ."*

All I can say is, "Thank you Universe! Thanks for putting Brene' Brown into my life, when I most needed her words of wisdom and also for the inspiring words of Theodore Roosevelt. I have no doubt that, *How One Parent Engaged Addiction*, is an example of me, Deni B. Sher—*daring greatly.*

My original sole (soul) purpose in sharing my journey had been to support emotionally and to offer insight and *hope* for other parents of addicted children. Today, I believe my daring greatly is also a beacon of light for anyone in a dysfunctional relationship, for anyone from a dysfunctional family of origin, and especially for those of us from families where parents or caretakers were alcoholics or addicts themselves.

Today, I believe this book also holds the key to freedom for anyone seeking to unlock and to identify dysfunctional behaviors, beliefs, and or symptoms of unresolved wounds from early childhood relationships. *Until we know what we do not know, we cannot change.* The possibility does exist, for those looking to find internal peace, truth, and wholeness, to benefit from my pain filled, yet liberating journey.

49
My Happy Endings

TO BRING YOU CURRENT AND TO TIE a 'bow' around my story, hoping it is received as a gift from me to you, Ryan went on to marry Ashley on January 15, 2012. Ryan and Ashley gave birth to a beautiful and perfect 9-pound, 2-ounce son, Tyler Blake, on June 22, 2012.

When Ryan first announced I was going to be a grandmother, I immediately sat down and wrote the following poem:

"Going to be a Granny"

And then I was told,
My dreams would unfold,
For I was to be a Granny!
I'm going to be a Granny,
Going to be someone's nanny,
Going to have another chance to love.
This is the time to right our wrongs.
This is the time to stop perpetuating pain.
This is the time to stop doing what's insane.
Give. Give your children the tools.
Stop. Stop rearing another generation of fools.
Let them know God is Love.
God is Spirit.
Spirit is everywhere,
Spirit is always there,
Spirit is in one's soul,
Spirit is in Earth and sky,

Spirit is in a tree grown high.
God is a Spiritual Power within you and me.
Let our grandchildren know—
It's okay to have a Higher Power—
A power greater, yes greater, than are *we!*

Ryan and Ashley have the opportunity to break the chains of familial dysfunction. As far as I am concerned, my son Ryan didn't stand a chance emotionally, after being born into a dysfunctional *family stew.* The story no longer needs to repeat itself. Tyler can be raised in a home without dysfunction. The choice to continue in recovery is theirs. Life is about choices. Life is about the battle between two wolves inside each one of us. My son and I are living proof that the wolf getting fed does win. A 'tipping' point resides within each of us, where we decide the victor.

And speaking of victors, I am thrilled to share that Michelle is healing from codependency. I left her a voice mail to please call, as I wanted her to read my book prior to publishing and to give me her blessings. She responded by text, giving me her email address. Then, I sent her a text asking if she was emotionally ready to read my book. She replied, "Emotionally I think I've dealt with everything. Will I cry? Probably. It was an emotional time. I don't regret anything, and it was all a great learning experience. He will always be special to me. I'm currently with someone who treats me like a princess, and I'm happy. My wish for Ryan is for his happiness with his wife and baby. My wish for you is to be a proud and happy grandmother."

My wish for Michelle is for her to continue being treated like the princess she deserves to be. Michelle was an angel in Ryan's life. We all need to be grateful for our Earth angels. They come in many forms; from a stranger in an elevator to a checkout girl at the grocery store; from the eyes of an animal to the eyes of a teacher; from the words of a poet on paper to the stroke of an artist's brush on canvas.

50

Who I Am

IN JANUARY 2013, WHILE LOOKING FOR random pieces of poetry written in my past, which might be appropriate in this book, I found something written back in 1999 while attending the Landmark Forum, that totally blew my mind. My friend Paul Fletcher, one of the two people who wrote the foreword to this book, and who enabled me to better understand tough love in 2005, had said something to me about two years before I finished this book. Paul said he thought I would become the Shakespeare of the new millennium. When he said that, all I could do was laugh. As flattering as it sounded, there was no way I compared myself to Shakespeare, or even felt worthy of his compliment.

Given what Paul said, here is the astonishing part. In the Landmark Forum, we learn about possibility thinking, and about *who* we see ourselves as the possibility of being. Fifteen-years ago, in 1999, this is what I wrote, when asked to write, "*Who do you think you are the possibility of being?*"

> "*Who I am is the possibility of being a messenger—a vehicle for divine inspiration to be channeled through me to the world in the form of the written word and received by the world in the form of books, theatre, cinema and public speeches. I am the possibility of being the Shakespeare of the new millennium, who will enroll the world in the possibility of transformation, where there is no hunger, no wars, and a true equality of life for all living people. And, this will be done through my words and declarations, which is who I am.*

Then written below I also wrote:
Possibility of compassion, creation, inspiration, motivation and kindness.

Amazing! I wrote those words over three years before doing tough love on Ryan! I do believe one person's words can create new possibilities. Should the words in this book foster change in a world full of dysfunction, addiction, codependency, and suffering, I will feel blessed. I am ready for change. I am ready for transformation. Are you? Let's make a difference. Let's help to save future generations from dysfunction and self-defeating behavior. Let's help to save future generations from escaping their feelings with drugs and alcohol. As Mahatma Gandhi once said, "We must be the change we want to see in the world."

In 2002, when I first began writing, I had no conscious memory of what I had written during the Landmark Forum. I always believed, however, since asking my Higher Power God, "How?" that I received both a plan and purpose. Discovering what I had written was one more affirmation that this book was meant to be. This book is the product of my possibility thinking. I became a vehicle for divine inspiration, channeled through me. The musical will become the product of my possibility thinking and vision. Should I enlighten other parents who struggle with an addicted child to give them *hope*, or provide insight into *Self* for anyone struggling to find wholeness—then I will have fulfilled my purpose.

*   *   *

I began part 3 with a quote from Melody Beattie. As I near the conclusion of my book, I would like to repeat her quote again for you. "Real power comes when we stop holding others responsible for our pain, and we take responsibility for all our feelings. Things change, not because we're controlling others, but because we've changed."

How I engaged my son's addiction: changed me. The surrendering of my ego to my higher *Self*: changed me. Accepting that codependency is an emotional illness and then examining my life in order to heal from the inside out: changed me. Owning my part in my son's emotional issues and his ensuing life of drug and alcohol abuse: changed me. Letting go of guilt and forgiving my wounded child *Self* for all of her poor choices: changed me. Understanding the influence my *family stew* had on my childhood: changed me. Understanding and finding forgiveness for my father's inability to parent: changed me. Taking the time to understand my mother and to examine the roles (both positive and negative) she played in my life: changed me. Not holding my high school sweetheart, Ricky, responsible for my pain: changed me. Letting go and letting God: changed me. Learning to say no: changed me. I have achieved "real power." I stopped holding others responsible for my pain. I took back responsibility for my feelings. Like a snake that sheds its skin, I shed the old, codependent *Self* for a new, healthy *Self.* I took back responsibility for my life.

Who I am today is the possibility of providing healthy parenting and grand parenting. I am the possibility of being a successful author, speaker, and mentor. I am the possibility of being an even more loving wife, mother, grandmother, and friend. I am the possibility of leaving earth a better place because of the lessons I learned and shared.

Adversity gave me strength. Experience gave me wisdom. My Higher Power God gave me spirituality and universal knowledge. My friends gave me their time and kindness. My husband gave me his love, trust, and support. And most importantly, my son, Ryan gave me my soul's purpose here on the Earth and the opportunity to recover my *Self.*

Who are you the possibility of being? Remember, anything and everything is possible!

51

Where I Am

AS OF FEBRUARY 2013 I STILL DON'T MAINTAIN the perfect relationship with Ryan, but we are working towards one. Ryan still harbors unresolved feelings of anger towards me, which sometimes crop up when we are together and even while speaking on the phone. But today I understand that I possess no control over Ryan or his anger. Ryan must work through his emotions the same way I must continue to work through mine. The only person, who can change Ryan, is Ryan. I am creatively visualizing him taking the time to read this book, where he can receive insight into his *family stew* and gain a greater understanding of how familial dysfunction operates.

Whenever we speak, he almost always ends the conversation with the words, "I love you, Mom." To my reply, "I love you too, Ryan." There are periods of time where we don't speak for days or weeks because I no longer respond to Ryan as a codependent. I have established boundaries for myself, and I learned to say no. I learned I need to take care of me, and Ryan learned the same for himself.

Detachment, as a former codependent mother, still feels like walking on eggshells at times, but today some shells get cracked! Ryan and I have our disagreements. It is part of the healing process for us both. Ryan is making choices and establishing boundaries that work for his sobriety. I need to respect those decisions. I am extremely proud of the internal, personal work Ryan did to turn his life around. I love my son. I don't always like his behavior, but I will always love him. Ryan doesn't always like my behavior either, but I know he will always love me, too.

After all, isn't being loved, understood and heard what all of us want and deserve? Acceptance and love seem so easy and yet, when we come from a dysfunctional *family stew,* we spend most of our lives seeking them—and usually in unhealthy ways.

*   *   *

It is now May 2013, and Tyler is just over ten months old. Over the past several months, Ryan grew further into his maturity both as a father and as a man. Recently hired by a major company, he is becoming one of their top producers. He told me during my recent visit, "Mom, my son's laughter is better than any drug I have ever taken!" I glowed inside while listening to those sentiments from my son, knowing I was witnessing another miracle.

He is a loving and responsible husband and an open, honest son. He has faced some of his deepest wounds and is working through them. I am so proud of Ryan's recovery progress. Ryan also shared that he visited his father sometime after getting out of rehab, and today they maintain a relationship. I had prayed for this to happen back in 2007. Another prayer answered. Another miracle revealed.

*   *   *

Eleven years ago Ryan flew home from Germany to begin a new life as a sober person. Eleven years ago he was not ready to be sober. Eleven years ago I took the first step in the process of recovery. Hard as it was—I applied tough love. I mounted my horse and went into battle. A battle hard fought and one that would change both of our lives forever.

The process of recovery is like riding a bucking bronco, but with each fall and each crisis I grew and moved forward. I kept getting back on the bucking bronco. As a parent of an addict, it is easy to give up, drop out, or eventually lose *hope*. All I can say to other parents of addicts is to keep riding that bucking bronco and do not give up *hope*. Recovery truly is possible. Easy? No. Possible? Yes.

At Anne Salter's suggestion, I will eventually be attending an intensive, family of origin recovery workshop to further deal with my own wounds. The more I can learn about me, the better prepared I will be to understand and relate to others. Life is about change. Once we change our thinking we change our lives. I will continue being my Michelangelo. I will also continue encouraging others to confront the family diseases of addiction and codependency— knowing recovery can happen!

*   *   *

I returned to visit with my son and his family in June to celebrate Tyler's first birthday. The week couldn't have gone any better. The joyfulness in my grandson's first birthday party was beyond words. The sparkle in Tyler's eyes, as he felt the love from everyone celebrating his life, will remain in my mind's eye forever. As I sat back and watched my son's joy in being a husband and father, I welled up inside with happy tears and that annoying lump in the throat one gets accompanying emotions. I truly was witnessing miracles. Seeing the inner glow of contentment shining through my son's face, as he held his wife in one arm and his son in another, was overwhelming. Ryan was at peace within himself.

*   *   *

Time passed. It is now September 9, 2013, and I am leaving to visit my son and his family to celebrate Ryan's thirty-seventh birthday. I stop to pause and to think how this day holds such new meaning. I get to celebrate not only the day of my son's birth thirty-seven years ago, but also the true miracle that he is still alive and sober. I do not take his life for granted. I give thanks to my Higher Power God. I am forever grateful.

I am eager to continue being a loving, kind, nurturing, non-toxic mother and grandmother. I get to spend more time with my adorable grandson and time building my relationship with my wonderful daughter-in-law and my resurrected son. Yes, my son resurrected. Ryan brought himself back from the deadening, numbing, destroying diseases of addiction and alcoholism. Ryan chose life!

Joyfully and gratefully I reflect on lyrics written ten years ago, inspired by my son's disturbing painting containing a gun. Lyrics I had written while visualizing Ryan's future—on the other side of pain. Today, those lyrics have actualized:

"On The Other Side of Pain"

I'm on the other side of pain,
I'm in control of my life again,
I've dug deep into my heart and soul.

I've seen the blackest black,
The wall has been at my back,
The gun has been pointed to my head,
I reached for life instead.
Like a baby starting to crawl,
Like a toddler wobbling to walk,
Like a newborn crying,
I started trying.
Today,
Today, I'm clean.
Today, I'm on my way.
I'm taking my parents,
Not letting the past stop my recovery.
One day at a time is my motto.
One day at a time is all I need.
One day at a time brings tomorrow.
One day, one step, at a time.

I visited my son and his family in October, and again over Thanksgiving and Christmas. I must tell you my visit in October was by far the best visit yet!! Ryan and I laughed so hard together we both had tears in our eyes. And our laughing sessions happened multiple times during my visit. Ryan and I connected in ways like we hadn't connected in fifteen years. It felt incredible. His anger towards me had changed to kindness, and his rudeness to respect. Yes, there is *hope*!

On Thanksgiving morning, Ryan, Ashley, and I sat around the breakfast table taking turns saying what each of us was thankful for in our lives. We went round and round and round several times while Tyler looked on from his high chair. Though I no longer wait until Thanksgiving to count my blessings, Thanksgiving evoked an even greater meaning for me. As the recovering, codependent mother of a loving, recovering son, the grandmother of a child I never envisioned, the mother-in-law of a dream come true daughter-in-law, and the wife of a healthy husband who survived lung cancer in 2012, my blessings are many.

Tyler started walking over Thanksgiving and by Christmas developed his walking ability. Watching him toddle was adorable. At seventeen-months, Tyler and I began bonding. Being with Tyler is like reliving Ryan as a baby. Tyler has the same sparkle in his eyes Ryan had and what is most wonderful is my son's eyes have regained their sparkle. I sit in wonderment as I watch Ryan's joyfulness. I value my time in the short but meaningful visits. Ryan and Ashley are amazing parents, who work hard and parent well. They are brewing a healthy *family stew*, and I cherish adding the few ingredients that only a grandmother can!

*   *   *

In November 2013, I attended the Miami Book Fair and enjoyed meeting and speaking with many authors. One particular author, Shirlee Scriber, wrote a book called, *Untangle,* with the subtitle: *"You Can't Save Others Until You Save Yourself."*

Her title moved me. The single word, *Untangle,* resonated with me so much, that it inspired me to write a short poem. I had spent the last eleven and a half years untangling my life, my emotions, and my relationship with my son. So, I wrote the following:

"Untangle"

Untangle
Untwist
Undo don't resist
Un think
Un ravel
Undo your babble.

Untangle
Unwind
Undo the tape in your mind
Un hurt
Un bleed
Undo your nasty deed.

Untangle
Forgive

Untangle
Let go
Untangle your *Self*
Let your soul flow.

Be free
Be love
Be God's blessings from above
Be that child born pure
Be that child once adored.

Untangle
Untwist
Undo don't resist.

Who we are today, as a family, is the possibility of successfully breaking the chains of familial dysfunction and untangling our lives forever. I put that thought into the Universe as I begin 2014 knowing all things are possible!

52

Even Eagles Need a Push

I WANT TO LEAVE YOU WITH SOMETHING I read in 2012, written by David McNally. http://www.davidmcnally.com. David wrote this to capture the essence of encouragement. When I first read it, it had a tremendous impact on me as a recovering codependent. I think you'll understand why.

"Even Eagles Need A Push"

The eagle gently coaxed her offspring toward the edge of the nest. Her heart quivered with conflicting emotions as she felt their resistance to her persistent nudging.

"Why does the thrill of soaring have to begin with the fear of falling?" She thought. This ageless question was still unanswered for her.

As in the tradition of the species, her nest was located high on the shelf of a sheer rock face. Below there was nothing but air to support the wings of each child.

"Is it possible that this time it will not work?" She thought. Despite her fears, the eagle knew it was time. Her parental mission was all but complete.

There remained one final task – the push. The eagle drew courage from an innate wisdom. Until her children discovered their wings, there was no purpose for their lives.

Until they learned how to soar, they would fail to understand the privilege it was to have been born an eagle. The push was the greatest gift she had to offer. It was her supreme act of love.

And so, one by one, she pushed them and—THEY FLEW.
THE PUSH...Sometimes WE NEED IT.
Sometimes WE NEED TO GIVE IT.
It can be the greatest gift you ever give. It will change a life forever.

*   *   *

When all is said and done—tough love was my PUSH.
I needed it, and I needed to give it—and then—WE FLEW!!

*   *   *

Thank you to my Higher Power God. Thank you to the Universe. Thank you for answering my, "How?" I am going to send my revised manuscript off today. I have edited it to its glory—again! I think it's ready. I think I'm ready also—to dare greatly. Who would have guessed you wanted me to write a book! I just know you also want me to write a musical! Amen.

Yes, this book has ended—but it could be your new beginning!

Step 1.

I am powerless to change anyone but my *Self.*

Step 2.

Be the change.

Namaste

Recommended Books

The following books provided insight along my journey:

Beattie, Melody. *The Language of Letting Go.* Center City, MN: Hazelden Foundation, 1990.

--------------------. *Codependent No More: How to Stop Controlling Others and Start Caring for Yourself.* Center City, MN: Hazelden Foundation, 1987.

--------------------. *Codependent's Guide to the Twelve Steps.* New York: Fireside, 1990.

Canfield, Jack and Mark Victor Hansen. *Chicken Soup for the Recovering Soul.* Deerfield Beach, FL: Health Communications, Inc., 2004.

Cartwright, Michael. *Believable Hope: Five Essential Elements to Beat Any Addiction.* Deerfield Bch., FL: Health Communications, Inc., 2012.

CoDa. *Co-Dependents Anonymous.* Phoenix, AZ: Co-Dependents Anonymous, Inc., 1992.

Conyers, Beverly. *Everything Changes.* Center City, MN: Hazelden Foundation, 2009.

Forward, Susan. *Toxic Parents.* New York: Bantam Books, 1989.

Frey, James. *A Million Little Pieces.* New York: Anchor Books, 2003.

Hasselbeck, Paul. *Heart Centered Metaphysics.* Unity Village, MO: Unity School of Christianity, 2010.

Holmes, Ernest. *The Science of Mind.* New York: Penguin Putnam Inc., 1966.

Maday, Michael, ed. *New Thought for a New Millennium.* Unity Village, MO: Unity School of Christianity,1998.

McNally, David and Mac Anderson. *Even Eagles Need A Push.* Naperville, IL: Simple Truths, 2009.

McQ., Joe. *The Steps We Took*. Little Rock, AR: August House, Inc., 1990.

Mellody, Pia. *Facing Codependence*. New York: HarperCollins Publishers, 1989.

Neff, Pauline. *Tough Love*. Nashville, TN: Abingdon Press, 1982 1996.

Ruiz, Don Miguel. *The Four Agreements*. San Rafael, CA: Amber-Allen Publishing, Inc., 1997.

Salter, Anne. *Family Stew: Our Relationship Legacy*. Bloomington, IN: IUniverse, 2012.

Seaward, Brian Luke. *Stand Like Mountain, Flow Like Water*. Deerfield Beach, FL: Health Communications, Inc., 1997, 2007.

Sheff, David. *Beautiful Boy*. Boston, New York: Houghton Mifflin Company, 2008.

Credits

THE AUTHOR WISHES TO EXPRESS HER thanks to the artists and license holders of the following books, and poems for their permission to use copyrighted work in this book. The copyright owners to the following reserve all rights:

Excerpt from *The Language of Letting Go*, by Melody Beattie, copyright © 1990 by Hazelden Foundation. Reprinted by permission of Hazelden Foundation, Center City, MN.

Excerpts from *New Thought for a New Millennium*, copyright © 1998 by Unity Village. Reprinted by permission of Unity School of Christianity, Unity Village, MO.

Excerpts from *Stand Like Mountain, Flow Like Water*, by Brian Luke Seaward, copyright © 1997, 2007 by Health Communications, Inc. Reprinted by permission of Brian Luke Seaward, Ph.D.

Excerpts from *Family Stew: Our Relationship Legacy*, by Anne Salter, copyright © 2012 by IUniverse. Reprinted by permission of Anne Salter.

Excerpt from *Even Eagles Need A Push,* by David McNally and Mac Anderson, copyright © 2009 by Simple Truths. Reprinted by permission of David McNally and Mac Anderson.

Recommended Websites

THE MOTHER OF TWO ADDICTED SONS created the Addict's Mom website in 2009. She developed a free site where mothers of addicts can share their feelings without shame, where mothers can get emotional support from other mothers of addicts, and where valuable resources for you and your addicted loved ones can be found. You can read what other mothers say without saying anything yourself, or you can participate in the many dialogs. The choice is yours. Http://www. addictsmom.com

There is also an Addict's Mom Facebook Group:
http://www.facebook.com/groups/theaddictsmom

Al-Anon:
http://www.al-anon.org

Alateen:
http://www.nar-anon.org/naranon/About_Nar-Anon/Narateen

Alcoholics Anonymous:
http://www.alcoholics-anonymous.org

Narcotics Anonymous:
http://www.na.org

Nar-Anon: http://www.nar-anon.org

National Association for Children of Alcoholics:
http://www.nacoa.net

And, please feel free to go to my website, where I intend to continue sharing more *hope* in blogs and in other on-line ways. I would like to enlist others to share their success stories on my site as we join in our fight against codependency, addiction, alcoholism, and family dysfunction.

www.HOPEaddictionBook.com
I can also be reached by email at:
Deni@DeniBSher.me

Acknowledgments

ALWAYS AT THE BACK OF MY MIND, while writing my story and focusing on the positive, was the ugly reality of how many parents have not been as lucky and whose children have lost their lives to the diseases of addiction and alcoholism. This truly breaks my heart. I easily could have been one of those parents. This reality kept me writing. This reality needs to change. And, that is why I write. Please accept my deepest and most sincere condolences for your loss.

First, I want to thank my dear husband, Arthur, whose gentle hands held my heart throughout my emotional journey. Without Arthur's deep love for me, and his understanding of my passion, I would not have been able to dedicate myself to this mission. Arthur has given me wings to fly and encouragement to write my story. He has no idea what I have written, so I pray he doesn't divorce me!!

Secondly, but most importantly, I want to thank my son for not giving up on himself and for choosing sobriety. I also want to thank you for supporting the publication of this book. It means so much to me, that you trust me to publish my side of our story and that you understand how important it is for me to share our story of *hope* with others. I also want to thank you for trusting me with your artwork. I love you so much and am so proud of the man, husband, father, and son you have chosen to become.

Thank you to my daughter-in-law, Ashley, whose love of God and love for Ryan opened him to the truth of his being and freed his heart to trust in love and to trust in *Self*. Ashley, you are a blessing in Ryan's life and an angel in mine. Thank you for giving me a perfect, healthy, and precious grandson! I love you like the daughter I never had.

Thank you to Karen Sugerman, Mitch Hinds, and Caesar Taveras for participating in moving my story forward through music. Life created my story, divine inspiration created my poetry and songs, and I thank you for your earnest commitment to resonate my soul through your music. Huge thanks also goes to the many talented singers, who graciously invested their time and talent to move *Tough Love – The Musical* forward.

Thank you to my dear friends Paul Fletcher, Alex Kronstadt, Ph.D., Anne Salter, LCSW, and Ron Mansclaw, MD, DDiv, who were put into my life over the past eleven years to help me better understand the disease of addiction, the recovery process, my *wounded child*, and what it means to be a codependent woman, wife, and mother.

Thank you to Michelle from the bottom of my heart, for the huge part you played in Ryan's recovery process. I love you and always will. I am so happy to know you have recovered from being a codependent girlfriend, and have gone on to find the happiness you so deserve. I still don't believe I'd have a son today if you hadn't been put into his life. Thank you for being you. *Everybody needs a Michelle*!

Thank you to my good friend Kathryn. If you hadn't bitched at me so much about my son and opened my eyes to see how destructive his addiction had become in my life, I may not have found the strength required to face the truth and to begin tough love.

Thank you to my childhood girlfriends Lynn Thompson, Linda Lingo, Mary Moore, Sue Braverman, Nancy Meschter, Zilla Cowart, Bobbie Mitchell, Linda Mazur, Kathy Lord and Karen Garton. These young girls helped to support my real *Self* while growing up. Today we continue to maintain our friendships into retirement. They knew me before I gave my *Self* to Ricky and were there for me through all my husbands!

I maintain one friendship from my days at Emerson College with Andrea Zintz, Ph.D. She too has been there through all of my husbands. I cannot thank Andrea enough for her supportive friendship over the years and for her participation as the lead vocalist in the recording of Karen's and my songs for *Tough Love – The Musical*.

Thank you to my dear friend John Weisenberger, who empowered and befriended me when I was in the computer business, and, who has always been there for me during the past twenty-five years whenever I needed to talk. You're a good man and a great poet.

Thank you to Reverend Frank Phillips, of Unity Church of Hollywood, Florida for your multitude of inspirational and motivational messages. As a spiritual being, I was led to Unity for a purpose. Your sermons on creativity, passion, worth, inspiration, motivation, choices, prayer, meditation, divine energy, truth, and love all spoke to me personally—on my journey. Reverend Frank, you taught me we can all experience heaven on earth by living a life of greatness while discovering the Spirit within.

Thank you to Pam McCue Newman, Claudia Cayne, Betty McClure, Jaime Potter, Pastor Melody Gustafson, Alex Kronstadt, Anne Salter, Ron Mansclaw, Sally Prichard, and Reina Sang, for taking the time to read my story before it was published. Your emotional support, editing suggestions, and written reviews mean so much to me.

Thank you to Elliot Goldenberg, Anne Salter and Linda Prospero for helping me with my early editing challenges.

I sincerely want to thank two talented graphic designers Vicki Lowe and Alex Pretelt, who both helped with my early graphic design ideas for the logo and cover of the first publication of this book. Though I ended up going an entirely different direction your work was awesome and your friendship most important.

Every writer needs a cheerleader. My cheerleader was my friend, Janice, who lives in New York, and who called me almost daily to make sure I was on task. Get ready Janice; the musical will be next. Thank you. Thank you. Thank you. Thank you for being such a "pushy" New Yorker, but most importantly, thank you for a very healthy and honest friendship. I'm so glad we met at ASCAP.

I want to thank all of the many angels who have crossed my path over the past eleven years to give me inspiration, understanding and light in some of my darkest times. I cannot possibly write every name on this page, but you know who you are!

I want to thank my father, Henry E. Boehm, who passed away in October of 2006 at age ninety-four. Thank you for giving me life and for doing the best you knew how in raising your only daughter. I always knew you loved me. I could see it in your eyes (when you were sober) and in how proud you were of me as an athlete. And today, I realize I also saw your unhappiness when drinking, but I didn't know then, what I know now.

I saved the best for last. I want to thank my adorable mother for the unconditional love and friendship she gave me throughout her life. Born Celeste A. Goldman on December 24, 1913, she passed on June 24, 2011, at the age of ninety-seven with the last name, Smith (after marrying her high school sweetheart when she was seventy-two). Mom always tried to be there for me and to guide me. She was a remarkable woman, who came from a wealthy, yet broken home, then married into dysfunction, and was a product of her times. She was as close to being an angel on earth as anyone can be. I miss you Mom. I carry you in my heart, and you live through me in my writing.

Celeste was also a poet, who loved to write. I leave you with a poem she wrote to me for Mother's Day in 1988.

"To Daughter Denise, from Mom"

Mother's Day is coming soon,
And since I am your mother,
The greatest joy that I can have,
It's love for one another.

Some gifts we give just can't be bought,
Like presents from the store.
This is the love right from the heart,
And, it lasts forever more.

It's not how much you spend that counts,
But the love that lies behind it.
Anyone can spend money,
But, it's really love that binds it.

I like to feel my gifts to you,
Are the things I always taught you.
And through the years you'll find it true,
More important than what I bought you.

There you go, Mother—now you're a published writer too!!

About the Author

DENI BOEHM SHER lives in Weston, Florida with her husband, Arthur. Possessing a love for writing, she returned to college at age fifty and received her BA in English at fifty-two. Her passion is to shed light on familial dysfunction, codependency, denial, enabling, alcoholism and drug addiction, through her personal experiences as an adult child of an alcoholic father, and as a recovering, codependent, enabling mother of an addicted son.

Deni's earlier education at Emerson College, where she majored in Children's Theatre, combined with her ten years of performance on stage in children's theatre, equipped her to write in a unique, positive, and creatively poetic style. Deni has portrayed such characters as Peter Pan, Cinderella, Brer Rabbit in *Brer Rabbit's Big Secret*, Androcles in *Androcles and the Lion*, and Charlotte in *Charlotte's Web*.

Deni loves theatre. She dreams of one day creating a musical called, *Tough Love - The Musical*, based on writings from within this book. She believes her spiritually inspired message of HOPE will effectively reach others through a staged musical production.

Deni also spreads HOPE, as a speaker. She is proactive in the prevention of addiction while working to take both shame and blame out of being in recovery. Deni wants teens and young people to know alcohol, drugs, and other vices are not the answer to emotional pain. She also wants teens to understand how easily addiction can happen—even to them!

Deni will gladly speak upon invitation.